I0057650

HOW I DID IT

HOW I DID IT

LESSONS FROM THE
FRONT LINES OF BUSINESS

Edited by Daniel McGinn

Harvard Business Review Press

Boston, Massachusetts

Copyright 2014 Harvard Business School Publishing
All rights reserved
Printed in the United States of America

No part of this publication may be reproduced, stored in or introduced
into a retrieval system, or transmitted, in any form, or by any means
(electronic, mechanical, photocopying, recording, or otherwise),
without the prior permission of the publisher. Requests for permission
should be directed to permissions@hbsp.harvard.edu, or mailed to
Permissions, Harvard Business School Publishing, 60 Harvard Way,
Boston, Massachusetts 02163.

The web addresses referenced in this book were live and correct at the
time of the book's publication but may be subject to change.

ISBN: 978-1-63369-481-1

Library-of-Congress cataloging information forthcoming

Contents

Doing Smart Deals

Finding a Strategy That Works

Introduction

For more than a century, business schools have been developing ways to teach students the basic tools of business—how to create and understand accounting documents, analyze cash flows, and appraise the strengths and weaknesses of strategic choices.

These tools and others like them can be vital to managers who are starting their careers, but their value typically diminishes as a person's responsibilities increase. The reason is simple: The higher an executive advances, the more likely the job will involve making complex decisions that rely less on tools, and more on wisdom.

That's especially true for chief executives. According to one rule of thumb, chief executives are never asked to make easy calls—if the decision was easy, it never would have reached the CEO's desk in the first place. It's the hard choices that come one after another, all day and every day.

It's not possible to teach the wisdom required to make these decisions, since wisdom is a function of experience. But it is possible to improve decision making over time by repeatedly observing and simulating decisions made by others. This is why quarterbacks sit in darkened rooms, watching films of opposing teams' defenses. It's why Navy Seals study after-action reports to understand what went right (and wrong) on past operations. It's also why, nearly a century ago, B-schools (led by Harvard Business School) began using case studies to try to expose students to real-life business problems in hopes that simulating and debating the choices made by managers would help aspiring leaders put theory into practice.

The essays in this book are a singular contribution to this tradition. Like case studies, they take readers inside the C-suite, but they go further, giving inside detail and perspective about the decisions made by the chief executives involved—told in their own words.

Beyond the bona fides of their authors—current and past leaders of companies including Google, Xerox, General Electric, DuPont, Burberry, and many others—the most striking element of these narratives is their candor. The public has a tendency to view top executives as polished, decisive, and infallible (and in fact some executives work hard to burnish this image). However, the CEOs in many of these essays admit to being uncertain or nervous. They get angry. They screw up. "We spent years trying and failing," writes the CEO of IMAX, describing his 20-year struggle to find a workable strategy. "We were wrong," writes the CEO of MacLaren, describing a stroller recall as "one of the most difficult times in my business life." "I remember thinking . . . 'We're screwed,'" writes Google's Eric Schmidt, describing his misgivings the morning the company went public.

Often, when CEOs agree to share a story with a business magazine, they're attempting to speak to a particular constituency: Their shareholders or potential investors, their customers, or even their employees. But when CEOs write for *Harvard Business Review*, they're typically concerned less with image or stock price and more with the duty they feel to pass along lessons to a future generation of managers—to provide a sort of virtual mentorship, and in that way to help improve the practice of management.

We hope their stories help prepare you for the hard decisions that lie ahead in your career.

—The Editors

HOW I DID IT

PICKING THE RIGHT PEOPLE

SOMETIMES THE BEST MANAGEMENT ADVICE IS ALSO THE most succinct. On that measure, it's hard to beat one of the core teachings of Jim Collins: "First *who*, then *what*." No matter what grand strategy a company pursues, Collins argues in *Good to Great*, its odds of success are long unless its managers ensure they have "the right people on the bus."

That's why many of the best executives spend the bulk of their time selecting, developing, and promoting the most talented people they can find—and encouraging the wrong people to opt to "spend more time with their families."

What's surprising about this work is how much disagreement there is over the right way to pick and groom people—whether entry-level workers or the next CEO. In several of the essays that follow, top executives explain why they disregard the procedures that HR types promote as "best practice."

One CEO explains why résumés and job interviews aren't a good indicator of potential—and why energetically checking references is the single most valuable way managers can identify real talent. Another boss explains why the traditional "horse race" for the corner office is a terrible way to pick a leader—and outlines how she spent a decade preparing her single handpicked successor for the job.

What's clear in all of these pieces is that people decisions loom large among the problems that keep CEOs awake at night—which means getting more of the right people on board can help everyone rest easier.

Gilt Groupe's CEO on Building a Team of A Players

by Kevin Ryan

Kevin Ryan is the founder and CEO of Gilt Groupe.

The Idea

Companies always say employees are their most valuable asset. Kevin Ryan thinks that few of them act accordingly. He believes a CEO's most important job is managing talent.

When I think about starting a business, my view is that the idea itself is worth between zero and very little. Most new companies already have competitors when they launch— and if they don't, they soon will. DoubleClick, where I was CEO from 1996 to 2005, had dozens of competitors within a year of its founding. Gilt Groupe wasn't the first flash sales company, and Google was by no means the first search engine to come along. Why have these businesses succeeded? It's not the idea—it's the people. Execution is what matters, and execution relies on human talent. Every company thinks it's doing a good job of managing its people. They all say, "People are our most important asset." But most companies don't really act that way. Here's a simple test: Ask the CEO if he or she spends more time on recruiting and managing people than on any other activity. For me, the answer has always been yes. That's a radical statement, so let me qualify it a bit. I don't think this test applies at a small company—say, 20 people—where the CEO may be doing a lot of the sales or directly overseeing operations. But at businesses that employ more than 50 people, the best use of a CEO's time is to bring in unbelievable people, manage them well, and make sure the company builds and maintains an A-caliber team.

Here's another test of a company's devotion to its talent: Is your head of HR one of the most important people in the company? I spend as much time with our head of HR as I do with our chief financial officer—and I'd never consider having the head of HR report to anybody but the CEO. That role is truly strategic, and the person in it needs a seat at the table.

It's clear to the people who work with me that I'm thinking about our talent most of the time. When we sit down for meetings, I frequently ask managers to review every one of their direct reports with me. I want continual updates. I also insist that as the CEO, I can talk with anyone in the company at any time. Some managers prefer that executives check with them before talking with their people. That's not going to happen here. I want to get to know our employees better and to assess their talent and potential. I also want to know if they have difficulties with a manager. I am evaluating talent all the time.

Addition by Subtraction

Part of building a great team is learning to recognize when individuals aren't working out and then letting them go. In general, managers are not rigorous enough about this. That's a problem, because often the only way to make room for better players is to get the weaker players to leave the organization.

Of course, it's essential for people to feel that the process is fair. But you have to be comfortable having a conversation with a low-performing employee that goes something like this: "You rank 10th out of 10 in performance. You're probably great, but this may not be the right job for you. We may not be the right company for you. I know you don't want to be in a situation where people think you're the lowest performer." Sometimes we can find a position in the company that is a better fit. Inevitably, the employee will question the judgment: "I'm not really the lowest performer." Then I say, "Evaluating talent isn't a precise science. But it's very rare that multiple managers think you're 10th out of 10 when you're really number two. Maybe you're number nine—maybe. But the real point is that I want you to be successful, and I don't think this is the right situation or career path for you." Sometimes I say the person can stay on for two months and look for a job at the same time, as long as he or she maintains a good attitude and continues to contribute. Sometimes the person feels burned or negative and needs to leave right away, with some severance.

I hold managers to the same standards when I ask them to build a team. Not long ago a senior person stepped into a new role. I said to him, "Five months from now, you need to have a great team. Earlier would be better, but five months is the goal. To do that, you'll need to spend the next month evaluating the people you have right now. I hope they're good. But if they're not, we'll make changes to replace them. If you need to promote people internally, we'll do that. If you need to go outside, we'll do that. You also need to make sure you retain your best people. I'm going to be really disturbed if I see that people we wanted to keep have started leaving your area."

In this case I saw all the signs I didn't want to see. At four months he hadn't filled a couple of key roles, and a couple of good people had left. We had a conversation. "Tell us what we can do to help," I said. "If you need us to double your recruiting resources, we'll do that." At six months he still hadn't built a great team, so I said, "We're done." After he left, people started to come forward and tell us how demotivating it had been to work for him and that they had come close to leaving as well. There are two lessons in that story: One, don't let a bad situation fester. A poor manager can ruin morale and damage a company's DNA. Two, no matter how well you think you know your organization, if you suspect something's wrong, it's probably worse than you imagine. You can't let those situations continue. They're just too destructive.

"Don't Hire Him"

I don't think there's a science to recruiting, but I do some things differently. The hiring process typically has three elements: the résumé, the interview, and the reference check. Most managers overvalue the résumé and interview and undervalue the reference check. References matter most. It would be a great experiment to not interview people at all—to hire simply on the basis of the reference check—and see what happened. I'm pretty sure that most companies would make better hires if they did that.

Résumés are good for establishing basic qualifications for the job, but not for much else. The primary problem with interviews is that it's impossible to avoid being influenced by people who are well-spoken, present well, or are attractive. All sorts of studies show how much appearance drives our perceptions of people. The résumé and interview also don't alert you to the biggest potential problems. When someone doesn't succeed in a job, it's generally not for lack of the technical skills—it's because of intangibles that don't come up in an interview. Is he attentive to detail? Does she work well with others? How does he treat his colleagues? References are really the only way to learn these things. The essential traits I look for are success and passion.

The truth is that successful people are rarely let go: They're hired by former bosses in other companies.

The presumption is that reference checks aren't worth much because people are scared to say anything negative. That's a valid concern, because there have been lawsuits. But the way around it is to dig up people who will speak candidly. Invariably, they're people you know personally or people you can network to find. You can't simply rely on the names a candidate supplies. Admittedly, this is hard if the person is 22 and just out of college—but for someone with 10 or 15 years of experience who has worked at two or three companies, you must have some mutual acquaintances. Search firms do this by making a lot of calls, and we try to do the same thing. We also look at LinkedIn profiles to find shared contacts.

A while back someone called me for a reference check on a guy named Fred. I didn't know the caller, so I was very guarded. I talked about Fred's strengths and weaknesses but emphasized that I liked him. The next day a college friend named Kevin phoned me. He said he was calling on behalf of someone I didn't know, a close friend of his, who was thinking of hiring another person who had worked for me. The hiring manager had asked Kevin to get the real story from me. If I didn't know the person making the call, I'd have given a lukewarm response similar to the one on the previous day. But this was a longtime friend asking for my candid opinion. I gave it simply: "Don't hire him." When you check references, you want to have a conversation as frank as that. It can take real effort to find someone who'll be straight with you, but it's worth it.

We don't always get this right. For one hire, an outside recruiter that helped with the search had checked some of the references. Ordinarily we try to do this ourselves. The man didn't work out—it was just a bad fit. After he left, I ran into a couple of people I knew: one who had worked for the guy at another company and one who'd done business with him as a banker. I hadn't realized that either of them knew him. They told me what they thought of him—which jibed exactly with our negative experience. Sometimes you don't hear an honest assessment until it's too late.

Recruiting is so important that we intentionally overinvest in it. We have 10 full-time recruiters on our staff—a lot for a company our size. We also frequently use external search firms, especially for senior positions. Sometimes a company will leave a low-performing person in a job because managers feel there's a shortage of time or energy to recruit his replacement. I don't want to be in that position.

As the CEO, I can't be involved in every hire we make. We hired 65 people last June—and interviewing every customer-support person would have been a bad use of my time. Even so, I interview many more people than CEOs usually do. I probably interview at least one person every workday. I also make it clear to my senior people that if they're making an important hire, I'm willing to call the person as part of the pitch. People love hearing from the CEO: "Steve, I haven't met you yet, but everyone thinks you're amazing. Is there anything I can do to help with your decision? Can I fly out to meet you?" They always say no, but the fact that you've offered shows you care. Recruiting is similar to sales, and sometimes the CEO's involvement makes a difference.

People talk about certain rules of thumb in talent management. One is that the great people in any company are usually underpaid. That's generally true, and you should skew your compensation system with performance pay to better reward them. Another is that A-level people generally hire other A-level people, but B-level people hire C-level people. I think that's true, too, but for a reason other than the usual one. B players hire C players not because they feel threatened by more-talented people but because most people don't want to work for a mediocre boss. Think about it: Have you ever heard someone say, "I just got offered a job. The person I'll be working for isn't very impressive, but I'm going to take it anyway"? That's not something talented people generally do.

Another piece of conventional wisdom is that people leave jobs mainly because they don't like their managers. That's also true. We did exit interviews when people left DoubleClick, and they were almost always leaving because of a manager. I talk about this with our team at Gilt all the time: If good people are leaving your group, that's your responsibility. I want all our senior people focused on that issue. It's especially important in the internet space, where good people are in high demand and have many choices. I think, too, that the hardest quality to find in a new hire is the ability to bring things to closure. Some people don't realize that analysis is useful only if it results in a decision and implementation.

Of all the duties facing a CEO, obsessing over talent provides the biggest return. Making sure that the environment is good, that people are learning, and that they know we're investing in them every day—I'm constantly thinking about that, yet I still don't feel I'm doing enough. If CEOs did absolutely nothing but act as chief talent officers, I believe, there's a reasonable chance their companies would perform better.

Originally published in January–February 2012. R1201A

Seventh Generation's CEO on Giving Up the CEO Seat

by Jeffrey Hollender

Jeffrey Hollender (inspiredprotagonist.com) is a cofounder and the executive chairman of Seventh Generation, a maker of environmentally responsible household and personal-care products.

The Idea

A founder of Seventh Generation describes how he knew it was time to go—and how he made that case to his team and his board.

It happened three years ago, but my memory of the moment I knew I had to step down as CEO is indelible. On the morning after a long business trip to the West Coast, I was returning to the Burlington, Vermont, headquarters of the company I had cofounded, Seventh Generation. As I walked through our offices, with their view of Lake Champlain and the Adirondacks' distant peaks, I resumed my daily ritual of seeking out associates with whom I didn't regularly connect. But this time I was struck by a startling realization: People were clicking away at their computers, huddling in conference rooms, or heading out for meetings—*and I had no idea what they were working on.* The experience unnerved me.

As the chief executive, I had long been intimately involved in many of Seventh Generation's inner workings. My team often found my preoccupation with the details both impressive and annoying. I would constantly bird-dog efforts to make our diapers absorb just one more gram of liquid. I'd focus relentlessly on new styles of perforation for our toilet tissue. I worked with our sales director on setting goals for every item we sold, right down to individual distribution channels and accounts. In meetings I took meticulous notes on each direct report, listing every commitment and project deadline. But something had changed.

Even as I shook off the jet lag, this new, discomfiting feeling of detachment persisted. Even worse, it escalated. I found myself baffled by two of Seventh Generation's most challenging strategic decisions: whether to sell our household and personal-care products at Wal-Mart, and whether to expand the brand outside the United States. For the first time in my career, I was at a loss for answers or ideas.

Intellectually, I was in denial. But in my gut, I felt ill prepared to take Seventh Generation—which in 2007 generated $93 million in annual sales—to its then stated goal of $250 million. Having steered the company for nearly two decades, I knew it was time to find a new CEO.

A Difficult Transition

Any senior leadership transition is fraught with challenges, none more so than when a company founder abdicates the top job. Each morning, as I sat in silence after my hour of predawn exercise, I'd reflect on executives who had bungled their transitions. Two glaring examples were from high tech: Michael Dell left too early, and Scott McNealy left too late. When Dell handed the reins of his namesake company to a trusted lieutenant, it was the world's largest PC maker; within three years rivals had clawed away much of Dell's market share, and its founder was compelled to return as CEO. Conversely, McNealy continued as chief of Sun Microsystems despite the company's stunted growth and falling share price. By the time he stepped down, Sun's eventual sale to Oracle was almost inevitable. But then there's Oprah Winfrey, who announced at the peak of her success that she would leave her iconic show in 2011, causing David Carr to write in the *New York Times* that her "gut intuition, about knowing when to say no and when it is time to go, is worth studying at every business graduate school in the country."

The tangible costs of a bungled transition can run to hundreds of millions of dollars' worth of squandered market share and submerged sales. But I was more concerned with avoiding damage to Seventh Generation's intangible assets: our associates' spirit and will, our stakeholders' trust, and our company's mission and reputation.

Seventh Generation aspires to do more than simply grow market share. Its purpose is to inspire a more conscious and sustainable world by being an authentic force for positive change. Profits are the score, not the game. But to fulfill the company's mission, we had to become bigger and more profitable. We needed a CEO who would use our financial imperatives to fuel our social and environmental imperatives—someone few executive recruiters are equipped to find. Not surprisingly, the more I thought about how best to proceed, the more questions arose: How quickly should I move? How public should I be? How would I get the board's support and associates' buy-in? How would I ensure that Seventh Generation's fierce commitment to social and environmental sustainability endured? Above all, was I doing the right thing? (Every family member and close colleague said no.)

Seventh Generation's directors wondered if they were about to lose the best investment in their portfolios: In 2007 alone, I had helped grow the business by more than 40%. Some staffers thought that no one who replaced me would have the same vision and values. Talented people signed on with Seventh Generation precisely because it explicitly promised to be a place where they could summon all their individuality and creativity—the very attributes that many companies insist be left at home. Associates worried that a new CEO would fill the place with corporate drones. My wife fretted that I'd end up at home, bored and depressed.

Nevertheless, we found a way to welcome the biggest change in the company's history. Last June, Seventh Generation got a new chief, Chuck Maniscalco, who until 2008 had been president and CEO of PepsiCo's nearly $10 billion Quaker, Tropicana, and Gatorade division. I remain at the company as executive chairman (Chuck reports to the board, not to me), and I've been devoting much of my energy to furthering Seventh Generation's mission, vision, and corporate-responsibility strategy. No one can predict the future, but early returns confirm that making the transition was the right thing to do.

Transition Tenets

It was tough to concede that I was the best person to guide our company through infancy and adolescence but not into full-fledged adulthood. I overcame lots of obstacles by following several transition principles involving community, transparency, mission, and corporate consciousness—all central to building a purpose-driven organization. As I learned through real-world experience, they're also valuable signposts for finding a new CEO.

Look unflinchingly at your own performance

For the better part of the past decade, Seventh Generation (with help from the author and consultant Carol Sanford) has been trying to develop its corporate consciousness—to make us more sharply aware of how we work and what we want to accomplish. Sure, the phrase exudes a whiff of the mystical (or at least the mysterious). But the idea is inherently tough-minded: Break ingrained habits of thought, kick over stale ideas, and avoid the easy path of simply repeating past successes.

In late 2007, when I first seriously considered recruiting a replacement, Seventh Generation was enjoying the best run in its history. In 2008 our sales approached $140 million, an unprecedented 51% jump over the previous year's record sales. To some it seemed the height of folly to bring in a new chief when the company was performing at its peak. Reed Doyle, a passionate, committed member of our product development team, summed up a lot of people's misgivings when he rose at one of our town hall-style meetings and let me have it. "How do we know," he inquired, "that you won't screw up our success by bringing in some corporate big shot?"

Actually, I worried that our success was vulnerable to other threats. Although we sometimes seemed to be moving with relative ease down well-worn roads, we were heading into new territory, populated by bigger, fiercer rivals. The company had historically been only marginally profitable, our significant growth masking our meager earnings; that was no longer acceptable for a company of our size. To compete with the giants of the consumer packaged goods (CPG) industry, we'd have to grow annual sales from $140 million to $500 million and eventually $1 billion, and earn double-digit operating profits.

As objectively as I could, I assessed my ability to lead Seventh Generation toward billion-dollar growth. Our ERP and other software systems had failed to keep pace with the company's expansion. My lack of interest in logistics was partly to blame for our inability to cut transportation and warehousing costs in half. And my senior managers would describe me as the CEO who never met an investment he didn't like: I saw only the upside, never wanting to dwell on the consequences of investments gone wrong.

When I was ruthlessly honest with myself, I couldn't help concluding that my limitations bled the benefits of my staying on as CEO. And I lacked the fire. Only when I began to think about taking on a greater cause, such as helping other companies weave sustainability into all their operations, did my pulse begin to quicken.

In the spirit of raising corporate consciousness—and to persuade the company's directors—I wrote the business case for my succession and presented it to the board. First, I outlined my greatest value to the company moving forward: to be out in public, increasing Seventh Generation's brand awareness and advancing our mission of creating a better world for future generations. Next, I argued that my lack of experience running a far bigger company reduced my effectiveness as a leader. Finally, I asserted that we needed a chief executive who knew how to build out a consumer brand while competing with huge CPG companies.

My presentation was met with stunned silence. I had shared my plans with a few board members ahead of time, but even they were at a loss as to how to respond to my passionate plea. Then, after a few polite questions—How quickly did I expect this transition to happen? What if we couldn't find the right person? How did I think the staff would respond?—the board found its equilibrium and agreed conceptually (though not wholeheartedly) that bringing in a new leader was the right decision. Its members wouldn't commit to a transition, however, until they were confident that we'd found the right successor. I thought that recruiting a seasoned number-two executive—a president who would oversee the company's operations but report to me instead of the board, and would become CEO in one to three years—would make for a smooth transition. But reality has a way of disrupting even the best-laid plans.

Dare to be transparent

Not long ago the founder and CEO of another values-driven company covertly recruited a successor, declining to go public until the day the new chief arrived. The sudden, unexpected change lowered associates' morale and productivity and made the new leader's job even more challenging. Secrecy is counterproductive, whereas transparency calms the chatter that so often accompanies significant change.

At one of our monthly all-hands meetings, I made the case to the entire Seventh Generation community for why I should step aside. At first people were skeptical, somewhat scared, and hungry for details. "How would we know that a new chief shared our values?" someone asked. "How do we know the new leader won't come in and flip the business for a quick profit?" someone else said. "Will we have a voice in the selection process—and how quickly is this going to happen?"

Our associates own close to 20% of the company; thus, I argued, what was best for the business was best for them. More than a few no doubt remained apprehensive about the changes to come—as I did. But I updated the staff on the search every four to six weeks and convened a team of senior and junior associates to meet with every serious candidate. Getting more minds into the mix would help us make a better decision, and we all felt that if the process remained open and transparent, we'd arrive at a good outcome.

Make the company's mission central in your search

Seventh Generation is organized around seven "global imperatives"—three of which are that we work to restore the environment, help create a just and equitable world, and encourage associates to think of themselves as educators dedicated to inspiring conscious consumption. If these goals sound impossibly utopian, that is part of the intent. Defining ourselves as evangelists for social and environmental sustainability sets the company apart.

Before we began interviewing, I created a spreadsheet to rate candidates on qualities in three categories: essential, important, and nice to have. Most essential was a commitment to fulfilling our mission of deeper business purpose—without which no one would make the first cut. Other must-haves included high-growth management experience, demonstrated strategic ability, and leadership capability.

Some might argue against my putting "values" at the top of the list—especially when we were heading into the teeth of a global recession. But I had already seen, in the course of recruiting executives to our senior management team, how our values helped us punch far above our weight class. Ambitious veterans who'd made their mark at heavyweights like Clorox, P&G, and Quaker Oats sought us out precisely because they wanted their work to make a positive difference in the world.

Chuck Maniscalco is proof of that. Just two weeks after he took over as CEO, he blogged that he had joined Seventh Generation because he was drawn to the company's mission. "I am at a point in my life of wanting, almost desperately, to give back," he wrote. But lest anyone think he's a softie, consider this: Out of the 70 candidates we reviewed, Chuck was the only one who wasn't interested in a number-two job. He made a persuasive case that to take the company where it needed to go, he would have to be the chief executive. I would have to immediately turn over the CEO post and redefine my role at the company. Considering all that Chuck had accomplished, and all that he could do for Seventh Generation, I knew I couldn't refuse.

The week before Chuck was scheduled to revisit Burlington for a final round of meetings, I convened with my senior managers and put three questions to each: Should Chuck be CEO or president? How quickly should we make the transition? What operational responsibilities should I retain for the first six months of his tenure? I thought they would ask me to stay at the top for as long as possible. I was wrong. With only one exception, each declared that it was time for me to move on—the sooner, the better. In their view, the transition was already under way.

As I reflected on their recommendation during my drive home, I was both saddened and angered. Part of me felt they'd been deeply disloyal. But at the same time, I knew they were doing what I always demanded—speaking the truth without political considerations. By the end of my half-hour commute, I knew that this 20-year chapter of my life was nearing its conclusion. I had to get ready to let go.

I'M NOW deeply involved in building initiatives to ensure that progressive businesses have more influence in shaping public policy. The most exciting of these is the American Sustainable Business Council, a challenger to the U.S. Chamber of Commerce. Chuck is fully engaged in running Seventh Generation. Time will ultimately tell whether we made the right moves. (I believe we did.) But I have no doubt that by using the transition principles above, we followed the right path.

Originally published in March 2010. R1003J

Xerox's Former CEO on Why Succession Shouldn't Be a Horse Race

by Anne Mulcahy

Anne Mulcahy was the CEO of Xerox from 2001 to 2009.

The Idea

Xerox named Ursula Burns its CEO in 2009, marking the end of a nearly drama-free succession process. That was no accident: The outgoing CEO had spent nearly a decade orchestrating a smooth transition.

In early 2007 Ursula Burns and I had dinner at a French restaurant on the Upper East Side of Manhattan. It was quiet and expensive—which was uncharacteristic for us. But we needed a place where we could talk. At the time, Ursula was a senior vice president at Xerox and the leading candidate to succeed me as CEO. We were about to announce that she was being promoted to president and would join the board of directors— a move intended to signal that the CEO job was hers to win. It seemed like a smooth transition on the surface. But it's fair to say that we were arguing behind the scenes, though I'd prefer to call it debating.

We were having trouble drawing a line between our roles for the period until she became CEO. We were playing the org-chart game, debating who would report to whom, and who'd have responsibility for what. Ursula rightly wanted as much responsibility as possible as soon as possible so that she'd be well prepared to lead Xerox. As president, she wanted most of the company reporting to her, and that just didn't work for me. We never let our team see that there was conflict between us, but there was—so we called a time-out. We asked our CFO to come to dinner and act as a facilitator. We talked honestly about how to provide the best transition experience for Ursula while being sensitive to the fact that it was hard for me to step back and give up power. And we talked about how, throughout the process, we would put the company first.

That dinner was just one moment in a long process that ended in July 2009, when Ursula succeeded me as chief executive. Ours was the first woman-to-woman CEO succession in the *Fortune* 500—and Ursula became the first African-American woman to lead a large U.S. company. I was determined to have a smooth succession, because I'd come into the job the wrong way: I'd taken over for an outsider who resigned after only 13 months as CEO. So I wanted Ursula to be as well prepared as she could. I wanted to move little by little, to make it almost a no-brainer when the time came. And that's how it felt.

That doesn't mean it was easy. Succession is very difficult, which is why companies so often fail at it. It takes a tremendous amount of discipline, focus, and support to do well. People have no road map for the process—they don't know what to expect or how to prepare for it. They also don't realize how hard succession is on the incumbent CEO. It's designed to make you able to go away without causing a big impact, and that doesn't come naturally. Giving up power and accountability is a challenge, but it's essential to preparing the future CEO for the role.

"Who *Is* This Person?"

Ursula's story is extraordinary, considering her background. She grew up in the projects, raised by a single mother who ironed and did chores to support her kids. Her mother used to tell her, "This is where you're going to grow up, but this is not what defines you." Ursula eventually received a master's degree from Columbia.

I first encountered her around 1991. She was serving as executive assistant to a senior Xerox executive, a developmental role for high-potential employees. I was running HR. Ursula stood out. In many meetings she was the most junior person present, and people in that role are expected to listen and be invisible. Not Ursula. She offered opinions. She challenged points of view. Among the senior team there was a sense of "Who *is* this person?" She was just so vocal. But I liked her authenticity and directness, even if she was a little rough around the edges.

During the mid-1990s I was chief of staff, one level above Ursula. She ran a product-development team. During those years I never looked at her and thought, *She could be CEO someday.* That's partly because she was young—still in her thirties. But I certainly knew she was smart and courageous, and that she'd do very well at Xerox if she stayed.

As Ursula rose in the company, she got on recruiters' radar screens. I don't know how many outside job offers she received, but I do know we came close to losing her around 2000. She'd received a great offer from a competitor, and she was a bit disillusioned with our company. An accounting scandal was just starting to unfold, and business results were tanking. She also felt that Xerox's value system and culture were changing. At the time, we had a relatively new CEO, Rick Thoman, who'd been brought in from IBM. Paul Allaire, Thoman's predecessor as CEO and one of Ursula's mentors, talked with her about whether she should leave. He told her a management change was likely (Rick resigned in May 2000) and asked if that would give her the confidence to stay at Xerox. She said it would. I became Xerox's president, and a year later I became CEO. I expanded Ursula's responsibilities to include manufacturing and the supply chain. I wanted her to be a significant member of my team, and I also wanted to give her an early signal that I believed in her and trusted her with a big part of the operation.

From the moment I stepped into the job, the board began discussing who might succeed me. At that point, in 2001, we focused on four candidates and were considering two scenarios. The first was: What if something unexpected happens tomorrow, and we need someone really experienced who can step in immediately? The second was: What if we had the luxury of developing someone naturally over a long period of time? Ursula fit the second scenario—she needed more time to develop.

Over the next few years she totally reengineered our manufacturing and supply chain. By the time she finished, our operating costs were probably a third of what they'd been five years before. She also overhauled our product-development process. My predecessor used to say that during the 1990s Xerox didn't launch products, it allowed them to escape. It was true: We brought out only a handful of products in that decade. But Ursula made that her mission, and by 2005 we were introducing 30 or 40 new products a year.

She also built a terrific team of people. Xerox had lost a lot of research and engineering talent during the 1990s, and Ursula groomed a new generation of technology leaders. She racked up an impressive list of accomplishments.

We had regular conversations about her progress. We're always very direct with each other; there's little subtlety. If I wasn't giving Ursula the assurance she needed, she'd be frank about wanting to be told "You're on track," which meant "You're a really good candidate for CEO." There were never any guarantees, but by mid-decade she was running half the company.

In the conversations I had with the other candidates during this time, I tried to be realistic about their status. I don't believe in having people face off against each other for the CEO job in a classic horse race. I know that's the General Electric model, but I didn't want to lose the three players who weren't going to get the job. I sent them honest signals about whether they were lead candidates or not, and what the possibilities would be if they didn't get the job of chief executive, so that they could feel good about their opportunities and the contribution they would make. I worked hard to avoid a contest that would be dysfunctional for the company.

Beware the Tapping Pen

Ursula had appeared before the board of directors in the past, but I made sure she had a lot of visibility in the boardroom over the next few years. She was on her feet a lot—that's the formal part of it. But board events also include dinners and lunches, and I would seat her next to the members she needed to get to know. We made sure she had a chance to engage with them at other social events, too, and she did very well.

I also tried to work with her on weaknesses. Earlier in her career she didn't have a good poker face—all her emotions were visible. That's a big thing for a CEO, because everybody is looking at you. You can destroy someone by showing your emotions, particularly negative ones. It just shuts people down. If you come into the office looking like you're having a very bad day, everyone reacts to your mood. As chief executive, you have to consciously set the right tone, and Ursula worked to develop that. I'm not perfect at it myself. My team will tell you that when my pen starts tapping in a meeting, it's time to run for the hills. But CEOs have to manage those unintended displays, because of how much impact they have on other people.

Something else Ursula needed to develop was an ability to engage her team. When you're really smart and tough and have a lot of responsibility, it can be hard to sit through a long process where everyone voices his or her views—especially if you've already reached a decision. A person like Ursula, who really hates to waste time, can be tempted to cut through the crap and reach a conclusion that seems obvious to her. But it's important to realize that if, as CEO, you make your call too early, your team won't feel that it owns the outcome. The process can seem like a waste of time, but it's important. Ursula is very good at it now, but it didn't come naturally to her early on.

Over the years we've worked together, some people have gotten the idea that Ursula and I are close personal friends. We're not. We don't socialize away from work. Our families don't get together. Misconceptions like this seem to be tied to women in leadership positions; people generally don't assume that male executives are best friends. People tend to look for characteristics in women leaders that would make them seem like really nice people and good friends so that those leaders won't fit the stereotype of ambitious women.

But we are good business colleagues, and we've been able to talk honestly and work through difficult issues. At dinner that night in 2007, we debated various scenarios for splitting responsibility. One involved flipping duties: I'd take over the parts of the company she knew well, and she'd take over the parts I was running. It sounded like a good developmental experience, but it was actually a pretty dumb idea. Putting your two top people on a learning curve isn't smart, and the CEO isn't expected to have intimate experience with every piece of the company.

Instead, we decided that Ursula would keep her current responsibilities and would take on all the corporate staff except the CFO. I kept customer operations and our geographic regions, with the understanding that she'd spend more time with the leaders of those units. It was a way of not moving too quickly but giving her access to everything. In some ways we were saying we'd run the company together—make decisions together with no definitive line of separation. We arrived at a really good place.

Smoothing the Path

Under the plan we came up with in 2007, Ursula would have been CEO by early 2009—possibly as early as mid-2008. In fact it took longer. Xerox had been facing securities litigation since 2000, and I wanted to settle that case before Ursula took over so that she could start with a clean slate. We wanted to get our services business up and running, and to have a road map for the acquisition of Affiliated Computer Services. A couple of our senior people were retiring, and we wanted to give their replacements time to get their feet wet so that Ursula wouldn't have a bunch of newbies on her team. I think she understood that there is no perfect time to become a CEO or to leave the position, but that it would be good to have some of those milestones behind her.

By mid-2008 the board had agreed that Ursula would succeed me. This was largely a formality; the process had been iterative. I'd been discussing our progress with directors over breakfast before every single board meeting, and Ursula was present for many of these discussions. The directors weren't still asking, "Is she ready?" or "Is this the right decision?" Their confidence in the answer had been established long ago. At that point they were concerned with timelines, communications, and how long I would stay on as chairman.

Looking back on the process, I think the succession conversation between chief executives and their boards needs to start a lot earlier than might feel comfortable. The board must make sure the discussion gets going—it's unnatural for a CEO to want to initiate it early in his or her tenure. And I think succession should play out over three to five years at a minimum, so the "early and often" nature of the conversation is crucial. Your actions have to support your plans. You have to give the candidates developmental responsibilities and visibility with the board. You also need to establish very clear guidelines with regard to timelines and expectations. I've seen lots of companies allow ambiguity on those points, and it's a problem. And although there may be exceptions, generally you shouldn't be CEO for more than a decade. You do a disservice to the company if you don't rotate the leadership.

There may be times when a company finds itself with two equally strong candidates who are in a horse race for the job. I'm glad that wasn't the case at Xerox. Having winners and losers isn't good for the company: You wind up losing top talent. (Of the three other candidates for CEO back in 2001, one has retired but two are still at Xerox.) If you can develop one very strong player and some peripheral candidates who could be groomed if necessary, and if you can put your energy into making sure that one person is absolutely the best person for the job, you'll be in a good place.

By the time Ursula took over, I knew we'd succeeded, because I was needed less and less. That came home to me most vividly at a meeting right after she was named CEO. Everyone was looking at her rather than at me. The whole team's attention had just shifted, without a lot of drama. That's the way it should be.

Originally published in October 2010. R1010A

Marriott's Executive Chairman on Choosing the First Nonfamily CEO

by Bill Marriott

Bill Marriott is the executive chairman of Marriott International and the author (with Kathi Ann Brown) of *Without Reservations: How a Family Root Beer Stand Grew Into a Global Hotel Company* (Luxury Custom Publishing, 2013).

The Idea

For decades Bill Marriott expected that his son would become the third generation to lead the global hotel company. But gradually he realized that he had to make a different choice.

When I became the head of Marriott, in 1964, many people were surprised. I was only 32 and had worked at the company full-time for just eight years. My father, who'd started the business in 1927 with a root beer stand in Washington, DC, before moving into restaurants and then hotels, had an experienced executive vice president working for him who many thought would succeed him. He was 20 years older than I was, and when it came to finance, he was brilliant. But he was a micromanager. He spent a lot of time marking up contracts, redoing the work of the company's lawyers. He didn't have good people skills and didn't understand the operation of the business. We had a senior director on our board who had been the chairman of three companies, and my father really relied on him. This director came to think that the executive VP was the wrong choice, and he urged my father to make me CEO. After all, I'd literally learned the business visiting restaurants with my father as a young boy, and I'd worked part-time in different jobs at the company since I was 14. My father was worried that I was too young, but Marriott was still small at the time—we had about $85 million in annual revenue—and I think he figured he'd be around long enough to bail me out if I got into trouble.

During my decades as president and CEO, the company grew immensely: At the end of 2012 we had 3,800 properties in 73 countries and territories, and our revenue last year was $11.8 billion. While I was leading the company, I often had several experienced nonfamily executives working with me. If something had happened to me suddenly, those deputies would have been qualified to step in. Some of them were probably viewed as potential successors, but I was in no hurry to give up the job. In 1989, when I was 57, I suffered a heart attack, and I began to think a little more seriously about succession. But I bounced back really quickly—I returned to work after six weeks—and I knew that I wanted to stay in the role for many years to come.

I have four children, and I had always hoped that one of them would succeed me as CEO, just as I succeeded my father. This is an 85-year-old company that until 2012 had had only two CEOs, and our family's involvement provides a great sense of continuity. Furthermore, our name is on the door, and that signals a level of personal accountability. I worry that too many businesses today have become depersonalized. We all shop at Target, but who is Mr. Target? Especially in the personal services business, in which the brand is guaranteeing a certain kind of experience, I believe that having someone whose name is synonymous with the brand, who stands behind it and cares about you, is a real advantage.

Not all my children were in the running to succeed me. My daughter, Debbie, is the mother of five, and although she worked at Marriott as a teenager, she stayed home with her kids for three decades. Today she works as Marriott's head of government relations, but she's been in that role only a few years. My oldest son, Stephen, has a debilitating disease—he's blind and mostly deaf. My youngest child, David, is just 39, and a phenomenal executive. He currently oversees all our hotels in the eastern United States, from Maine to New Orleans. He has tremendous potential, but at the moment, he is still learning.

That leaves my son John, who is 52. Like all family members who have joined the company (including me), John started at the bottom, as a cook in the kitchen. He went on to work in nearly every part of the business over the next 30 years. He spent most of his adult life preparing to succeed me as CEO. He devoted his heart and soul to learning the business. If I'd followed my own heart, I probably would have chosen John as my successor.

But as time went on, I realized that it wasn't the right fit—not for John, and not for Marriott. As personally disappointing as that was to both of us, I had to make the right decision for the company.

From Litigator to Manager

I first met Arne Sorenson, who eventually succeeded me, in 1993. Marriott was involved in a big lawsuit, and Arne was one of the lawyers who represented us. He was 35. He was obviously very smart and articulate. My first real experience with him came on the day he prepared me for a deposition. The case involved a lot of incredibly complicated financial details, and Arne helped me first to understand and then to explain them so that they sounded simple. I was really impressed that he could explain something so complex in a way that anyone could understand.

After the case wrapped up, Arne and I kept in touch. About three years later he came to work for us. But he wanted to try something new, not law. We brought him in to head our mergers and acquisitions team. I didn't have much direct contact with him in that job, but I did get to know him a bit better. In 1998 our chief financial officer left, and although Arne wasn't an obvious choice for that position, we moved him into it. In that job he presented to the board at every meeting. The directors became very supportive of him, and he performed well.

Beyond his performance, the most important thing Arne did during those years was develop his people skills. At Marriott our culture is focused on people, because treating one another well is essential to creating an atmosphere in which everyone treats guests well, and that's the most fundamental element of our business. Litigation does not have as a primary goal making people feel good. When I think of a litigator, I don't see someone who's putting his arm around people, coaching and counseling and loving them, supporting and promoting them. So that was a concern.

But even though he'd spent years filing lawsuits and conducting cross-examinations, Arne has a broader background, as I came to learn. His father was a Lutheran missionary, and Arne was born in Japan while his parents were doing missionary work. He grew up very active in his church. I believe there were people skills in his DNA, even if they weren't immediately apparent. During his time at Marriott, I watched him become very patient with people. He's often thoughtful, and he's a good listener. He combines that with a firm and commanding leadership style.

I recognized that Arne had great potential, but he didn't have any experience in the operations side of the hotel business. So in

2003, with the support of the board, we made him president of our European operations, which at the time consisted of more than 150 hotels. He remained based at our U.S. headquarters, in Bethesda, Maryland, but he spent one week every month visiting hotels in Europe, and he really began to understand the business from the bottom up. In 2009 Arne was promoted to president and chief operating officer. The job gave him broader exposure to employees away from our headquarters—to general managers and frontline workers. I checked in with some of those people from time to time, and it was obvious that Arne had quickly become well respected and well liked by everyone in the field.

During those years, Arne was an attractive executive for other companies that needed new leadership. I know that some of our lodging competitors tried to hire him for very senior roles. If you believe the conventional wisdom about family businesses—that talented nonfamily executives won't stick around, because they feel they have little chance of being promoted to the most senior jobs, which are reserved for family members—you'd think he would have been pretty excited about those opportunities. But in my experience, fears about retention are overblown: If you treat people well, they'll want to stay. That's especially true at Marriott, where we fill most jobs from inside, which gives people an awareness of the potential to move up. As far as I know, Arne didn't seriously consider leaving. He really liked working in the Marriott culture, and he wanted to stay near Washington, where he'd lived since college and where he and his wife were raising their family.

It Wasn't a Horse Race

As Arne was learning the business, my son John continued to move up through the company. In all, John spent three decades at Marriott. He ran restaurants, ran the food and beverage operations of hotels, and was the general manager of the Crystal City Marriott in Virginia. He held important jobs in finance and brand management. He oversaw all our sales efforts as an executive vice president, and then he became president of North American Lodging, which gave him total responsibility for our largest business. In 2002 he joined our board.

John performed very well in all those roles. He worked extremely hard, and he knew the business from A to Z. I was determined to mentor him and to give him all the tools he would need to succeed. But as he moved from running hotels to working at headquarters, he seemed less happy. He'd enjoyed being in the field; now the pressure built on him to be in the office every day, attending long back-to-back meetings and focusing on administrative work. Every company develops some level of bureaucracy as it grows, and for a senior executive, managing that bureaucracy is an important part of the job. As I watched John adapt to this role, I could see that he wasn't having much fun.

I began to think about Arne as a potential CEO. But that didn't make it a horse race between him and John. I don't believe in horse-race succession—it's disruptive, and the person who loses inevitably ends up leaving the company. I didn't want that. Arne and John didn't act like rivals, and I'm sure that if John had succeeded me, Arne would have given him a chance and stayed on in a senior role. And although succession is ultimately the board's decision, I believe that if I'd pushed, the directors would have been willing to give John a chance too.

But the more I looked at the situation, the more I realized that John is a natural-born entrepreneur. He doesn't have the temperament to run a company the size of Marriott today, with 3,800 properties and 18 brands. He doesn't want to be tied to his desk. Over time we both came to the conclusion that, wonderful as it would have been for me to hand Marriott off to my son, he wasn't the right choice. So in 2005 John became vice chairman of the board and left his executive position at the company. Since then he has founded a medical testing company, which is going to be very successful, and he also serves as the CEO of JWM Family Enterprises, a family trust that he founded, which owns and operates 16 hotels. Although I miss working with him on a daily basis, in some ways our relationship is better now that we've gotten the question of succession out of the way.

By 2011 I was approaching 80. I don't believe that anyone who's 80 should be running anything. Many companies have mandatory retirement at 65, and a lot of CEOs today are retiring in their fifties. Arne had already begun to handle some of the day-to-day jobs typically done by a CEO, and I decided it was time to make the transition official. I didn't find it difficult. Although the announcement, in December of 2011, was treated as big news because Marriotts had been in the top job for nearly 85 years, it wasn't much of a surprise to people who knew the company. Arne was clearly the right choice, and it was time.

Confident and excited as I am to have Arne as our CEO, I continue to believe in the advantages of having a Marriott family member in that job. And if a family company chooses its first nonfamily CEO, that doesn't necessarily mean no family member will serve as its top executive in the future. I look at Ford Motor Company, which family members ran from its founding until 1979, when a series of nonfamily CEOs took over. Then, in the late 1990s, Bill Ford came on as chairman and served as CEO from 2001 to 2006, when he brought in Alan Mulally as the chief executive.

So when I look to the future, I think about the possibility that my youngest son, David, will someday be the CEO. He knows the business, and people love working for him. Arne has a lot of respect for David, and David has a lot of respect for Arne. But Arne is only 54, so it's premature to think too deeply about who might succeed him.

It's been more than a year since Arne officially took over, and I'm quite happy with how the process has turned out. I care too much about Marriott, which has been my life's work, to make a risky choice. And John is far happier in what he's doing now than he ever could have been running a $12 billion company.

My wife and I had dinner with John and his wife recently, and I mentioned that I'd spent the day in a 10-hour management meeting. John just shook his head and laughed. That isn't the life for him.

Originally published in May 2013. R1305A

Honeywell's CEO on How He Avoided Layoffs

by David Cote

David Cote is the chairman and CEO of Honeywell.

The Idea

When the Great Recession hit, many companies "restructured" and laid off thousands of workers. By asking employees to take unpaid leaves instead, Honeywell positioned itself for the recovery.

When I arrived at Honeywell, in 2002, the company had gone through a challenging period. In 1999 it merged with AlliedSignal and shortly afterward closed on the acquisition of a company called Pittway. The three cultures were never integrated, Honeywell had repeatedly missed earnings, and the company had announced cumulative write-offs of $8 billion. Having been in the chemical industry for more than 100 years, it had environmental liabilities that had never been dealt with. Honeywell had gone through three CEOs in four years and had had a lot of turnover at the managerial level as well. Virtually no pipeline of new products existed, because managers had been disinvesting to boost profits.

In my first five years here, we worked to fix many of those problems. We instituted more-conservative bookkeeping and addressed our environmental liabilities. We invested in new products and services, and we expanded abroad. The share of our revenue coming from outside the United States increased from 41% in 2002 to 54% in 2012. We built our management bench strength to the point where 85% to 90% of our top-level vacancies are filled by internal candidates; previously only 50% had been. Most important, we established a "One Honeywell" culture in which we focus on business acumen, listening to the customer, and doing what we say we're going to do. By the end of 2007 we had reestablished our credibility with investors, our share price had more than doubled, and we were significantly outperforming the S&P 500 and our peer group averages.

In September 2008, though, we began to see a shift in our business. Suddenly orders were being canceled, and no new ones were being placed. It soon became obvious that the U.S. was in a recession and that we, as a big industrial company, were going to see our results soften. The only businesses in our portfolio that held up well were defense, aerospace, and energy efficiency. Everything else was down.

Businesses like ours have two primary costs: the material we use to make products, and people. In a recession, material costs (direct costs) drop naturally—you just buy less stuff as your incoming orders decline. You can also work around the edges by seeking opportunities to lower indirect costs such as travel and other non-business-critical expenses. Cutting the costs of people, which in an industrial company usually account for 30% to 40% of total costs, is more difficult. Companies typically react by "restructuring": They cut, say, 10% of the workforce, take a big charge against earnings, and move on. We did do some restructuring in 2008–2009, but I've never been fond of that approach to a recession. So we made sure that any restructuring we agreed to during that period would be permanent—in other words, not solely in response to the recession but, rather, what was best for business efficiency and profitability over the long term—and would have no impact on our ability to outperform in recovery.

As my leadership team began looking at options, we kept coming back to the idea of furloughs: Workers take unpaid leaves but remain employed. The conventional wisdom is that because furloughs spread the pain across the entire workforce, they hurt everyone's morale, loyalty, and retention, so you'd do better to lay off a smaller number, focusing on weak performers. They're also a challenge logistically. To implement them, we needed to comply with individual state laws and also laws in other countries where we do business. The process didn't go perfectly. Looking back, I recognize some clear mistakes we made, and if I had to do it again, I'd do a few things differently. But on the whole, our decision to use furloughs rather than layoffs was a success.

The False Promise of Layoffs

When I arrived at the company, I thought we had too many people. Over the next five years we managed to keep employee numbers flat—even as sales increased at a compound annual growth rate of 10%—and we eliminated some lower-performing employees by doing more-rigorous performance reviews and not filling jobs that were vacated through normal attrition. When the recession hit, our head count still wasn't as low as it could have been, so if we did layoffs, we wouldn't be "cutting into bone." But we opted for furloughs, for several reasons. Most managers underestimate how much disruption layoffs create; they consume everyone in the organization for at least a year. Managers also typically overestimate the savings they will achieve and fail to understand that even bad recessions usually end more quickly than people expect. We wanted to be ready for recovery as soon as it came, whether it was soft or V-shaped, and furloughs were one way of positioning us for any outcome.

To understand that reasoning, look at what really happens when you do layoffs. Each person laid off gets, on average, about six months' worth of severance pay and outplacement services. So in essence, it takes six months to start saving money. Recessions usually last 12 to 18 months, after which demand picks up, so it's pretty common for a company to have to start hiring people about a year or so after its big layoff, undoing the savings it began realizing just six months earlier. Think for a minute about the costs of a layoff the way you'd think about a traditional investment in a plant or equipment. Imagine going to your boss and saying, "I want to spend $10 million on a new factory. It will take us six months to break even on it, and then we'll get to run the factory for six months. But at that point we're going to need to shut it down." You'd never do that— yet when it comes to restructuring costs to lay off employees, everyone seems to think it makes sense.

That's because when faced with a recession, managers find it hard to look ahead toward recovery. If you worry that a recession is going to last forever, you may believe that the savings achieved by a layoff will be permanent. But that's not really how it works. I've been a leader during three recessions, and I've never heard a management team talk about how the choices they make during a downturn will affect performance during the recovery. But in 2008 and 2009 I kept reiterating that point: There will be a recovery, and we need to be prepared for it.

Both layoffs and furloughs can create behavioral issues and costs, and you could argue that furloughs are tougher in some ways. But one fact remains: Layoffs are much more disruptive to an organization in both the short and the long term. Even employees who stay are extremely distracted, because they've lost friends and are worried about their own jobs. To me, that's no way to run a railroad.

The Challenges of Furloughs

We told our businesses to ask every worker to take a series of unpaid weeks off during the first half of 2009. The number of weeks varied by business—the average furlough was three to five weeks, taken in one-week blocks—and business leaders reassessed their situations every few weeks to see if additional furloughs were necessary. This approach presented its own difficulties. Some states have very strict laws about what constitutes work, so we sometimes had to take away people's smartphones and laptops to ensure that they didn't check office e-mail during a furlough. In some foreign countries, government regulations and approvals prevented us from doing furloughs at all. But in most places the program went pretty smoothly, at least in the beginning. During the first week or two we received positive feedback: People felt good about making sacrifices, because they knew they were helping to save jobs—maybe their own, maybe a colleague's. As the furloughs kept going, however, their attitude began to change. Some people complained, "I can't live on this salary." Some concluded that they wouldn't have been among the people laid off, so they started to resent the sacrifice.

We also faced challenges when our top executives—my direct reports—felt that they, too, should be furloughed, as a symbolic gesture. To me this was mistaken solidarity and shortsighted. I told them we couldn't afford to have leaders absent during this period. I also reminded them (and our employees) that as leaders, they received more than half their annual compensation in the form of a bonus, so although employees were losing five weeks' pay, on average, leaders would be losing far more. "Trust me—on a percentage basis, you're going to be severely affected," I told them. The bottom line was that we needed them to stay at work.

By the summer of 2009 people were pretty anxious. They wanted to know how many more weeks of furloughs might be necessary. We still didn't consider layoffs, but we did begin looking at benefits costs, to see if we could find ways to save more money without putting people out of work. I tried to explain to everyone—both employees and my top executives—that we had three constituencies whose interests we needed to balance: customers, investors, and employees. Penalizing customers wasn't an option, and product programs had to go forward. So the pain would have to be divided between investors (in the form of lower returns) and employees (in the form of reduced pay). Finding the right balance was a challenge, but I think we accomplished that.

Prepared for Recovery

The economy stayed soft for most of 2009. During the first nine months of the year, our unit leaders had difficulty making their sales forecasts because demand kept weakening. However, despite lower sales in 2008-2009, the company stayed highly profitable and held its segment margin rates, which is very difficult to do in a recession.

During the fourth quarter of 2009 our sales forecasts stopped going down, and by January of 2010 my team and I were starting to talk about a recovery. As orders began to pick up, it was clear that we were well prepared in comparison with our competitors: Our inventory and delivery times were better, and because we had held on to our people, we found it easier to win new business.

We watched our turnover very carefully as the economy rallied. The rap on furloughs is that they penalize top performers and cause them to leave. But in fact our "regrettable turnover" (the number of employees we'd like to retain who nevertheless choose to leave) decreased significantly. That makes sense to me. Generally speaking, not everything is about money: People aren't mercenary, and they want to be part of something successful that is bigger than themselves. We'd had a good track record since 2002, we had a lot of employees who believed in what we were doing, and we communicated it clearly. People could see that things wouldn't stay awful forever, so they hung in.

Even so, I believe that we made two mistakes in implementing our furlough program. The first was how we let employees know about the sacrifices I would be making. Very early in the recession I decided that I would not take a bonus for 2009. At the time, my annual bonus was around $4 million, so that was significant. When employees asked me in town hall meetings how the recession would affect my compensation, I always gave the politic corporate governance response: "That's not my decision—it's up to the board." Everyone would have been better served if I'd just said that I'd already decided to forgo my bonus.

The second mistake was that when we decided to let individual units determine how many weeks of furlough they needed, we should have made it clear that we didn't want them imposing standardized furloughs across their businesses. For example, some of our units furloughed workers in China, where revenue was still growing. Employees in emerging markets have a lot of opportunities, and ordering furloughs in a fast-growing market created some HR problems and organizational angst that we could have avoided.

Still, I believe that our decision to use furloughs instead of layoffs was the right one and that we managed to get about 90% of the implementation right. I hope we never have to do it again—but if we do, I'll make sure we hit 100%.

Originally published in June 2013. R1306A

BUILDING THE RIGHT CULTURE

"CULTURE" IS ONE OF THE SQUISHIER CONCEPTS OF management. It can be hard to define, even harder to quantify, and it often has nothing to do with what's in the employee handbook or the corporate mission statement. But research shows that culture can often be an important driver of company performance.

In the essays that follow, leaders tell how they worked to create cultures that drive performance—or fix broken cultures that imperiled a business. One describes building (from scratch) a company where a telephone rep feels it's perfectly okay to spend six hours on a single customer call. Another describes what it's like to be hired into a company that's had seven CEOs in the past 10 years. One faced an unusually grim managerial dilemma: What to do when 40 employees were killed on the job at your company last year? Another describes going undercover as a mystery shopper to understand why his company's employees were scoring high in existing performance measures even as sales fell.

Many management tasks are fairly discrete: You choose an employee, set a budget for ad spending, do (or don't do) a deal. Changing a culture can be immensely harder—it's a task for which no spreadsheet analysis will help. That's why one of the best ways to learn how to do it is to hear from others who have tried and succeeded.

Zappos's CEO on Going to Extremes for Customers

Tony Hsieh is the CEO of Zappos and the author of *Delivering Happiness: A Path to Profits, Passion, and Purpose* (Business Plus, 2010), from which portions of this article have been adapted.

The Idea

In search of high-caliber employees to staff its call center, Zappos relocated the entire company from San Francisco to Las Vegas in 2004. Here's why the move made sense.

In the 11 years since Zappos was founded, we've had to make some big decisions. One of the most significant came in early 2004, over lunch at Chevys, a chain Mexican restaurant in San Francisco. We hadn't expected to make a life-changing choice over a plate of fajitas, but when you're part of a fast-growing company, a lot of decisions arise at unlikely moments.

Zappos was then nearly five years old. I'd gotten involved with the company as an investor after LinkExchange, which I'd cofounded, was sold to Microsoft in 1998. At first I thought that selling shoes online sounded like a poster child for bad internet ideas. But the founder of Zappos, Nick Swinmurn, explained that shoes were a $40 billion market in the U.S. and that 5%

of them were already sold by mail order. What had started as just one of several dozen angel investments ended up as a job: By 2000 I had joined Zappos full-time. The company had survived the dot-com crash, and our gross merchandise sales were growing—up from zero in 1999 to $70 million in 2003. But for most of those years we had been short of cash and struggling to cope with growth.

In early 2004 our biggest problem was customer service—specifically, finding the right employees to staff our call center. A lot of people may think it's strange that an internet company would be so focused on the telephone, when only about 5% of our sales happen by phone. But we've found that on average, our customers telephone us at least once at some point, and if we handle the call well, we have an opportunity to create an emotional impact and a lasting memory. We receive thousands of phone calls and e-mails every day, and we view each one as an opportunity to build the Zappos brand into being about the very best customer service. Our philosophy has been that most of the money we might ordinarily have spent on advertising should be invested in customer service, so that our customers will do the marketing for us through word of mouth.

But that requires the right staff members—and our inability to find enough dedicated, high-caliber customer service reps near our San Francisco headquarters was turning into a huge problem. It's hard to find people in the Bay Area who want to make customer service a career. Culturally, it's not part of the Silicon Valley mentality. The high cost of living also plays a role: In San Francisco you can't afford to buy a home on a call center rep's salary. So most of the people working the phones for Zappos were temps, and they weren't always providing the *wow* experience our customers deserved.

How About Outsourcing?

By late 2003 we'd started looking at different options for expanding our call center. We initially considered outsourcing it to India or the Philippines, and we met with a few outsourcing companies. We got the whole sales pitch and listened in on sample calls. You could tell on the ones from India that the people talking were from another country. Accent aside, they just didn't understand the nuances of American culture. How would they be able to help a customer who asked, say, for shoes like the ones Julia Roberts wears in *Eat, Pray, Love?*

We were reluctant to outsource the call center, because we'd had bad experiences with outsourcing in the past. In fact, one of the big lessons of Zappos's first few years was that it never makes sense to outsource your core competency, especially if your aim is to be maniacal about customer service. In its earliest days, Zappos fulfilled orders with drop shipments: We didn't carry any inventory; instead we relied on shoe manufacturers to ship products directly to our customers.

That system never worked very well. We didn't have 100% accurate information about our vendors' inventory, and because their warehouses were all over the country, delivery times weren't predictable. So we stopped drop shipping and began buying inventory from manufacturers, but we outsourced the warehousing and shipping to a separate company in Kentucky. That didn't work well either. As an e-commerce company, we should have considered warehousing to be our core competency from the beginning. Trusting that a third party would care about our customers as much as we did was one of our biggest mistakes. If we hadn't reacted quickly by starting our own warehouse operation, that mistake would eventually have destroyed Zappos.

So we agreed that Zappos employees would staff the call center. But finding them in San Francisco remained a problem. One option would have been to set up a satellite call center, staffed by Zappos employees who were operating someplace far away. As we thought more about it, though, we realized that it wouldn't be matching our actions to our words. If we were serious about building our brand around being the best in customer service, customer service had to be the whole company, not just a single department.

We decided we needed to move our entire headquarters from San Francisco to wherever we built the call center, whose staff we had recently named the Customer Loyalty Team, or CLT. We talked about lower-cost cities where housing would be cheaper and there would be a bigger supply of workers who might think being a phone rep for a fun, growing company was a viable career choice. We did a lot of research into real estate, wages, and the cost of living in various cities, and we narrowed down the list of possibilities to Phoenix, Louisville, Portland (Oregon), Des Moines, Sioux City, and Las Vegas.

Over lunch that afternoon at Chevys, we talked through our choices. Could the company afford the huge costs associated with moving its staff? How many of our employees would be willing to relocate to a new state? Would the potential upside be worth the disruption to our young company? What would be the best decision for our culture?

You Can Call Us Anytime

If we moved, it would be only the latest effort in Zappos's drive to achieve world-class customer service—a goal that has led us to run our business in a way that sets us apart from many of our competitors. In the United States we offer free shipping both ways to make transactions risk free and as easy as possible for our customers. A lot of them will order five different pairs of shoes and then send back the ones that don't fit or that they simply don't like—free of charge. The additional shipping costs are considerable for us, but we view them as a marketing expense. We also offer a 365-day returns policy for people who have trouble making up their minds. (Originally our returns policy was only 30 days, but we kept increasing it at the urging of our customers, who became more loyal as we lengthened the returns period.) Our returns run high—more than a third of our gross revenue—but we've learned that customers will buy more and be happier in the long run if we can remove most of the risk from shopping at Zappos.

Our customer service orientation is also apparent on our website. On many websites the contact information is buried at least five links deep, because the company doesn't really want to hear from you. And when you find it, it's a form or an e-mail address. We take the exact opposite approach. We put our phone number (it's 800-927-7671, in case you'd like to call) at the top of every single page of our website, because we actually want to talk to our customers. And we staff our call center 24/7.

Looking at every one of our interactions through a branding lens instead of an expense-minimizing lens means that we run our call center very differently from others. For instance, most call centers measure their employees' performance on the basis of what's known in the industry as "average handle time," which focuses on how many phone calls each rep can take in a day. This translates into reps' worrying about how quickly they can get a customer off the phone—which in our eyes is not delivering great customer service. Most call centers also have scripts and force their reps to try upselling to generate additional revenue.

At Zappos we don't hold reps accountable for call times. (Our longest phone call, from a customer who wanted the rep's help while she looked at what seemed like thousands of pairs of shoes, lasted almost six hours.) And we don't upsell—a practice that usually just annoys customers. We care only whether the rep goes above and beyond for every customer. We don't have scripts, because we want our reps to let their true personalities shine during every phone call, so that they can develop a personal emotional connection with each customer, which we refer to as a PEC.

When one of our reps found out that because of a death in the family, a loyal customer had forgotten to mail back a pair of shoes she'd planned to return, the rep sent her flowers; now she's a customer for life. Once, at a shoe sales conference in Santa Monica, after a long night of barhopping, a small group of us headed up to someone's hotel room to order food, but room service had closed at 11. When we couldn't find a place that delivered food after midnight, a couple of us cajoled a woman (who didn't work at Zappos) into calling a Zappos rep for help while we listened in on speakerphone. The rep was a bit confused by the request, but she quickly recovered and put us on hold. Two minutes later she told us the five closest places in Santa Monica that were still open and delivering pizzas.

There's a lot of buzz these days about social media and "integration marketing." Our belief is that as unsexy and low-tech as it may sound, the telephone is one of the best branding devices out there. You have the customer's undivided attention for five or 10 minutes, and if you get the interaction right, the customer remembers the experience for a very long time and tells his or her friends about it.

Usually when marketing departments do their ROI calculations, they assume that the lifetime value of a customer is fixed. We view it as something that can grow if we create positive emotional associations with our brand. To that end, most of our efforts at customer service actually happen after we've already made a sale. For example, for most of our loyal repeat customers, we do surprise upgrades to overnight shipping, even when they have chosen the free ground-shipping option. Our warehouse is open around the clock every day, which is costly. The most efficient way to run a warehouse is to let the orders pile up, so that when a worker walks around picking up orders, the picking density is higher and the worker has less distance to walk. But we're not trying to maximize picking efficiency. We're trying to maximize the customer experience, which in e-commerce involves getting orders out to customers as quickly as possible.

What We're Learning from Amazon

In the debate about moving our headquarters, we settled on Las Vegas. We didn't consult with our board or our investors— we just told them we were doing it. (It may have helped that Nevada has no income tax; some of them probably figured we were moving for tax reasons.) Las Vegas wasn't the cheapest option we considered, but we thought it would make our current employees the happiest. It also made sense for other reasons. It's an all-night city where employees are used to working at any hour, which would help us find people willing to take the overnight shift at our call center. And because so much of the city's economy is focused on hospitality, Las Vegas has a customer service mentality—employees there are used to thinking of people as guests.

Two days after the lunch at Chevys, we held a company meeting and announced that we were relocating to Las Vegas. We would pay the moving costs for any employees who came along, and we'd help them find new homes. When the announcement was made, everyone in the conference room was in a state of shock. We told everyone to take a week before making a decision one way or the other.

We had about 90 employees in San Francisco at the time, and I had guessed that maybe half of them would decide to uproot and move with the company. A week later I was pleasantly surprised to learn that 70 were willing to give Vegas a shot. In their minds it was all about being adventurous and open-minded. The move cost about $500,000 altogether, which was a significant amount of money for us at the time. It also cost us some good people: Our star software developer loved San Francisco and decided not to leave. Some of those who did move were taking a real leap of faith. One employee had been with Zappos only 10 days (and married for only 15) when we announced we were moving. He came with us—and, luckily for him, so did his wife.

Although our timing could have been better (we moved at the height of the real estate boom in Las Vegas, and subsequently property values dropped across the board), the move paid off in several ways. When we arrived in Vegas, we had no one to lean on except one another. Our company culture, which had always been strong, became even more so. As we grew, we made sure we hired only people we would enjoy hanging out with after hours. As it happened, many of our best ideas arose while we were having drinks at a local bar.

By 2008 we had hit $1 billion in gross merchandise sales. But the economic slowdown made for a crazy year. Even though we were still growing, we realized that our expenses were too high for the revenue we were bringing in. We had planned on faster growth, and discovered that we'd overhired. Late in the year we decided to lay off 8% of the staff. It was one of the hardest decisions we've ever had to make.

In 2009 we agreed to sell ownership of Zappos to Amazon. Amazon has always described its goal as being the most customer-centric company in the world, but its approach is more high-tech than ours, with a focus on using web design and functionality to make the shopping experience so easy for customers that they don't have to call the company. Ours is more high-touch—we try to make a personal connection. Since the sale, we've learned from Amazon's technology: We've started to track some metrics Amazon tracks, and we're learning how it thinks about warehouse operations. We've also expanded far beyond shoes. Now Zappos sells a wide assortment of clothing, housewares, cosmetics, and other items.

Today we have more than 1,800 employees. We offer starting pay for call center reps of around $11 an hour—typical for reps in Vegas—but because Zappos is known as a great place to work (we made *Fortune*'s "Best Companies to Work For" list for the second time in a row this year), we have no shortage of applicants. Last year 25,000 people applied for jobs with us, and we hired only 250. Someone told me that statistically it's harder to get a job at Zappos than it is to get admitted to Harvard, which says a lot about the strength of the culture we've created here.

Looking back, I attribute most of our growth over the past few years to the fact that we invested time, money, and resources in three key areas: customer service, company culture, and employee training and development. The move to Las Vegas helped us make progress in each of the three. If you'd like to hear what our telephone reps sound like, just pick up the phone and give us a call.

Originally published in July–August 2010. R1007A

HSN's CEO on Fixing the Shopping Network's Culture

by Mindy Grossman

Mindy Grossman is the CEO of HSN, Inc.

The Idea

When Mindy Grossman became HSN's eighth CEO in 10 years, she encountered dirty offices and downtrodden employees. Her solution? White paint, new chairs, and a strategy to reinvent the brand and re-engage the workforce.

In 2006 I'd been working at Nike for six years, and I loved it. I worshipped that brand. Nike's CEO, Phil Knight, was an inspiration. But I'd been commuting between my family in New York and my job in Portland, Oregon. I was traveling outside the U.S. 25% of the time. I was in my late forties, I wanted to be a CEO someday, and Nike had recently appointed a 50-year-old CEO and a 49-year-old president. They deserved the jobs, but I was left without the best succession opportunities. I'd had a lot of recruiters come at me, but nothing felt compelling. Eventually I gave the recruiters a laundry list of what I was looking for: I wanted to run a direct-to-consumer brand. I wanted a company that was poised to take advantage of technological changes and the shifting ways in which people shop.

I wanted an entrepreneurial atmosphere but not a start-up. I wanted a company that I could transform and grow. And they said, "Oh, really? Is that all?"

Six months later I got a call from a recruiter who was looking for a CEO of IAC Retailing. I said, "That's great. What the hell is it?" It wasn't even on my radar. It turned out to be Barry Diller's retail portfolio, which was composed of Home Shopping Network (the core of the business), a shopping channel in Germany, a small and struggling auction business in the UK, and a portfolio of e-commerce catalog brands called Cornerstone. I asked the recruiter to give me a week to study the business. I'd never watched a home shopping channel, and if I was going to have lunch with Barry Diller, I wanted to know what I was talking about.

So I started channel surfing. HSN wasn't easy to watch. It was very hard-sell. The aesthetics were dated. The products weren't aspirational and didn't seem very relevant. I could see from the numbers that HSN wasn't growing and was a very distant number two to QVC. At the time, I was an aficionado of Food Network and HGTV. So I'd flip back and forth between HSN, QVC, HGTV, and Food Network, trying to get ideas. The only thing I liked on HSN was Wolfgang Puck selling cookware. He was funny and engaging. He gave you recipes. Even if you didn't want to buy anything, you could watch Wolfgang for an hour. And I had this "aha" moment: I realized that HSN really needed to become more of a lifestyle network that would inspire people through products.

So I had lunch with Barry, and I gave him that pitch. I had no television experience, no direct-to-consumer experience, and no experience in most of the product categories HSN sold. But I got the job. When the announcement was made, my friends couldn't believe it. They thought I'd lost my mind. I was moving from one of the world's most aspirational brands to a company many people associated with selling ThighMasters. But if I was ever going to take a big risk, this was the time to do it.

In retrospect, I didn't really know what I was getting myself into. HSN had had seven CEOs in the previous 10 years. I didn't realize how troubled the culture was or how great the scope of the retention problems. IAC had recently acquired the Cornerstone brands, and the integration with HSN was an unmitigated disaster. I'd never been to HSN's headquarters, which was in Saint Petersburg, Florida. If I'd visited there before I accepted the job, I might not have taken it. The place was dirty, the people seemed downtrodden, and I had the sense that the organization was frozen in time. When a company goes through so many CEOs that quickly, all people are doing is waiting for the next one to come in.

Finding the Right Talent

Before I went down to Florida, the head of HR called and asked if I had a first-day agenda in mind. "What do other employees do on their first day?" I asked. She said that ordinarily they went to new-employee orientation. "Then I'll go to new-employee orientation," I said. "Are you kidding?" she replied. I wasn't.

The next morning I flew down, got my little ID badge, and went into this big room. They made us go around the circle and introduce ourselves. First there was a merchandising assistant, then a TV production person, then a quality-control person. "Hi," I said. "I'm Mindy. I'm the new CEO." Can you imagine? But it ended up being the best way to spend a first day. Like every other new employee, I was shown the production set. I listened to customers in the call center. The next day I held a town hall meeting. Going through orientation had introduced me to every part of the company very quickly, and it gave me some credibility.

As I grew to understand the business, it became clear that it was fundamentally broken. To fix it, I needed to dramatically alter the company's culture. I also needed to understand and reposition the brand and then devise a product strategy that made sense. Not only did I have to do all those things at the same time, but we had to change the tires while the car was running. This was a 24/7 TV operation, so we couldn't close the store while we prepared to relaunch.

In order to focus on HSN, I had to eliminate some of the distractions. We closed the failing UK auction business. We sold the German shopping channel. We had a small U.S.-based shopping channel on DIRECTV that was very down-market, selling mostly clearance merchandise, so we closed it. I put another executive in charge of the Cornerstone brands.

The next step was to assemble the right talent around me. Too many people who come in as CEO of a poorly performing company assume that none of the incumbent executives are worth retaining. That's not always the case. Sometimes the talent is there but it's not being led well. I was fortunate: Some of HSN's executives were great. The CFO had kept the company together through sheer force of will because she really believed in it, and I knew she'd make a great partner. The head of operations was terrific. The people in charge of HR and cable and satellite operations were solid. But other groups were uninspired. Companies lose some of their best employees when people are beaten down; then they overpromote junior people because they can't persuade outsiders to sign on.

That had happened at HSN. We had weak teams in television, marketing, merchandising, programming—the lifeblood of the business. I knew I needed people with television experience who understood both storytelling and women, our primary customers. I needed somebody on the digital side who understood that HSN couldn't be just a television shopping channel anymore—it had to be a shopping destination across multiple screens. So I set out to find the right people. I found one working for IAC in the UK, where his creative talents weren't being utilized. Another was running a little business we owned called Gifts.com, and I put him in charge of digital. To head up programming, I hired someone who'd worked at Lifetime and VH1—he understood women and he understood storytelling.

I knew we needed to increase engagement for all employees below the executive level as well. I wanted people to be proud of where they worked. I hired a consultant to conduct employee engagement surveys; suffice it to say the scores were subpar. I decided that within the next year I wanted to raise them by five points. The consultant said that wasn't realistic, but I was committed. I did a lot of town hall meetings at all our locations, and I started to divide the employees into three groups: the "evangelists," who knew that HSN could be a great business and just needed the right leadership to make it happen; the "blockers," who were perpetually negative—the only solution was to get rid of them; and the "wait-and-sees," who were in the middle and would either jump on the bandwagon or not. I had to make some quick decisions: embrace the evangelists, get rid of the blockers, and let the rest of the people know they had a finite amount of time to get on the wagon.

Cleaning House

I also tried to change the physical environment to help drive the cultural change. I didn't have much money for renovations, but I was determined to do something. One of the first weeks I was there, I brought in Dumpsters and told everyone to take a day off from their regular work and just throw things away—we had all this furniture and stuff that was broken or dirty or just clutter. Then I had all the buildings pressure-washed and painted white. I'd been living in New York City when Rudy Giuliani became mayor, and the first thing he'd done was get rid of all the graffiti. This was my way of getting rid of graffiti.

Next I looked around and realized that we had 40 different kinds of office chairs, many of which were in disrepair. So I bought several thousand Herman Miller Aeron chairs. Office chairs are an easy way to let people know you care about them. I must have received 100 e-mails about the chairs the first day they were there. People really want a nice environment to work in, and things like that make a difference. When the consultants surveyed employees a year later, our engagement scores had increased to 73—almost 10 points higher than the industry norm and higher than the consulting firm had ever imagined possible.

While all this was going on, I was also working to reposition HSN as a brand. I brought in brand strategy consultants to learn about consumer perceptions of the network. I started at HSN in May of 2006, and by October we had rolled out a new brand image, a new tagline, a new vision statement, a new customer manifesto, and new advertising. I made it clear that I had zero intention of chasing QVC and that we were going to set a completely new path for HSN—one that would create a new lifestyle experience for consumers. When I look back, I still don't know how we got it all done so quickly.

Once we had decided on a new positioning for the brand, we had to adjust the product mix. In my first year we stopped selling $150 million worth of brands that didn't fit the new strategy. At the same time, we worked hard to lure new brands and new personalities to sell products. I went to the Consumer Electronics Show, which I'd never attended before, and personally worked to get higher-end brands to sell on HSN. I signed a two-year deal with Sephora in the beauty category. We expanded our culinary lineup by adding Emeril Lagasse and Todd English.

In the spring of 2007 we put on a two-hour fashion show that was organized by Stefani Greenfield, who'd worked at DKNY and Esprit before founding Scoop, a hot chain of fashion boutiques. Stefani persuaded Theory, J.Crew, Stuart Weitzman, and other brands to participate. Veteran HSN employees thought this was crazy, because they thought it was too high-end. "We're never going to be able to sell this stuff," they said. I said, "You don't understand. We are never going to ignite our fashion business if we don't have fashion." The shows turned out to be very successful, and Stefani now runs Curations, which sells exclusively through HSN.

By the middle of 2007 we had relaunched the channel, relaunched the website, embarked on a complete campus renovation, and redesigned everything, down to the fonts on our business cards. By then it was clear that we were starting to turn the business around.

Then, one Sunday night in November, my husband answered the phone and said it was Barry Diller. I thought, "Barry is calling me at home on a Sunday night? Uh-oh." Barry said he'd decided to split IAC into five separate companies. Four of them—including HSN—would be spun off and become publicly traded. "You're going to make a spectacular public-company CEO," he said.

I spent the next few months raising financing just as the markets were imploding. Picture me with my CFO, walking into all these banks and telling them we're in turnaround mode and trying to sell them on the concept of home shopping. They thought I was crazy, too. We went public in August of 2008, a few weeks before Lehman Brothers collapsed. By December our stock was down to $1.43 a share, and our market cap was lower than our receivables balance. My toughest job was keeping the organization focused and motivated.

We've grown every year since then—at this writing, our stock price is about $35, and our market cap is close to $2 billion—and I believe we've proved the fundamental resilience of our business model. HSN is one of the few networks that can be a complete consumer destination—for shopping, for sharing, for gaming, for information, for entertainment. I want to be where our shoppers go as soon as they wake up—whatever they're looking for.

Overall, the company has been performing well. We've exceeded expectations. We've gained tremendous credibility as a business for the future—not just a mature business with no growth opportunities and no excitement, which is what HSN was when I arrived. Five years ago people never would have dreamed that we'd have the greatest chefs in the world on HSN, or that we'd have Jennifer Lopez or Queen Latifah or Mariah Carey or Iman on our channel, or that we'd be in the front row at Fashion Week. If the turnaround hadn't worked, I'd have been another in the long line of CEOs who failed at HSN—and I'd probably be remembered as the one who bought all those fancy office chairs. But more than five years later our culture is fixed, and I know there's much more growth potential to be unlocked here. Every day I'm making changes to try to achieve that.

Originally published in December 2011. R1112A

Anglo American's CEO on Getting Serious About Safety

by Cynthia Carroll

Cynthia Carroll is the CEO of Anglo American plc.

The Idea

Mining involves risk, and some executives believe fatalities are inevitable. But after nearly 200 on-the-job deaths in the five years prior to her arrival, Carroll decided to take a public stand to create safer working conditions.

When I became the CEO of Anglo American, in 2007, I encountered plenty of challenges. For decades the company had been made up of unrelated businesses, and had been organized and managed accordingly. I believed it needed a clear vision, guiding values, an overarching strategy, common business objectives, and, above all, a safe working environment for its employees. In my experience, a strong safety performance translates into a strong business performance.

Over the previous five years Anglo American had suffered nearly 200 fatalities. Some company veterans insisted that deaths were inevitable at such a large mining company, because ours is simply a dangerous business. I fundamentally rejected that assumption. My priority was to see how things worked with my own eyes. So I began a tour of our operations, visiting mines in Australia, Chile, Colombia, Venezuela, and South Africa.

There were safety concerns at all the operations I visited, but one of them had a particularly poor track record: our platinum business in South Africa, which at the time employed more than 86,000 people. Conditions there are extremely challenging. Various cultural groups have to work closely together with no common language. The literacy rate is very low, and the work takes place several hundred meters underground, where it's dark, hot, wet, and steep. In some areas the miners have only enough room to kneel.

When I visited the operations, my conversations with local managers were frustrating. Safety was improving, they assured me, but it would never be perfect. My goal of zero harm was simply not achievable. The head of our platinum operations at the time insisted repeatedly, "Cynthia, you just have to understand..." As I talked to people and examined the facilities, I wondered how much authority someone who is underground for hours on end, with a shift supervisor right behind him, really has. I questioned whether a line worker had the power to put up his hand and say, "I'm not going to do this, because it is unsafe."

I met with shift supervisors and mine managers—the people we trusted to keep everyone safe. I wondered if they were the right people for that responsibility. Could they engage with the entire workforce? Could they motivate the miners and make them receptive to a different way of thinking? I was bothered by what I'd seen, and I pondered these questions during the helicopter ride back to our Johannesburg offices.

I had just landed when the CEO of our platinum division pulled me aside. "I have some bad news," he said quietly. "We've had another fatality." Just hours after I'd visited the mine, one of our workers had been killed after he slipped onto a conveyor belt.

That was it. I refused to accept that fatalities were an inevitable by-product of mining. There was only one way to send that message throughout the company. We would shut down the world's largest platinum mine, at Rustenburg, which employed more than 30,000 people. And we would do so immediately.

The CEO of the platinum division probably thought that my directive was meant mostly as a public relations gesture—that after a perfunctory safety check we would resume production as swiftly as possible. That was not what I had in mind. I wanted an indefinite shutdown, during which we would fundamentally overhaul our safety procedures with a top-to-bottom audit of our processes and infrastructure followed by a complete retraining of the Rustenburg workforce.

No such shutdown had ever before been done in the mining industry, and the costs would be enormous. This was not a popular decision. In fact, the platinum CEO left the company a few weeks later.

A Traditional World

When the Anglo American board hired me, the directors were looking for a change agent. I doubt that most employees knew what kind of change agent I would turn out to be. In its nearly 100 years of operation, the company had been led by South Africans—all men—and steeped in traditional views of how to run a mining business. As neither a South African nor a man, and with a history of managing capital-intensive multinational industrial companies, I was brought in to provide a fresh perspective and a different kind of leadership. I had my work cut out for me.

Part of the challenge was scale and reach. Anglo American is the world's most diversified mining company, by both geography and commodity mix, with 90% of our operations in developing countries. We are the largest producer of platinum (about 40% of world output) and of diamonds (through De Beers). We are also a major producer of copper, nickel, iron ore, and coal for both steelmaking and power generation. We operate on six continents with 150,000 permanent and contract employees.

Part of the challenge related to tradition. Anglo American was born in South Africa in 1917, and although it had grown into an international company over time, it retained a culture of strict hierarchy and a rigid, top-down management style. This was a very traditional world, and I was in an unprecedented position to influence change. For just one example, until very recently women hadn't been allowed to visit underground at mines in South Africa, let alone work there.

Most important, however, was the question of the industry's role in the 21st century. The commodities we produce are vital to economic growth and the technological revolution, and we must keep these precious resources flowing. But we must also contribute to society as a whole. The communities in which we operate should benefit from our presence on a sustainable basis, and, above all, our workers must be safe. To realize these goals requires a strong and transparent collaboration between the mining industry and its stakeholders: governments, unions, communities, shareholders, customers, suppliers, and NGOs. That is not an approach the industry has been known to take in the past. Standards within it still differ greatly, and mining companies have traditionally operated in something of a vacuum, their reputations affected by numerous legacy behaviors.

Inviting Public Scrutiny

The decision to shut down Rustenburg and stop production for seven weeks was a turning point for Anglo American, and over time it has led to an overhaul of safety practices in mines across the world. In the short term, the move prompted complaints and resistance within the company. Many employees were not prepared to change, and almost all the managers at that mine were replaced. Ultimately that was a good thing, because ensuring that we had the right people in crucial roles was an important step in creating safer working conditions.

After we scrupulously examined all our safety procedures and issues, we had to retrain more than 30,000 workers before any of them could produce a single ounce of platinum at Rustenburg again. Small-group meetings and face-to-face communication between executives and individual employees were used to identify what had gone wrong in the past and to instill personal and group responsibility. Leaders also engaged with the entire workforce at once, in sports stadiums.

Within weeks of getting Rustenburg back on line, I reached out to both the National Union of Mineworkers and the minister of South Africa's Department of Mineral Resources. My goal went beyond changing practices at a single mine: Anglo American's safety record wasn't out of line with those of its competitors, and I was horrified by safety statistics for the industry as a whole. The minister was surprised by my overture. Mining companies have historically had combative and mutually suspicious relationships with both host governments and labor unions. Like some of my employees, he questioned the wisdom of taking a public stand on safety.

"Are you sure about this?" the minister asked me. "You're going to be exposing Anglo American to scrutiny, and you'll have to make commitments that you can't turn back on." I believed that the exposure and the commitments would actually be very helpful, because they would put greater pressure on the company—and the industry—to change.

Our partnership with the government and the union was unusual but necessary. Making mines safer would be so complex and have such widespread ramifications that a single organization couldn't do it alone. Even a decision as small as how many hours were appropriate for a safe shift needed agreement from the government, the unions, and the company. If we were really going to change things, we had to collaborate. Our initiative became known as the Tripartite Alliance.

We had an initial public summit to which we invited industry heads and the media. It was an uncomfortable experience: Facts and figures relating to the industry's death toll were discussed openly, and everyone had to face a harsh reality. But once those facts were on the table, we were ready to move. We formed a working group that included industry executives, government officials, and labor leaders. The ground rules were simple: All three parties would be considered absolutely equal in this alliance—in determining the agenda and how the work was to be carried out. The working group would begin by studying global best practices in safety. We ultimately toured mines on four continents, and we also visited industrial operations outside the mining sector.

Changing Body Language

Over the next six months members of the group began opening up in a way they hadn't previously. At one point a well-known businessperson in South Africa, who had become involved in our discussions, told me, "We're used to putting on boxing gloves with Anglo American, and here you just come in and tell us what you think, and expect the same from us. That's something completely new." I could tell we were making progress from how our body language evolved. When we first began meeting, we would sit on far sides of the room or the table. By the spring of 2008 we were much more relaxed. We had formed close, trusting relationships and become partners and friends.

Eventually the group came back with key recommendations, including establishing universal safety standards. But even after we'd agreed on what was safe, each of the stakeholders would need the capacity to manage safety. Because the people who would be implementing the safety program would do a far better job if they were involved in setting the standards, we included lower-level managers, union leaders, and government representatives in the planning as well. Anglo American committed to training for all employees. The company invited senior leaders from both the union and the Department of Mineral Resources to attend our executive risk management and safety program (to date 3,000 leaders have been through it), and since 2008 we have trained 12,000 line managers, supervisors, and frontline employees.

These changes put pressure on the entire industry, and some competitors were unenthusiastic, to say the least. I got calls from other CEOs who said, "It's going to take us more time. We're going to have to spend more money. You're creating obstacles and challenges for all of us." But I believe it was the only way forward for the mining industry.

MINING HAS never been more complex than it is now. Standards for environmental risk and safety differ around the world. Labor issues, increasingly assertive host governments, and stronger campaigning in local communities play a role. It's our job to challenge ideas that are wrong or unreasonable—such as the notion that mining is just inherently dangerous. Our focused approach on safety has brought significant benefits to our overall performance at Anglo American. I have always said that safety is a leading indicator of wider performance—if you get

safety right, then other things will follow, from stronger relationships with unions and governments to greater productivity
and efficiency across the board.

Our work has made a huge difference. In partnership with
the Department of Mineral Resources and major labor unions,
Anglo American has improved its safety record considerably.
In 2011, 17 employees lost their lives at Anglo American operations, compared with 44 in 2006, the year before my arrival—
a reduction of 62%. Time lost owing to injuries is down by
more than 50%. This has had a positive effect throughout the
industry: Fatalities in South African mining as a whole have
declined by about 25%.

That's not to say our work is done. We recently held a companywide remembrance of workers who had been injured or
killed. It breaks my heart every time I get a phone call saying
that there's been a fatality. This is a continuing struggle, and we
can't afford to lose focus.

We're not perfect. But I'm determined to reach my goal of
zero harm.

Originally published in June 2012. R1206A

HCL's CEO Explains How He Persuaded His Team to Leap into the Future

by Vineet Nayar

Vineet Nayar is the CEO of HCL Technologies and the author of *Employees First, Customers Second: Turning Conventional Management Upside Down* (Harvard Business Press, 2010).

The Idea

To transform HCL, CEO Vineet Nayar got employees to acknowledge the crisis, pioneered a unique "employees first" culture, kindled people's passions—and danced.

Imagine waking up to find yourself perched on a window ledge outside your corner office. The building is on fire. The windows won't open. The ledge narrows to nothing on both sides. You could stay put and pray that someone will rescue you. Or you could leap—you hope—to safety.

That's the metaphorical choice I faced five years ago, when I was appointed president of the Delhi-based IT services provider HCL Technologies. Although the company's revenues were growing by about 30% a year, it was losing market share and mindshare. Our competitors were growing at the rate of 40% or 50% a year, and the

IT services industry was changing rapidly. Customers didn't want to work with an undifferentiated service provider that offered discrete services; they wanted long-term partners that would provide end-to-end services. Could HCL become such a company?

History will tell you it did. By 2009 HCL had changed its business model, nearly tripled its annual revenues, doubled its market capitalization, been ranked India's best employer by Hewitt—and pioneered a unique management culture that I call Employees First, Customers Second (EFCS).

How did I do this? I didn't. One hundred senior managers and 55,000 employees, the people of our company, accomplished the transformation. How did I persuade them to do it? I spoke the truth as I saw it, offered ideas, told stories, asked questions, and even danced. Most important, I made the leap myself.

Acknowledge Point A and Identify Point B

I realized that no one would jump into the future until the organization acknowledged that we needed to do so. So I spent the first few weeks of my tenure visiting HCL's offices around the world, meeting senior managers in small groups and at larger gatherings. I discussed the company's current situation—Point A, I call it. Some people sensed no danger; they could see only our track record, the booming IT services market, and our past successes. Many had no opinion; they wanted to wait and see. A few believed that the situation was dire and HCL should have changed a long time ago.

These meetings had a disruptive effect—not because I'm a great orator who oozes charisma but because I presented facts and articulated opinions that had not been aired before. Although we didn't give a name to these conversations then, we codified the process and came to call it Mirror Mirror. I had held up a mirror to the company in a new way, forcing people to see the reality of our situation. Gradually, it became impossible for anyone to argue that everything was fine. Now, whenever the environment changes, we use the Mirror Mirror exercise to rethink HCL's position.

I also met many customers during my travels, and it was from them that a potential Point B—where we should land—began to take shape. What struck me was that customers didn't talk much about our products, services, or technologies; they spoke mostly about HCL's employees. The value the company offered lay in the interface between customers and frontline employees—that was our value zone.

However, we weren't organized as if that was the case. HCL was a traditional pyramid, in which frontline people were accountable to a hierarchy of managers. The hierarchy usually made it more difficult for employees to add value. I began to wonder if we could turn the organization upside down, so that senior management—the heads of enabling functions such as human resources and finance and even the CEO—could become accountable to employees. This concept gradually grew in clarity and strength, and blossomed into the EFCS approach that underlies almost everything HCL now does.

Collaboratively Develop a Strategy

I had told everyone that we would set a strategy collaboratively—and I meant it. In July 2005 I convened a meeting of our top 100 managers and proposed that HCL transform itself from an IT services vendor into an end-to-end global IT services partner that could compete against the likes of IBM, Accenture, and EDS.

I didn't care if we adopted this exact strategy; I reasoned that if these smart and experienced people rejected my proposal, they would come up with another approach as good as or better than mine. I asked the managers for their views in order to identify the "Yes, buts...." These are the caveats and concerns that arise when any initiative—but especially one that entails change—is proposed. "Yes, buts..." are at the very heart of collaboration; if you don't respond to them, you'll never get the people who have questions or doubts to play with the team.

The "Yes, buts..." took three forms. Some managers feared that by taking on the major global players, we would forsake the position we had built over the past decade and would lose everything. Others raised issues I hadn't thought of, asking, for example, "The IT analysts favor the established players—how can we get them to recommend HCL?" A third group supported the proposed strategy and was exasperated with the status quo. These managers wanted us to act boldly, and often to ignore others' objections.

I said very little during these discussions. I did not want to provide answers, offer justifications, or make new suggestions; I wanted alignment to emerge on its own. Three days of debate later, we agreed to adopt the strategy I had proposed. Everyone was on board—at least in theory.

Bridge the Gulf

During this period I also held informal meetings with frontline employees, engaging them in discussions about the kind of company they wanted to work for and how they saw their jobs. These meetings became more formal in 2006, with a series of companywide meetings we called Directions. (We still hold them.) They involve thousands of employees and take place in large venues around the world. I usually make some provocative remarks about the company's future and then open up the meeting to questions, conversation, and discussion.

But I felt that at the very first meeting it would be counter productive if I marched up to the podium in a suit and tie and expected people to open up to me. Only the boldest or the craziest would speak.

I had to remove the gulf between employees and executives. So I walked to the center of the stage and looked out at some 4,000 faces. I said nothing. A popular Bollywood number suddenly blared from the speakers. I started to dance. I wiggled. I danced into the aisles. I pulled people up from their chairs and danced with them. HCLites, as we call ourselves, still chuckle about my performance.

After a few minutes the music ended, and I went back onstage to make my remarks. Those words sounded very different coming from a sweaty man who had just proved in public that he couldn't dance than they would have coming from the emperor at the podium. Two hours of purposeful and animated discussions followed.

I went on to repeat that performance about 25 times that year, dancing my way around the world. I don't know whether people thought my dancing showed I was crazy enough to believe in EFCS or whether it disarmed them enough to accept change. I do know that by the year's end the change initiative had gathered momentum.

Use BODs for Change

Transformation requires action, not just words, but I don't believe in large-scale technology initiatives or massive reorganizations. We triggered change at HCL through small-scale catalysts that I call blue ocean droplets (BODs)—a phrase borrowed from the ideas in W. Chan Kim and Renée Mauborgne's *Blue Ocean Strategy*. I used four BODs at HCL:

Sharing financial data

At the time, employees had access to the financial information that pertained to their projects but didn't know how either their business unit or the organization was doing. Nor could they compare the performance of their team to that of others. We decided to share financial data extensively, within and across groups. The goal was to help people better see where we stood and to increase trust by greatly increasing transparency. Once people saw that I was willing to show them how the company was performing, they began to shed their mistrust of top management.

The smart service desk

I set up an online system that allows anyone in the organization to lodge a complaint or make a suggestion by opening a ticket. We have a defined process for handling tickets (for instance, a manager has to respond to every ticket), and the employee who opened the ticket determines whether its resolution is satisfactory. Not only does the system help resolve issues, but it effectively puts managers in the service of frontline employees.

The comprehensive 360-degree

Although HCL had a 360-degree performance review system in place, employees rarely reviewed managers because they didn't know what they stood to gain by doing so. I decided to allow anyone who had provided feedback to a manager to see the results. Employees would be more likely to participate, I thought, and managers would celebrate positive results with their teams. I knew I couldn't force managers to make their reviews public; I could only encourage them to do so. The best way to do that was to lead by example. In 2006 I posted the results of my 360-degree appraisal on the intranet for all the company to see. Most managers followed suit. If they didn't, it suggested they had something to hide.

The online planning process

Rather than reviewing the business plans of my 100 managers, as had been the case earlier, I asked the managers to make video recordings summarizing their plans and post them on an online portal, where other managers could review them, share feedback, and discuss changes. This made a difference in how managers formulated and communicated ideas. Consequently, plans became more specific and executable.

Calculate the Passion

As we improved the working environment for employees, it became clear that middle-level managers had lost some of their power. I thought about conducting an employee-satisfaction survey to see how to improve their lot, but I worried that satisfaction is a passive state, unlikely to lead to change. Engagement isn't much better; it doesn't necessarily lead to change either.

I wanted passion. We developed a new survey, the Employee Passion Indicative Count, to identify the drivers of passion in the workplace. This led to the creation of Employees First Councils, groups that focus on specific passions, from art and music to philanthropy and social responsibility. The councils help employees break down the barriers between their personal and professional lives and bring more meaning to their work. These groups had one unexpected benefit: Some sprang up around business issues, such as cloud computing, which channeled personal passion into company innovation.

Because of these changes, I was able to transform managers in the enabling functions from *petits fonctionnaires* into contributors to the business and the organizational culture. It's rare for these HCL employees to leave the company today, even though they are in great demand, because their work has become more meaningful and exciting.

Provide Transparency for the Board

When I arrived at HCL, in 2005, the chairman, Shiv Nadar, and the board already sensed that the company was heading for trouble. Shiv, HCL's founder and a legendary figure in Indian business, didn't have to be convinced that change was essential. I told him I needed a free hand. "Of course," he said. Shiv never once asked me what my approach might be. That was a good thing, because I didn't know at that stage.

Shiv and the board thought carefully about their role during the change process. They wanted the opportunity to discuss issues with me before we made major decisions, but they didn't want to get involved in day-to-day operations. I wanted their support and to tap into their collective experience. The best way to achieve both objectives, I found, was to be transparent. I constantly sent the board progress reports, held extra meetings, and ensured that more people than usual participated in the process. Senior executives and directors together came up with several new ideas and approaches, and over the next five years the board voted in favor of every proposal I brought before it—unanimously.

I didn't worry much about the stock market in the early stages of my transformation efforts. What's the point of making promises to analysts and shareholders who have heard it all before? I wanted first to show results and then to explain how we had achieved them.

Near the end of the year HCL started to win contracts that would have been out of reach for the company a year before. The first was from Autodesk, in November 2005. In January 2006 we won a large five-year contract with the consumer electronics chain DSG International—the largest IT services deal that any Indian company had ever secured.

That same year HCL closed five outsourcing deals worth a total of $700 million while competing with the world's biggest IT service providers. That's when the buzz began. The *Economist* wrote: "IBM and the other multinationals are becoming increasingly nervous about the fifth biggest Indian outsourcer, HCL Technologies."

THE MOST DIFFICULT decision to make about transformation is when to start. We began when HCL was still growing at a healthy clip. We may appear to have been early, but I'm convinced that if we hadn't made our move then, HCL wouldn't be so successful today.

When the global downturn began, we started discussions again about Point A. Rather than engage in layoffs or restructuring, I asked employees for ways to help us get through the bad times. They offered many suggestions. Some of them related to cost cutting, but most of them focused on how to increase revenues. Most important, HCL's employees felt that we had included them in determining how to weather the storm—unlike other IT companies, where, because management didn't take an inclusive approach, employees felt uncertain about their future and that of the organization. It's not accidental that while those companies' revenues fell, HCL grew by about 20% in the worst year of the recession. In 2008 we closed orders worth twice as much as those of the previous year and hired hundreds of employees globally, including in the U.S. and the UK.

I believe that many CEOs today are standing on a ledge, so to speak, unaware or unwilling to admit that the edifice behind them is on fire. Some are banging at windows, trying to summon help. Others have frozen in place. Only a few are thinking about boldly moving toward the edge. Having been in that position, I believe there is only one thing to do. Leap.

Originally published in June 2010. R1006J

Tsingtao's Chairman on Jump-Starting a Sluggish Company

by Jin Zhiguo

Jin Zhiguo is the chairman of Tsingtao Brewery.

The Idea

Western executives may complain that their organizations are bureaucratic, inbred, or risk averse, but few companies display these attributes as vividly as the ones controlled by the Chinese state. Here's how a fledgling CEO instituted reform.

In 1995 I was the assistant managing director of Tsingtao's first brewery, and we'd had a very good year. To celebrate, I took our employees on an outing to Laoshan, a beautiful mountain near the plant, for a day of hiking. While climbing the mountain, I received a message on my pager from my boss: "Get back now." I rushed to the office, where I was told that Tsingtao's management had decided to give me a new assignment. They wanted me to go to Xi'an, more than 800 miles away, to run the Hans Brewery. I was to start the new job in three days.

Tsingtao had just acquired Hans, and the deal wasn't working out very well. On my first day at Hans, I found a financial statement lying on my desk that said, "Daily production: 1,000." At first I thought this meant 1,000 cases of beer, which wasn't bad.

But when I met with the staff, I learned that it meant 1,000 bottles. This was a company that employed more than 1,000 people—so it was producing less than one bottle of beer per employee per day. My stint at Hans began with this moment of great disbelief.

At the time, that kind of underperformance wasn't unusual in Chinese businesses. Until China began its economic reforms, in 1978, most companies were state owned. The government determined production plans; few managers paid attention to customer needs or traditional marketing. The tracking of metrics such as costs, productivity, and efficiency was rudimentary. There was no mechanism for consumer feedback, so managers didn't know (and didn't really care) what customers thought. Some of the practices that Western businesses take for granted, such as holding employees to high standards of performance, didn't apply. By the early 1990s many state-owned enterprises had improved their productivity in response to aggressive market competition from Western brands, which were popular with consumers, but Hans still had far to go. I set out to revolutionize its culture over the next five years to effectively compete with private enterprises—and when I became president of all of Tsingtao, in 2001, I tried to expand those practices to the entire company.

Customers Are My Boss

I was born in 1956 in a shabby rented room. My parents were orphans with limited financial resources. Growing up in such a family, I was under tremendous pressure. According to Chinese tradition, because I was the eldest son, I would be expected to support my parents when I grew up. That made me focus on working hard from an early age.

I remember one morning I watched my mother preparing fermented flour so that she could make steamed buns when she returned home from work. In order to give her a surprise, I ran home immediately after school and steamed the buns myself—something very unusual for a boy my age. When my mother came in and saw what I'd done, she was so excited that she ran all the way back to her factory with buns in her hand to show off to her colleagues what a great son she had. I'll never forget the joy on her face. I'm still that boy today. Whatever I do, I always try to give people a pleasant surprise, and I always try to take care of my team or my company as if it were my family.

When I arrived at Hans, I couldn't understand why it was failing so miserably. As a state-owned enterprise, it had capital and technologies at its disposal. It should have been able to use them to compete against Yellow River Beer, which was privately owned, and Baoji Beer, a township enterprise. What had gone wrong?

The biggest culprit, I learned, was the brewery's local leadership. At state-owned enterprises, managers are appointed because of their connections to the Communist Party—they don't need to work hard or perform to achieve promotions. In a culture like that, a person's success is determined by how well he pleases his superiors, not how well he meets consumers' preferences. As a result, Hans managers spent most of their time knocking on the doors of their bosses and trying to make a favorable impression, and very little time paying attention to the local beer market. My first job was to change that attitude.

I've always been a hard-core believer in the concept that customers are my boss. As beer men, we need to get out in the market and gain a firsthand feel for it. I began going to restaurants and food stands after work, sitting and talking to people about beer. When they left, I would count the number of empty bottles on their tables and take note of the brands. I talked to restaurant owners and asked the ones who didn't carry Hans why it wasn't on the menu. I encouraged my salespeople to gather this kind of information as well, by giving each of them a three-yuan daily beer allowance.

By dining and drinking with ordinary Xi'an citizens, we came to understand how they perceived our brand. It turned out that local beer drinkers had a saying: "Hans is bitter, Yellow River is light, and Baoji has lots of sediment." None of the beers was perfect, so I decided that we should aim to be not bitter, not as light as Yellow River, and sediment free. From those evenings I also learned how much the Xi'an people like spicy food, such as hot pot and barbecue. Lighter beers pair better with that cuisine, so I decided to reduce the alcohol content in Hans from 12% to 10%. Finally, because of their spicy diet, people preferred chilled beer, but most beer distributors delivered the product warm and left restaurants to chill it themselves. I decided that we would turn an empty hop house into a large refrigerator and begin chilling our beer at the brewery. China didn't have refrigerated trucks in those days, so we arranged for a fleet of three-wheeled carts to transport the beer, covered with thick quilts, to every customer. Our carts became known around the city.

Those changes worked. When I arrived in Xi'an, Hans was losing 25 million yuan a year. At the end of our first year we had earned 10 million yuan. Over the next few years our market share surged, and by 1999 we had reached our target: profits of 50 million yuan a year. Hans had become Tsingtao's most profitable brewery, and our profits offset the losses incurred by many of its other local breweries. Meanwhile, production had gone from 1,000 bottles a day to 790,000.

Pancake M&A

In 2001 Peng Zuoyi, the president of Tsingtao, died from a heart attack while swimming. I considered myself the best candidate to replace him, but at least 11 other candidates held higher positions in the company. The board conducted a companywide secret-ballot survey of managers, asking "Who's the best candidate for CEO?" I received more than 70% of the votes. When I was told the results, I felt a burst of happiness and gratitude. I also felt the weight of the responsibility. My wife didn't want me to accept the job, out of concern that overwork might threaten my health. But I had spent 25 years at Tsingtao, and I owed all my talents to the company. It was facing a life-or-death situation, and I felt I must step forward.

The company had wildly overexpanded during the late 1990s. In 1993 Tsingtao had done an IPO on the Hong Kong Stock Exchange, becoming the first-ever Chinese company to be listed there. Afterward the government was still its biggest shareholder, but we now had private shareholders as well, and they expected good returns. My predecessor had felt compelled to do something strategic with the money we'd raised, and the capital markets had exerted great pressure on him to expand. Within a few years Tsingtao owned 47 local breweries. At the peak of its expansion spree it bought two breweries in one week.

In its M&A decisions Tsingtao had focused too much on the capacity of potential acquisitions and not enough on market demand. The belief was that acquiring breweries would provide easy access to new markets, but that wasn't necessarily true. Just as I had in Xi'an, I worked to persuade managers to look closely at the markets. Tsingtao needed to make decisions—including those about production capacity—with an eye toward what consumers wanted, not simply on how much it could produce. In 2002 we acquired only two more breweries. I shut down several others. The economics of keeping them open just didn't make sense.

I tried to explain my approach to M&A to employees by using a street vendor as a simple metaphor. There was a woman near our headquarters who cooked two dishes: pancakes and steamed buns. She used the same dough for both. For pancakes she stretched it light and thin to cover as much area as possible. For steamed buns she kept it thick. Before I became president, Tsingtao had been making pancakes—trying to cover many regions but without depth or meaningful market share. I wanted to make steamed buns—to have a more substantial presence in fewer areas.

Consider how we went about doing this in Wenzhou, one of the most developed cities in China. In 2004 Tsingtao had only one distributor there, with annual sales of 2,000 kiloliters (about 528,000 gallons). We set up an office in Wenzhou to manage distributors and expand the market. Then we divided the region into four territories and put each in the hands of one distributor. Actively managing our efforts in the region, instead of simply signing up a distributor and leaving the rest to him, made our sales soar: We sold 4.08 million kiloliters in 2005, 4.54 million in 2006, and 5.91 million in 2009.

A Team of Wolves

I used a different metaphor to communicate our shift from a government-run company to a business that serves consumers. In the era of the planned economy, companies had been like dogs—the government was the owner, and it would determine what and how much we ate. Our job had been to watch over state-owned assets, and we could expect a warm meal if we obeyed orders.

In the market economy we had to fight for our meals—like wolves. Wolves survive by fierce competition: In their bloody fights, the winner commands the highest respect.

Having worked for a state-owned enterprise, our people weren't used to competing for jobs or to being replaced for a subpar performance. In my first six months as president I replaced seven of the eight general managers who were running big departments at Tsingtao and more than 20 general managers at our breweries. Many of these people had been supervisors or colleagues of mine. To be honest, I found the firing process extremely difficult. When you're at a company for a long time, you know everyone. But I believed that the market should rule, and that only those who performed well should be able to stay. I stuck to that belief. I needed to create a team of wolves who wanted to compete.

Some of the changes we made may sound basic, but in a traditional Chinese company they were innovative. For instance, until 2002 Tsingtao didn't have an HR function, so we implemented one. We began tracking our talent, actively recruiting, and focusing on retention. We worked harder to find the right people for the right jobs. We also revised our incentive systems. Salespeople were given clearer targets, and the compensation system was set to reward them for meeting goals. Finally, our leaders became role models for the cultural change. In Xi'an, I had emphasized that we needed to be customer oriented, and I had modeled that by going out every evening to eat barbecue with common citizens. As the leader of Tsingtao, I continued to emphasize that employees should spend time listening to customers. Slowly this value seeped into the culture.

Over time Tsingtao began to adapt to being market driven. It prospered, just as Hans had. As the changes took root, I altered my leadership style. A 2002 joint venture we formed with Anheuser-Busch was one reason for that. During the negotiations I had asked that we establish a system of knowledge transfer so that Tsingtao could learn Anheuser's best practices. We exchanged personnel, and I spent two weeks every year shadowing Anheuser's CEO. I went to board meetings and management reviews and learned the company's decision-making process. It was a revelation.

To my amazement, Anheuser-Busch executives worked according to strict plans. Appointments, meetings, and visits were highly organized. The CEO would not touch on any specific matters and rarely attended events without prior arrangement.

He simply looked into strategy and left the day-to-day business to other people. That is not how a Chinese CEO manages. Chinese CEOs spend half their day signing papers. Watching Anheuser-Busch work gave me a lot of inspiration. I began to understand that a company cannot base its success on the competence of several high-performing leaders. It must develop a system that generates success by itself.

I began to build this system at Tsingtao. My cell phone became a test of its effectiveness. If the phone didn't ring for a long time when I was out of the office, I knew the system was working. In 2008 I became the chairman of Tsingtao. Even before that ascension, I had begun to think of my evolving role in terms of soccer positions: I was becoming less of a forward, who's the key to the offense and is involved in most plays, and more of a goalkeeper, who serves a protective function while other players act as the aggressors.

The cultural shift at Tsingtao has produced strong financial returns. In 2001 our share price was roughly 10 yuan. It rose as high as 47 yuan before the global financial crisis and is now in the low 30s. In February 2010 Reuters reported that the company was the fifth largest beer seller in the world; that year we sold 6.35 million kiloliters of beer and had revenues of 19.9 billion yuan. In the first half of 2011 revenue and profits grew by more than 20% over the prior year.

My ultimate objective is to build within Tsingtao Brewery a platform on which everything runs so smoothly that my presence or absence will have no bearing whatsoever on the business. I hope that when I leave, my successor will retain this system so that the company can survive and grow on its own, no matter who serves as CEO.

Originally published in April 2012. R1204A

Office Depot's President on How "Mystery Shopping" Helped Spark a Turnaround

by Kevin Peters

Kevin Peters is Office Depot's president for North America.

The Idea

The office products retailer was measuring customer service using metrics—such as the cleanliness of bathrooms—that didn't drive sales. Its new president is trying to fix that by retraining the staff and transforming the company.

When I became the leader of Office Depot's retail stores in the United States, in 2010, the first thing I tried to do was figure out the meaning of a puzzling set of facts. Our sales had been declining, and although that's not unusual in a weak economy, they had declined faster than the sales of our competitors and of retailers in general. At the same time, the customer service scores our third-party mystery-shopper service was reporting were going through the roof. This didn't make any sense. How could it be that we were delivering phenomenal service to our customers, yet they weren't buying anything?

To understand these contradictory data points, I decided to do some mystery shopping myself. I didn't wear a suit. I didn't wear a blue Office Depot shirt like the ones employees wear in all our U.S. stores. Instead I wore a faded pair of jeans, a T-shirt, and a baseball cap. I didn't tell anyone I was coming to visit, and in most cases I didn't let anyone know afterward that I'd been in the store. What I wanted was to experience Office Depot in the same way our customers do. Over the next several weeks I visited 70 stores in 15 or more states.

At each location I followed the same routine. First I pulled into the parking lot and just watched customers go in and out for a few minutes. When I went into the store, I'd spend 20 to 30 minutes observing what was going on. I'd talk to customers, in the aisles and as they were leaving the store. Some of the most interesting conversations took place when I followed people out who weren't carrying shopping bags and asked them why they hadn't bought anything. Some of them gave me an earful.

I could tell you a lot of stories about the things I saw, but two scenes stand out in my mind. In one store I watched an employee argue with a customer about whether or not we carried a calculator that her son needed for first grade. An employee arguing with a customer—it was unbelievable.

At another store, I parked and saw an associate leaning up against the brick facade smoking a cigarette. Meanwhile, customers were walking out without any bags. This employee did nothing—he just watched them leave empty-handed. At that point I had a tough decision to make: Should I blow my cover and alert the store manager, or should I stay silent? I sat in the car a few minutes, thinking it over. Finally I decided, I just can't let this go.

I went into the store and looked at the stanchion that stands at the front of every location, displaying the name of the manager and his or her picture. Guess who the store manager was?

Yes—the guy smoking outside the store. So I went up to him and introduced myself, and we had a good long talk. He was ashamed of his behavior—and he was sweating during the conversation. He promised he'd do a better job of taking care of customers, and I promised to keep in touch. Even today we exchange e-mails every month to discuss his performance.

Get In, Get Out

During most of my visits, though, I managed to stay incognito, and I came away having learned a big lesson: Our mystery-shopping scores were correct. You know what was flawed? Our scoring system. We were asking the wrong questions. We were asking, Are the floors clean? Are the shelves full of inventory? Are the store windows clean? Have the bathrooms been cleaned recently? Think about that for a moment: How often do you go to the bathroom while shopping for office supplies? It turns out that customers don't really care about any of that. Those factors don't drive purchases, and that's why our sales were declining. It would be easy to blame our associates for ignoring shoppers, but under the system we'd built, they weren't doing anything wrong. They were doing exactly what we'd asked them to do—working to keep stores clean and well stocked instead of building relationships with customers.

My conversations with customers gave me three insights into how we should transform our business to become more competitive: One, we had to reduce the size of our stores. They were too large and too difficult to shop in. Two, we had to dramatically improve the in-store experience for our customers. That meant retraining our associates to stop focusing on the things our existing system had incentivized them to do and focus on customers instead. Three, we had to look beyond office products to provide other services our customers wanted. They wanted copying, printing, and shipping. They wanted help installing software and fixing computers. We needed to expand our offerings if we were to remain relevant to our customers.

Talking directly with dozens of customers also reminded me of a cold, hard fact: They have many choices. Office products are a $300 billion industry, and the top three players—Staples, Office Depot, and OfficeMax—account for less than 10% of that. Approximately 65% of our customers are small and midsize businesses, and buying office supplies doesn't add value to what they do. It's a chore. They want to get in and get out—they care about convenience above all else.

Less Stocking, More Selling

On the basis of that feedback, we began to transform our business. It's probably one of the most challenging journeys I've taken in my life. We started by designating two test stores, one in Chicago and one in south Florida.

Many of the changes we made were done behind the scenes, in parts of the business that customers don't see. We altered the way our supply chain operates so that we could accept deliveries from vendors even when no one was in the store to sign in the merchandise. We began separating stock onto U-boats (the narrow stocking carts we use in aisles) assigned to different parts of the store and delivering the U-boats to an optimal spot—marked with an X on the floor—to minimize the labor required by associates to stock shelves. We also divided the store into zones and began having the same associates stock the same sections repeatedly. Becoming expert in one area of the store allowed them to restock faster, reducing labor.

Many people think that in order to improve service, you need to hire more frontline workers. But in fact, by finding ways to reduce the time employees spend on functions such as stocking shelves, we've been able to repurpose their time for selling to customers. Each of our stores employs 18 people on average; by finding ways to work smarter, we've been able to save 80 hours a week—the equivalent of hiring two full-time salespeople but at no added cost.

Once our associates had more time to serve customers, we needed to ensure that they knew how. We simplified our sales process from five steps to three—it's now called ARC, for "Ask, recommend, and close"—and trained them to implement it. We taught them to ask customers open-ended questions. Our research indicated that in certain departments—such as furniture—sales go up by more than 100% when associates with really good product knowledge are assigned to those zones. So in addition to sales training, we invested in product training.

When a retailer delivers poor service, many people are quick to blame the employees. In my experience, it's more complicated than that. We have 22,500 associates in our retail organization; one of the things we did as part of our change program was to have every one of them take a test built on the Myers-Briggs Type Indicator to help us understand their skills, behaviors, and attributes as they relate to serving customers. An interesting thing we found was that we'd been hiring people who were most comfortable with their backs, rather than their bellies, to the aisle. Roughly one in five associates preferred performing tasks on merchandise over interacting with customers. A challenge we faced in rolling out these initiatives was how to help those workers become comfortable with the ARC culture—or, frankly, to help them find other meaningful jobs within the company if they couldn't acquire the right selling skills.

Smaller Is Better

You can't drive changes like this overnight. Our business has been around since 1986, and that's a long time for employees and customers to establish expectations and behaviors. These changes won't be completed in the next month or the next quarter—maybe not even in the next year. In addition to the two "lab" stores in Chicago and Florida, we've rolled out 30 pilot stores, and we're seeing encouraging evidence of an improvement in sales. We're also hearing positive anecdotal feedback from customers and associates. (There has been a dramatic improvement at the store where I caught the manager smoking outside: Today it is one of the top performers in the company.) We hope that by the end of 2011, 325 of our stores will be utilizing the new system.

We've also made progress in shrinking the size of our stores. Today they average 24,000 square feet. We've already had success with new stores of 15,000 to 17,000 square feet. We are introducing a small-format store that's about 5,000 square feet. It carries only 5,000 SKUs—compared with 8,500 SKUs in our traditional stores—but because they're our most popular products, they represent 93% of what we sell in a traditional store. This format will allow us to be in downtown markets like New York City or in remote markets where we wouldn't consider putting a large-format store.

As we work to make these changes, I still try to visit our stores as frequently as possible. It's really the only way you can know how your business is doing. You have to see how customers are being treated, and you can't rely on reports or scores or hearsay—you have to experience it yourself. If you think your company is doing well with customer service, ask yourself, Am I really sure? Do I know what the customer experiences?

What I pay attention to most of all is how many people are leaving the store without a shopping bag. I'd be glad if people came to our stores to browse, but this is not a browsing industry—people are shopping with a very specific purpose in mind. If they don't make a purchase, something has gone wrong. If we can reduce this "balk rate" by just 10%, it will have a meaningful impact on both our top-line revenue and our margins.

You also have to make sure you're measuring things that really matter to customers. I can tell you from firsthand experience what happens when you measure the wrong things. I always try to remember that we need our customers more than they need us—and we'd better act like it.

Originally published in November 2011. R1111A

TELLING THE RIGHT STORY

ONE OF THE BIGGEST CHALLENGES OF BEING A CEO IS THAT no matter how strategically you manage your time and set priorities, you can never anticipate the specific challenges you'll face tomorrow. Stuff happens, and leaders often face pressure to quickly fashion a response.

That's especially true when a company's image and reputation are at stake. How do you respond when your family business—one known for its history of social responsibility—is accused of harming precious rainforests and contributing to global warming? How can a cash-strapped start-up convince big-name athletes to wear and promote a new brand of athletic gear without writing checks? Even less time-pressured decisions can fall far outside a traditional leader's comfort zone. For instance, how should a CEO convince a skeptical board that the company's new bet-the-farm ad campaign will feature . . . a quacking duck?

By their own admission, many of these leaders were caught flat-footed by a crisis, and it often took two or three tries before they crafted the right response.

The stories told by these leaders illustrate why there is no standard formula for shaping a company's image, particularly when messages must be shaped from a defensive crouch at a company under attack. Of all the decisions that managers must make, these more than most rely on instinct, intuition, and improvisation.

Under Armour's Founder on Learning to Leverage Celebrity Endorsements

by Kevin Plank

Kevin Plank is the founder and CEO of Under Armour.

The Idea

Celebrity endorsements used to be fairly straightforward: a face in an ad, a logo on the TV screen. But that world is rapidly changing, and Under Armour's CEO is nimbly navigating it.

I started Under Armour in 1996, when I was 23 years old and just out of college. The idea for the product was pretty simple. I had played football in high school and college, and I'd hated how the T-shirts I wore under my shoulder pads became soaked with sweat. It wasn't just uncomfortable—I really believed the extra weight hurt an athlete's performance. I saw the need for a shirt that would stay dry. I looked at all sorts of fabrics and eventually settled on one that would wick away moisture and stay light even if the wearer sweats heavily. I asked a tailor to turn the material into a T-shirt, and I produced a bunch of prototypes. Then I set out to sell them.

To do that, I turned to my network. I had attended St. John's College High School, in Washington, DC, which has a power-house football program. At least eight of my high school team-mates went on to play Division I football at places like Syracuse, Wake Forest, and Virginia, and two of them made it to the NFL. After high school I spent a year at a prep school called Fork Union Military Academy, which was another factory for ath-letes. Among my Fork Union teammates, 23 signed to play Divi-sion I football in college, and one of them—Eddie George—won the Heisman Trophy. Four years after we graduated from Fork Union, 13 of my former teammates were drafted into the NFL. In college I walked on to the football team at the University of Maryland, and 20 or 25 of my teammates during my four years there went on to play professional football.

This is a piece of the Under Armour story that most people don't appreciate. They focus on the innovative product. But I wasn't just a guy who created a new kind of athletic wear. I had friends inside the locker rooms of more than a dozen professional football teams. Although Under Armour has become a $1 billion brand by selling to consumers, I created it as a product for elite athletes. And when I was laying plans for the business, my con-tacts among these NFL players were a vital part of my strategy.

But knowing these guys didn't necessarily make navigating the world of celebrity endorsements any less complicated. What began as an informal word-of-mouth brand-building strat-egy has evolved into a multimillion-dollar expense item that requires elaborate negotiations and constant attention to the return on investment. But it's also a lot of fun.

Managing Freebies

Simply getting my first products into players' hands was chal-lenging. This was pre-Facebook, and I had to work to track down the guys I went to high school or college with. When I did reach them, I was careful in my approach. A lot of people ask these guys for help, and I didn't want to sound like the obnoxious third cousin who tries to borrow $500. So I wouldn't say, "Do me a favor and wear this shirt." Instead I'd say, "I have this neat product and this cool company I'm working with—you should check it out." If they sounded interested, I'd say, "Hey, let me send you a couple of shirts. If you like them, wear one—and give the other one to the guy with the locker next to yours." It was a grassroots approach. I tried to emphasize that if an Under Armour shirt could help these athletes improve their performance just a little bit, they'd be able to earn even more money. I positioned wearing it as a tool to help them rather than a favor to me.

I thought that once a few players on a team began wearing the shirts and talking them up, the team would feel obliged to buy them for everyone, the way it buys other equipment. That was the business model I had in mind, and in fact, that's what happened. Our first order came in 1996, from the Georgia State football team, and soon after that we made big sales to the Atlanta Falcons and the New York Giants. I was still giving free shirts to individual players in the hope that they'd spread the word, but I made the money back with sales to teams.

Then, in the summer of 1997, the equipment manager for the Miami Dolphins called. "Hey, Kev," he said, "a couple of our guys have your shirts, and we love them. If you do me a favor and send me 150 of them, I'll make sure every Dolphin— including Dan Marino—is wearing one on Sunday." I told him I couldn't give away that many shirts for the promotional value: It wasn't in my budget. "Are you crazy?" he said. "The exposure will be unbelievable." He was right—the Dolphins game would be nationally televised, and with the Under Armour logo visible on the neck of every shirt, our brand would be in front of millions of people.

That was a defining moment, one of those decisions that determine the future of a company. "Look," I said. "I like you very much, and I do have the shirts in stock. But I can't send them to you free—I just can't. We make a good product, we charge a fair price, and other teams are paying for them. If I give them away to you, I'll need to do it for everybody, and I can't keep up with that game." He was apologetic, but he said he didn't have the money, and he hung up. I was kicking myself. Had I done the right thing? I considered sending the shirts down anyway, despite what I'd said.

That phone conversation took place on a Wednesday, and the game was on Sunday. On Thursday he called me back. "Okay, I have an idea," he said. "We'll pay for the shirts, but you'll bill us on a 45-day cycle, which will help me take the money out of next month's budget." We shipped them overnight.

When you deal with products for which endorsements are important, you have to make decisions like that all the time. When is it worthwhile to give away your product, and when do you stand your ground and demand a fair price? As Under Armour grew, that calculation became even more difficult. Star players began asking to be paid to wear our gear. By 1998 Barry Bonds had become a big advocate of our product. We didn't know how he was getting the shirts (we weren't sending them to him), but he was wearing them all the time, and he really liked them. Some of our guys asked him if he'd be willing to do a photo shoot for us. "You know, I love your product—I'd love to," he said. It was a very big deal for us. We flew a photographer down to spring training to do the shoot, and I went with him.

Barry came down to the set that morning and said, "I'm not going to do it." He had his manager with him. I pleaded with him: "Barry, it will take five minutes—let's just get a picture of you in the shirt." He told me he wanted $5,000 to let us take the photo. At the time, we weren't paying any players to wear Under Armour, and I told him that. We came up with a compromise: We'd give him $5,000 in merchandise and a promise that if we ever began paying players to wear the brand, we'd pay him whatever we were paying our top-earning athlete. (In 2001 we gave him $5,000 for his charity as well as $5,000 in merchandise; he was still our top-earning athlete that year.) He looked at me, grabbed hold of his manager, and said, "Kevin, if you ever screw with me, I'm going to kill this guy." Everyone laughed. We took the photos and put one in our catalog. It was cool. But as time went on, we were constantly dealing with things like that. Celebrities became even more important to our business after 2000, when we began selling apparel at retail.

"What's Up with the Stock?"

One thing people don't realize about endorsements is how few athletes are instantly recognizable—and how effective an endorsement can be from someone who's relatively unknown but has the right personality. Many of the early athletes we used only looked famous—they were big, athletic, strong. Eric Ogbogu was a teammate of mine at Maryland who played with the Jets, the Bengals, and the Cowboys. He looks like a million bucks. But out of 800 players in the NFL, there are only about 10 that most people would recognize with their helmets off—and Eric wasn't one of them. Nonetheless, we put him in an Under Armour ad screaming, "We must protect this house!" The catchphrase became really well known, and Eric became famous as the Under Armour guy. The point is that you don't need to have Tiger Woods in a commercial for it to be effective.

At a certain point in our evolution, it began to make sense to pay athletes to promote our brand. Once we'd established a big consumer business—and especially as we've expanded into new categories, such as footwear—the value of endorsements became clear. Consumers know that Under Armour is an authentic brand that was built on the field. Athletes' endorsements reinforce that, and they provide us with a bigger platform to communicate our product stories. We are strategic with our partnerships—our athletes talk about the benefits of our gear because it helps them perform. Today our most prominent athlete is Tom Brady, the Patriots quarterback, whom we signed in November 2010. We've never disclosed how much we pay him, but Tom's deal is unique in that it includes equity in the company. It's a great arrangement, because I want our biggest partners rooting for Under Armour. One day last summer our stock took a pounding, and I received a text from Tom: "What's up with the stock? I'm buying more tonight." That's exactly what I want—an athlete who has truly bought into our success.

Sometimes we decide not to spend money on particular athletes, and that can be a hard decision, too. Recently the endorsement market for players selected in the NBA draft has been really high. In 2010 John Wall was the number one pick, and another company paid more than $5 million for an endorsement deal with him. He hadn't even dribbled a ball in the NBA yet! The number two pick was Evan Turner, out of Ohio State. We wanted to sign him. We figured a deal with him was worth $150,000 a year. Another company came in and paid him more than $2 million a year. To us, that didn't make sense.

Often these deals aren't just about the money. You need to find out who is on the other side of the table and whom you should be talking to. There's the athlete, of course, but sometimes a friend or a handler or the mom or dad is the key decision maker. You have to build trust and explain your story. These athletes have everybody in the world coming after them. Your job is to break through the clutter and the noise and show them why your brand would be a good fit.

Once we have a top athlete on board, we look to him for more than just endorsements. Ideally, he'll help us drive product innovation, too. One of our top athletes is Brandon Jennings, who's in his third year in the NBA and plays for the Milwaukee Bucks. When the NBA locked out last summer, Brandon didn't feel like going home to LA, so we offered him an internship. He had an office at our Baltimore headquarters. He worked out here and ate in the dining hall. His official title was Curator of Cool. He hung out with our designers. A guy like that helped them come up with new ideas.

Sometimes when we enter a new category, we have to pay more to get athletes to wear our gear. We were signing up baseball players to wear our cleats before we even made baseball cleats, so it was a leap of faith by them. Deals like that are more difficult. But when we enter a new category, we work hard to get it right as quickly as possible. When we launched football shoes, everyone said we couldn't compete. But within a few years we had Tom Brady winning the Super Bowl MVP in our shoes, and Cam Newton, the number one NFL draft pick, led Auburn to the 2011 national championship in a pair. We launched basketball shoes in 2010, and I guarantee that within four or five years our athletes will be winning championships in them, too.

When we started out, the way companies used endorsements was fairly simple: You put the athlete in an ad or hoped your logo showed clearly on TV during games. In the past few years that's changed, too. As athletes continue to build their own brand identities, they seek endorsements that reflect their lifestyle and values. A successful endorsement should facilitate a conversation between the brand and the athlete and between the athlete and the consumer.

Today social media give us infinitely more opportunities to tell our story. Most of our athletes are on Twitter, and our marketing department has social media experts. They're usually 25, with two years of experience, but they know more about this stuff than anybody else. Looking at how communication has changed in the past few years, with the emergence of Facebook and mobile technology, it's hard to say how the endorsement business is going to change over the next decade. I do know that we'll continue to embrace those changes.

Originally published in May 2012. R1205A

Aflac's CEO Explains How He Fell for the Duck

by Daniel P. Amos

Daniel P. Amos became the CEO of Aflac in 1990, making him one of the longest-tenured CEOs in the *Fortune* 500. Since 2001 he has also been Aflac's chairman.

The Idea

Ten years into an ambitious advertising campaign, Aflac still had low name recognition. Would a noisy duck do any better?

The Aflac Duck is a rock star in Japan. That's the only way I can describe how big he has become there. In a down economy, Aflac Japan's sales increased by 12% in 2003, the year we introduced the duck. Today we insure one out of every four Japanese households and are the leading insurance company measured by number of policies in force. We took that title from Nippon Life, which had held it for more than 100 years.

In 2009 our Japanese marketing team introduced a new incarnation of the duck for a new insurance product. It's a mix of our duck and the traditional Asian good-luck white cat, Maneki Neko. The cat duck has become so popular that our newest commercial was voted number one in Japan. A giant plush version of Maneki Neko Duck toured the country by bus, drawing crowds as big as 20,000 in city after city. At each event we set up tables where we were able to sell policies to enthusiastic fans.

How did we even get to this point? What made our white duck a sensation in Japan when the original Aflac Duck commercial aired there? More important, how has it helped drive revenues up by 44% since 2003? Aflac's revenues in 2008 were $16.6 billion, with 70% of that coming from Japan.

No one is more surprised than I am.

Making a Name for Aflac

The Aflac Duck was created to increase the company's name recognition in the United States. When I first became CEO of the American Family Life Assurance Company, in 1990, I reviewed all of our operations and decided to sell or close the ones that were underperforming in order to focus on Japan and the United States, the two biggest insurance markets in the world. I took the $8 million we saved by closing those operations and launched a name-awareness ad campaign in the United States. Our name recognition at the time was about 2%. Nearly a decade later it was still below 10%. At that rate, I realized, I'd be retired before we reached 25%. We had to do something dramatic.

Keep in mind that the company's name was originally American Family Life Insurance Company. "Insurance" was changed to "assurance" as the result of a gentleman's coin toss between our former CEO and the head of a Wisconsin insurance company of the same name. But I could see that we still had trouble distinguishing ourselves from the scores of other companies whose names began with "American." A radical name change would have been impractical, because we would have had to give up all our insurance licenses and reapply for new ones in every state. So rather than try a brand-new name, we decided to go with our acronym, Aflac.

In the late 1990s, we thought it was time for some new television advertisements, so we invited several agencies to pitch us at the same time in a creative shoot-out. We reviewed at least 20 different concepts and set out to test the best. The top two agencies were allowed to submit five ads each for testing.

One of the agencies was the New York–based Kaplan Thaler Group, whose creative guys came up with the idea of the Aflac Duck because they'd been having a hard time remembering our name. One day, one of them asked, "What's the name of the account we're pitching?" A colleague replied, "It's Aflac—Aflac—Aflac—Aflac." Someone said that he sounded like a duck, and the idea was born.

Kaplan Thaler decided to risk pitching the duck, hoping that we wouldn't be offended by the commercial's making fun of our name. With some trepidation, we agreed to let the agency test the commercial, along with some other concepts, to determine which of them was the most memorable.

Our previous commercials had consistently underperformed other financial services ads, which earned, on average, a 12—meaning that 12% of people polled recalled the company's name after watching the ad. In six years only one of our commercials had earned a 12.

In the Kaplan Thaler testing, one of the highest-scoring concepts featured the actor Ray Romano, whose hit television show, *Everybody Loves Raymond,* was then at the height of its popularity. At the end of the commercial, some children who were playing with blocks spelled out "Aflac." The ad scored an 18—more than 50% better than we had been doing. I considered it a bird in the hand.

But that darn Aflac Duck scored a 27.

We had a dilemma: Should we go with a commercial so bold—or with the gentle Ray Romano commercial that performed much better than our traditional ads? I asked one of my CEO friends, who said, "Nobody ever got fired for doing 50% better. Go with the safe choice."

But I couldn't ignore that 27.

A Duck in the Hand?

When I tried explaining to people what we were thinking about, no one got it. "Well, there's this duck," I'd say. "And he quacks *Aflac*." The response was always the same: a silent stare. So I stopped telling people. I didn't even tell our board; I just said we were trying something very bold and creative for our advertising campaign. It's difficult to explain, I told them, but we've had it tested, and the numbers are amazing.

Having gotten my college degree in risk management, I was committed to making the decision the way I'd been taught: Don't risk a lot for a little; don't risk more than you can afford to lose; and consider the odds. We were going to invest $1 million in the initial ad campaign. That's a lot of money, but we could afford to lose it, and I knew the odds. I decided that we'd run the commercial for two weeks and monitor every second. If it went badly, I was just going to pull it. At that time, we weren't sophisticated enough to realize exactly what we were doing. We were just going to test for name recognition afterward.

The first Aflac Duck ad debuted on New Year's Day, 2000, on CNN. It ran four times an hour. I knew that businesspeople would be watching CNN all day to see if the Y2K virus had wreaked havoc. So it was a great slot for us to gain maximum saturation. I watched it myself, over and over, still not sure if this would work.

Success was immediate—in fact, it was overwhelming. Our first day on the air, we had more visits to our website than in the entire year before. Within weeks we were getting requests for a stuffed-animal version of the duck. We didn't know how to manufacture ducks, but we quickly came up with a plan and decided that all the proceeds would be donated to the Aflac Cancer Center, in Atlanta. Within just a few months we had generated $75,000 for the cancer center.

I'm not sure I really believed that the duck was a success until a few months later. We were sponsoring an event at Disney Studios in connection with the Democratic National Convention in Los Angeles. We didn't know whether it would be a good idea to put ducks on all the tables—the kind of thing we'd ordinarily do as an event sponsor. This was a crowd of 500 movers and shakers. I didn't want to be embarrassed if no one took the ducks. I paid almost no attention to what anyone was talking about that afternoon; I was just watching to see if ducks were left on the tables.

By the end of the event, they were all gone. I spotted the head of Disney Studios with a bulge under his jacket. When I jokingly asked him what was going on, he said, "I want you to understand that Donald is always the king around here. But I want to take one home to my kids." That was it for me: the confirmation of confirmations. I knew we had a winner and we had to play it for all it was worth.

What remained to be seen, however, was whether we would achieve our business goals. That question was answered swiftly: In the first year our sales in the United States were up by 29%; in three years they had doubled. Our name recognition was up to 67% after two years of running the commercials. We increased our ad spending in proportion to growth. Today it's at $65 million, and our name recognition is higher than 90%.

The Duck Goes Global

When I decided it was time to bring the Aflac Duck to our Japanese market, I assumed, on the basis of the duck's tremendous success in the United States, that my idea would be eagerly received. But although I was excited about the notion of synergy and consistent global branding, our Japanese marketing director was not.

Aflac had been in Japan since 1974, and we were one of the most profitable companies operating there. But the marketing director felt no burning need to change his strategy. Although the Aflac Duck had become integral to who we were in the United States, he could not imagine that a white duck would sell insurance in Japan.

I'm not sure he understood the connection—maybe because in Japan a duck doesn't say "quack-quack," it says "ga-ga." Not to mention that in Japan the company was known by its full name: American Family Life Assurance Company. I began to understand the challenge for him. He did, however, halfheartedly agree to dub a U.S. commercial into Japanese and see how it did. Not surprisingly, it didn't do very well. I learned a valuable lesson from this experience: If you don't have buy-in from the people you're leading, your ideas won't work.

For a year and a half, I let my idea go. But it stuck in my mind. So I tried again. I told the marketing director that I wasn't going to force him to do this, but if he could find a way to make the duck work in Japan, I'd pay him a $50,000 bonus at the end of the year. Miraculously, angels must have come down and spoken to him, because lo and behold, he decided it might be a good idea to try the duck.

Once I had his buy-in, Aflac Japan helped make the appropriate cultural adjustments. First of all, the comedian Gilbert Gottfried's voice, which we used for the American duck, didn't work in Japan. People thought the duck was yelling at them. So we used a softer voice. And in the United States, people identify with the boisterous Aflac Duck who struggles to be heard. However, in Japan it's extremely rude to ignore people—or ducks, for that matter. So the Japanese duck interacts with people. He's a sage financial adviser who helps protect families.

Duck Wranglers Needed

Making a commercial in Japan with a real duck wasn't easy, because the Japanese weren't used to using live animals in ads. We had to fly in several people from our U.S. operation and a duck-wrangling crew for the commercial shoot. I'm pretty sure our Japanese colleagues thought we were *toppyoushimonai* (crazy) for doing all this. But they were committed to making it work in spite of their doubts.

The Japanese Aflac Duck ads exceeded our wildest expectations. Various versions of the jingle from the commercials became the number one downloaded cell-phone ringtone in Japan. Following our lead in the United States—where the duck has a Twitter account and 165,000 Facebook fans, and YouTube is filled with parodies of Aflac commercials—Aflac Japan started marketing to the social media and created a website that allows people to rework the song the duck sings in Japanese commercials. In the website's first two months of existence, 100,000 people posted spoofs. (By early November 2009 that number had reached 200,000.)

So, how committed am I to the Aflac Duck? Well, in aid of branding, I wear only ties that have ducks on them. If I see a duck tie in a store, I buy it in every color. When we designed an addition to our corporate headquarters in Georgia, I told the architects that the only thing I insisted on was a duck pond. After all, when people came to headquarters, they wanted to see the Aflac Duck.

Recently, when I was talking to our executives in the United States, I described how the duck had morphed into a cat duck to introduce a new product in Japan. It reminded me of how, when

I was first interviewed in Japan about our commercials, people asked me repeatedly to explain why we had picked a duck. I kept telling them that a duck says "quack-quack" in America. But no one got it. So I just started saying "Ducks are cute."

As I explained the cat duck to the U.S. executives, I had a similar feeling. All I could say was "Trust me, this works in Japan." By the end, every last one of them wanted a cat duck to take home. I swear, the Japanese are on to something with this cat duck campaign, but I haven't figured out how to make it work in the United States. I'll keep thinking.

Originally published in January–February 2010. R1001L

Timberland's CEO on Standing Up to 65,000 Angry Activists

by Jeff Swartz

Jeff Swartz is the president and CEO of Timberland.

The Idea

After Greenpeace pressured Timberland to pull out of Brazil, CEO Jeff Swartz chose instead to engage with the activist group and Timberland's Brazilian supplier in hopes of making a positive difference.

You can tell a lot about how your day is going to unfold by the number of e-mails that are waiting for you. I'm a pretty early riser—4 AM most days—so I typically start out ahead of the game when it comes to e-mails. But on June 1, 2009, they kept coming, and coming, and coming.

The first one accused Timberland of supporting slave labor, destroying Amazon rain forests, and exacerbating global warming—all in the first sentence. The second was a repeat of the first, as was the next, and the next. I had a funny feeling it was going to be a long day.

The fan mail was from Greenpeace supporters reacting to a newly released Greenpeace report about deforestation in the Amazon. The gist of the report was (a) Brazilian cattle farmers are illegally clear-cutting Amazon rain forests to create pastures, and (b) the leather from their cows might be winding up in shoes—including Timberland's. (A) plus (b) equals (c): New Hampshire–based bootmakers are desecrating the environment. Take them to task. And take us to task they did. The senders didn't threaten a boycott but said they were "concerned" and urged us to work with Greenpeace to find a "permanent global solution" to both deforestation and climate change.

As a CEO, I'm used to getting angry e-mails—most of them along the lines of "You support something I oppose; therefore you're an idiot." But these were different. Even though their text was a form letter pulled off the Greenpeace website, it was well written and informed. And it was coming from a potent activist organization, suggesting a problem I wasn't intimately familiar with. Even in my early-morning haze, I knew that was a bad combination.

Throw away the Monday morning to-do list—we've got us an issue here.

That morning our IT department set up a system to automatically reroute all the activist e-mails from my inbox to a separate folder—not so that I could avoid them (although it was nice to have my inbox back), but because we wanted to make sure each one got a response.

Next on the agenda was figuring out *how* to respond—not just to Greenpeace's allegations, but to the angry senders, who totaled 65,000 over the next few weeks. I figured if that many people were taking the time to send an e-mail, there must be at least half a million not sending e-mails who were also pissed off. That's a big number. Our brand's reputation was at stake.

My first response to the e-mails was to be pretty angry myself. Of all the environmental problems Timberland has been actively committed to addressing, deforestation tops the list. We've planted a million trees in China; we host community regreening events in cities all over the world. Our logo is a tree, for crying out loud. How much more ridiculous could this campaign be? It would have been laughable—if not for the 65,000 Greenpeace supporters who were buying into the allegations and making clear their expectation that we'd come up with an acceptable solution. The "or else" was implied, but we've all seen videos and news articles about big corporate bullies that fall victim to Greenpeace's wrath. I didn't want Timberland to be painted as either a corporate bully or a victim.

The Origin of Hides

Some members of our team, justifiably, thought our primary goal should be to figure out how to end the conversation—meaning get the angry activists to go away. Only about 7% of our leather is sourced from Brazil, so it would have been relatively easy to find another source that didn't come with strings such as deforestation issues and Greenpeace reports attached. This option became more compelling as other companies, including some of our competitors, started issuing statements in which they vowed to immediately stop buying leather from the region in question. "Let's just do what they're doing and say 'We're out,'" some colleagues advised.

I'm a third-generation CEO. I'm not the first guy into a fight. But I'm also not one to take the politically correct, cut-and-run route when I think something is worth staying and talking about—in this case, the reputation of our business and a serious environmental issue.

As much as I didn't want to admit it, Greenpeace was asking a legitimate question: Where was our leather coming from? Second on the list of things I didn't want to admit was that we didn't know the answer. We—our company, our industry—had until then never been asked, or asked ourselves, that question. Sure, we cared whether the leather came from a cow, a goat, or a pig. But where did the animal graze before it went to the slaughterhouse? I'm a bootmaker, not a cattle rancher. That's not a question that was keeping me up at night—at least not before that June.

The fact is, the origin of hides has never been easily traceable: They're treated as a waste product by slaughterhouses, which are mostly interested in the meat. In some parts of the world, hides are sold in batches of two or three by guys on the side of the road. They're not tracked the way other materials—pharmaceuticals, for example, and most food products—are. The lack of traceability in our materials supply chain is almost archaic. But the thought of tracing one hide back through the tannery to the slaughterhouse to the cow to the herd to the pasture to the land—multiplied by however many hides make up the 7% of our leather that is sourced in Brazil—is enough to make your head hurt.

I was willing to suffer the headache—and impose it on my team—because I thought Greenpeace had raised a good question and that there was value in trying to answer it. I also saw this issue as a battle for the hearts and minds of environmental activists—the ones who believe that private enterprise by definition sucks and the world would be better off if companies burned down. I wanted to confront that notion head-on, to convince them that if they *really* want to help the rain forest—to make a sustainable environmental impact—they need the help of companies like Timberland. I wanted them to know that it's possible to be a profitable global business and also be actively engaged in protecting the environment.

Frugality Drives Sustainability

To understand how we responded to Greenpeace, it helps to understand the role that stakeholders—and issues like the environment—play in how Timberland operates. It also helps to understand that activist groups like Greenpeace have a unique operating model of their own.

Our environmental sensibility stems from being a frugal Yankee outdoor company. In Timberland's first factory, my grandfather used to walk around picking up the bobbins that fell off the machines to reuse them; every time, he'd say, "That's a penny." Leather came wrapped in thick green paper, and instead of throwing the wrapper away, my grandfather would smooth it out and make patterns from it. He wasn't recycling to save trees—he was thinking about not having to pay for the stock to cut a pattern.

Today we do a variety of things to minimize our use of resources—because my grandfather's frugality runs deep, and because we'd rather leave a light footprint on the earth than a heavy one. Our efforts to be environmentally responsible— from powering our facilities with renewable energy to calculating the carbon footprint of our footwear—made Greenpeace's allegations hard to swallow. Furthermore, we actively participate in cross-brand collaborations to address industry issues, and we host stakeholder calls once a quarter so that anyone concerned about the impact of our business can share questions and criticisms with us. It's not always comfortable to be bumping elbows with our toughest competitors or to sit in the hot seat during those calls. But we benefit from outside perspectives. That's another reason why Greenpeace's guerrilla tactics—accuse first and engage later—felt like such an affront.

For Greenpeace, guerrilla tactics are supremely effective— something I was naive about when all this began. There's no question the organization cares about saving rain forests, but it also cares about recruiting new members and collecting membership fees. Making headlines by attacking companies helps it do that.

If Greenpeace wanted to start a dialogue with the footwear industry about how our supply chain might be hurting rain forests, I strongly feel that someone there should have picked up the phone. The organization could have convened the industry's CEOs to talk about these issues and craft a solution—and then held a press conference where it took credit for getting us to address the problem. There isn't one executive in our industry who wouldn't have wanted to be at that press conference. But phone calls and press conferences aren't as sexy as an attack campaign and wouldn't have riled up Greenpeace's member base, which is part of what drives its revenue. So it came at us instead, leading us to waste a ton of energy fighting a goopy mess rather than making meaningful progress.

We called Greenpeace within a few hours of receiving the first e-mail, but it took days to get someone knowledgeable about the issue to come to the phone. While we waited for the organization to talk to us, our supplier tried to get some answers. To illustrate its claim that ranchers were illegally clear-cutting the Amazon forest, Greenpeace published pictures from Google Earth showing cows grazing in places that had been forest just a month before. In conversations with our supplier, we learned that it didn't actually know where ranchers were pasturing their cattle—so Greenpeace might be right. Hmm ... not the answer I was hoping for.

My next question for the team: If our supplier didn't know where the cattle originated, could we start figuring it out? Could we track where specific cows were grazing? Our engineers concluded that the task was arduous but not impossible; although there wasn't a system in place to capture and manage that data, there *could* be, given enough time and resources. What would make it impossible, they said, was if the companies further up the supply chain—the cattle ranchers and the slaughterhouses—were unwilling to go along with it.

It's called a supply chain for a reason: There are a lot of links—ranchers, slaughterhouses, tanneries. In the scheme of things in Brazil, we're a very small player with very little leverage. To its credit, Greenpeace understood this. So it didn't come after shoe companies only—it also targeted companies that buy beef, including Wal-Mart and other grocery chains. It applied pressure to Brazilian politicians, who turned to Brazilian law enforcement, which began going after the ranchers who were breaking the law. Greenpeace effectively brought a coalition of pressure against every link in the chain simultaneously—a powerful tactic, and one it knew would work.

Our supplier had little choice but to take this seriously: All its customers were asking the same hard questions at the same time. We didn't have to threaten to cancel our contracts—the threat was implicit. The supplier knew it was going to have to step up.

Crafting a Response

Dealing with the supply chain would take weeks, if not longer—but in the meantime, we had 65,000 love notes to respond to. Bill Clinton likes to say that when it comes to winning votes, you need to consider two kinds of people: the Nos and the Maybes. Now, the Nos are against you all the way; you can't win their votes, so you shouldn't waste time trying. Every election, he says, is won or lost on the Maybes—they're your fighting chance. Even though we had no way of differentiating Nos from Maybes, given the cookie-cutter e-mail, we knew we had to craft a response that had the best possible chance of winning the Maybes (provided there were any in the bunch)—those who might, just might, see that we were trying to do the right thing.

Our response ended up evolving over time. Writing an e-mail response may seem like a no-brainer, but we worked really hard to get it right. For instance, if an e-mail had come from an Italian internet address—even if the message was in English—we replied in Italian. And we watched how many senders replied. We never expected that everyone would write back and say, "Wow, we never realized you were great guys!" but we did hope to hear from activists who appreciated our response. And some of them did.

By July, we'd begun to make progress in working with our supplier and in consulting with our competitors and with Greenpeace. Although Greenpeace had hoped that we'd simply come out with a high-level statement agreeing with its position, we wanted to really understand the problem—and to make sure our supplier had a system in place that could be implemented and sustained.

On July 22, Nike announced that it would require its Brazilian leather suppliers to certify in writing that their hides hadn't come from deforested areas. Now, Nike is huge—a much bigger player than we are in terms of leather sourcing—and its suppliers would have to start mapping and tracking ranches all over the country. A few days later—seven weeks after the e-mail onslaught began—we reached a similar agreement with our supplier.

Implementing the agreement has been just as hard as we expected—even harder. Our leather supplier was acquired by a larger company last fall, which has predictably slowed things down. But our supplier has committed to certifying, in short order, that the hides it buys from large cattle ranches aren't coming from deforested areas—and to having smaller ranches mapped by 2011.

At the end of July 2009 we issued a statement praising Greenpeace for bringing the matter to the industry's attention, and it was able to declare victory. In return, it issued a statement saying that Timberland had taken a leadership position on the issue, which was as gratifying as praise from an organization that has painfully put you through the paces can be.

Here are some things I learned from the experience.

When angry activists come at you, don't stand there with your arms folded and your mind closed

You may not agree with their tactics, but they may be asking legitimate questions you should have been asking yourself. And if you can find at least one common goal—in this case, a solution to deforestation—you've also found at least one reason for working *with* each other, not against.

On the other hand, don't greet them naively with open arms

For every common goal, half a dozen personal agendas are in play. Greenpeace's include selling membership subscriptions as well as saving the world. If that weren't true, the organization would be making more phone calls and fewer sexy headlines.

In times of tension, watch and listen

That's when you learn just how committed you are to your principles—and how committed your team and your partners and even your competitors are to theirs.

Did any of this make a difference for the issue of deforestation in Brazil? The jury's still out and probably will be for a while. But I believe there's real value in the outcomes we've already seen and in the lessons I'll take with me as I continue to work to make Timberland a more responsible and sustainable organization— the same path I was on before the first e-mail came in, and the same path I'll be on tomorrow.

Originally published in September 2010. R1009A

Maclaren's CEO on Learning from a Recall

by Farzad Rastegar

Farzad Rastegar is the CEO of Maclaren USA.

The Idea

Though Maclaren USA had spent months carefully planning a recall, when the news leaked a day early, the company was unprepared. What followed taught its CEO some valuable lessons.

Like many CEOs, I subscribe to a daily e-mail service that notifies me when my company is mentioned in the news. On the morning of November 9, 2009, a Monday, the first headline I saw was "Maclaren Stroller Recall."

The story, from the New York *Daily News,* went on to explain that Maclaren USA, a business I've run since 2001, was recalling one million strollers following finger injuries to 12 children. The information about the recall was true. But I hadn't expected to read about it in the paper that day.

Maclaren had been planning to release a statement to the same effect on November 10, following guidelines set by the U.S. Consumer Product Safety Commission. But the news had somehow leaked out ahead of schedule—and in my opinion, the spin was unfair and inaccurate. Maclaren had not been ordered to take faulty strollers off the market. We were voluntarily responding to an increase in reports of children's fingertips being caught, pinched, bruised, or cut, primarily in the saddle hinges of two of our models. Some cases had involved laceration or distal amputation. These incidents took place only in the United States, involved only two of our models, and had occurred not when the strollers were in use, with the children strapped in, but when caregivers opened the devices without realizing that their charges were close enough to reach in. For several months we had worked with the CPSC on a plan to make owners more aware of the danger and to provide protective hinge covers for all our models (including those not associated with the reported incidents) to anyone who wanted them—unquestionably the right thing to do. But the news story provided none of this context. Nor did it explain that practically *all* strollers on the market have similar hinges.

That morning I immediately got dressed, headed into the office, and called my senior executives and the recall project team to talk about a response. My first concern was correcting what was now a rapidly spreading misperception. Other news outlets had picked up the story; customers were already calling us, many of them understandably upset or worried. We had hoped that the recall would build awareness about the wider risks of operating a stroller—not just about hinges. Instead we would have to start defending our brand. But we were reluctant to speak publicly without CPSC approval. We contacted the agency to see if we could release our statement early. The regulators took a few hours to come back to us with a yes, but by then we were already playing catch-up.

We also had a larger, more damaging problem. The experts advising us, including the CPSC, estimated that in the first 30 days of the recall we would get 50,000 requests for hinge covers, representing 5% of the one million strollers we had on the market. To be safe, we had prepared for more than twice that; hired extra people to handle calls, e-mails, and fulfillment; and arranged for cloud-computing capacity so that our website wouldn't be overloaded. On November 9, however, none of this was ready to go. It was a colossal oversight; we should have anticipated a leak, or at least been prepared well in advance.

As the news spread, prompting thousands of concerned parents to contact us, our communications systems first jammed and then crashed. Callers got a busy signal. E-mails went into the ether. Our website froze. The showroom at our headquarters in South Norwalk, Connecticut, was closed, because Monday is a day off for the on-the-floor sales team, so when a television crew from the local ABC affiliate showed up, peered into the dark windows, and then started to leave, I had to run down from my second-floor office to catch the reporters.

Communicating through personal mobile phones and e-mail addresses, my colleagues and I assessed the situation. Our IT team was working feverishly to bring our systems back. We immediately realized that we would need more of everything. We had hired 10 extra people; we would need 40. We'd produced 125,000 hinge covers; we would need more than triple that number. We were in triage, dealing with one issue after another, and the frustration was deep. We'd been preparing to execute on the recall for months. We were like athletes forced to play the big game a day early—in the rain. Everyone was out of breath. And things stayed that way for at least two weeks, until nearly all customer communications had been recovered and we were airlifting additional hinge covers from our production center.

Safety First

Having a safety recall at Maclaren—let alone one that went off track—was particularly painful for me. My first experience with the company had been as a parent, years before, after a stroller

I'd bought for my daughter, a top-of-the-line brand, collapsed in the middle of New York City's Fifth Avenue. My London-based sister-in-law recommended that we get a Maclaren instead, a brand then available mainly in the UK. We did, and I was so impressed with its quality that I started to do some research on the company. Founded by Owen Maclaren in 1945, the business was based in Northamptonshire and employed nearly 500 people. I was working in my family's investment company at the time, looking for opportunities. This seemed like the perfect one. We acquired the company, and I became the CEO of the U.S. business.

Maclaren's top priority has always been safety. Everyone talks about how expensive and fashionable our strollers are relative to other umbrella models on the market, but that's because they are made with the strongest and best materials and tested to the highest standards in the industry, even in the absence of regulatory requirements in the United States and many other countries. A child is a child no matter where he or she lives, and safety should never be compromised. Parents the world over get exactly the same models as parents in America.

Largely because of this commitment to quality, Maclaren has had great success. It is a leading brand, with engineering and licensing headquarters in Hong Kong, a design center in the UK, outsourced manufacturing, and a network of distributors, many of them independently owned, in various regions. This structure has served the company well in a number of ways. Centralized product and brand management ensures consistent quality, while local sales and communications teams can decide what strategies work best for their markets. But during the U.S. recall crisis, the lack of an overarching management body made global coordination difficult.

Unwelcome Delay

After we discovered the rise in reports of finger injuries in the U.S., we appointed an investigative team to look into the matter. Then, after much consultation and brainstorming with my counterparts around the world, consistent with Maclaren's global approach to product development, we decided that the company must take action in two ways. First, we would enhance or add warnings on all our strollers and in all our instruction manuals worldwide. Second, we would approach regulatory bodies in the U.S. and other markets where appropriate.

We sent a report to the CPSC on July 9 and asked for a meeting. Several weeks later the agency gave us a date—August 12—so we pulled our engineers and executives from their summer vacations and convened. We made a pitch for releasing a protective hinge cover in time for the annual industry trade show in Las Vegas in September. As a voluntary recall, the process could have been completed in three weeks. However, we finally had to settle with the CPSC on a go-live date of November 10. Our technical review and testing of the hinge cover design were completed by September; in our view, the back-and-forth with the CPSC was slow. Perhaps the delay involved a debate over how to deal with a potential industrywide risk when only one brand had exposed the problem. Or maybe the agency had broader concerns about how to regulate a consumer product category that has no mandatory minimum standards in the U.S.—even though it is second only to toys in causing injuries to children under five. Maclaren's aim was not only to execute the recall but also to make parents more aware of the safety issues. In the months leading up to November we had invested in many things: product safety experts, producing and transporting hinge covers, consultant project managers with MBAs to oversee the recall, extensive outreach to retailers, and the aforementioned additional staff and technical support. We did not invest in crisis management or communications advice. Given our reputation for safety and our work with the CPSC, we thought the PR would handle itself and that our money would be better spent supporting the recall.

A Sensationalist Leak

We were wrong. If we had hired the right advisers, we might have learned how easily an early, sensationalist leak could occur and then prepared a comprehensive response strategy for any scenario. We had in fact raised the question of confidentiality with the CPSC, because according to its regulations, retailers had to be informed about the recall in advance. They were supposed to wait until our announcement before releasing any information—but unfortunately, that guideline was no guarantee. When the news broke, our reaction was completely ad hoc. Aside from the interview with the local TV crew, I spoke to no press representatives that day. When I got home, my wife pointed me to a thoughtful blog post by Julia Kirby on the HBR website, and because I was so impressed with the clarity of its analysis, I responded to it. A few days later I gave an interview to the *Financial Times*. But even this limited outreach was criticized in the press ("Why does Mr. Rastegar have time for interviews in the midst of a product recall?"), so my colleagues and I decided, mistakenly, that I should stop talking. Instead our marketing manager, Charlotte Addison, who had started her job only weeks before the recall announcement, fielded press calls and worked to get our message out on parenting websites. It was a struggle to keep up with sometimes erroneous and sometimes vicious reporting.

Undoubtedly, a PR expert would also have predicted the vehement emotional response and the global fallout. In Canada,

Britain, Europe, and Japan, reporters, regulators, and parents were asking why Maclaren hadn't "recalled" its strollers from their countries, too. We had in fact asked the CPSC about the need for global action. Its response was that the injuries were in the United States, Maclaren USA was an American company, and American protocols must be observed. We had misgivings about that approach, but we followed the CPSC's lead. In hindsight, that was a bad decision. For one thing, the term "recall" has different meanings in different countries. For example, in the U.S. it means any corrective action, including one like issuing hinge covers, but in the UK it is a faulty product that must be returned for a refund or replacement.

The negative reaction was like an explosion from one market to the next. And because of Maclaren's decentralization, it was difficult to craft a global response. The Canadian distributor didn't want to do anything. The UK business was desperate to talk to the press. When the European Commission requested a meeting, I was the person dispatched. Eventually we decided that Charlotte would be the global point person for the press, and I would handle dealings with regulators.

We did hire a big PR firm in the middle of the crisis, but that, too, turned out to be a mistake. The firm's advice—which ranged from making an apology to limiting my personal appearances in the media because of my "foreign" accent (I'm of Persian origin)—was out of line with my desire to defend the fundamental safety of our products and to communicate directly and openly with our customers.

Valuable Lessons

As I look back at the period following that initial *Daily News* article, I think it was probably one of the most difficult times in my business life; certainly it was the worst in Maclaren's history.

But good did come of it. I've learned a lot about myself, my role as CEO, and what it means to lead a growing global company.

First, I have a new admiration for all our stakeholders—retailers, customers, and employees. I am constantly humbled by how intelligent, reasonable, and supportive they are. Even during the crisis, many parents blogged testimonials, and stores such as Mothercare in the UK issued statements of support. Meanwhile, our employees performed exceptionally well under enormous pressure, and many of the extra hires have stayed on. Our business did take a hit in the U.S. right through February 2010, but we think that was owing more to postrecall policy problems with a few big retailers than to customers' refusing to buy Maclaren's products. Overall, our sales around the world have remained strong, and our brand continues to enjoy passionate support from customers. Everyone at the company has been reminded how important it is to stay true to our safety-first values.

Second, the recall demonstrated to Maclaren's senior management team that the company must become more cohesive. We are working on an initiative called One Maclaren, with the goal of owning nearly all distribution under a single global umbrella by the end of 2011.

Third, and most important, we have realized that Maclaren must play a bigger leadership role in the industry, mobilizing other brands, manufacturers, retailers, and regulators around the world to work toward mandatory minimum global standards with common definitions, harmonized procedures, and uniform protocols. In the United States strollers remain one of the very few major consumer goods categories with no regulations. We have already approached our key partners and are preparing a set of proposals. The CPSC is moving toward regulating more children's products and has set a timetable for implementation. The safety of children, however, is an international issue.

Thanks to the recall, we have realized that Maclaren is a tiny company with a giant name. We can have an impact on our industry; we can keep our children safe and make their parents more aware. We were never in an advocacy position before, but we are now—and obsessively so.

Originally published in January–February 2011. R1101A

Duke Energy's CEO on Learning to Work with Green Activists

by James E. Rogers

James E. Rogers is the chairman, president, and CEO of Duke Energy.

The Idea

When James Rogers became CEO at then-ailing PSI (now Duke Energy), he was determined to listen to all its stakeholders. But environmentalists posed a particular challenge: The green movement had long viewed the energy industry with skepticism.

"How can you advocate for a low-carbon future when your company is among the largest emitters of carbon dioxide in the United States?"

I'm asked this question a lot. It reminds me of a time about two decades ago, when I was 42 and in my second year as a CEO, trying to lead a utility back from the brink of bankruptcy. The effects of acid rain from burning coal had become clear. Much of our industry denied the facts and resisted any regulation of sulfur dioxide emissions. My company took a different path.

I believe that a price on carbon is inevitable, and utilities that take a long-term view will be part of the solution. Smart public policy can serve the interests of both business and society. It pays to be collaborative and build a consensus. But that isn't easy.

100 Days of Listening

I wasn't sure I had what it took to be a CEO when, in 1988, I interviewed for the job of leading Public Service Indiana, which had just written down a $2.7 billion loss on a half-constructed nuclear plant. PSI generated most of its electricity by burning coal in a number of aging plants in America's heartland.

At the time, I didn't consider myself an environmentalist. I was a lawyer with a background in energy, and I was looking for something with greater challenges and more responsibility. PSI, once a highly regarded utility with deep local ties, had plenty of challenges: Its finances were in disarray, morale was damaged, and leadership had lost the confidence of regulators, shareholders, and customers.

I spent a week preparing for my job interview with PSI's board of directors and developed a plan I called "100 days of listening." The idea was to meet with the company's many stakeholders before taking action. That would help me to identify the issues, set priorities, figure out whom I could trust, and start repairing and rebuilding relationships. The other candidates had far more industry and leadership experience, but none of them came prepared with a plan. I was given the job.

All the members of my management team were much older than I was, and all of them advised me not to meet with any environmentalists. It was an emotional time for PSI's veteran executives; their largest construction project had just been killed by the very groups I was planning to talk to. Internal opposition to my proposal was so strong that I considered changing course. But that felt like a cop-out: I had proposed a plan, and now I needed to execute it. Plus I was curious about the environmentalists' point of view, and I believed in the power of collaboration to address tough problems. I decided to follow my instincts.

My management team was not pleased. Some of its members thought I was naive. Had PSI not been on the verge of bankruptcy, its dividend suspended and emergency rates in effect, I might have faced a mutiny during my second week on the job. On a Saturday morning I drove 100 miles south to the Ohio River Valley, where our abandoned nuclear plant was located. There I sat down for coffee in a diner with leaders from the environmental groups that had blocked the plant. I started by telling them I was new to the job and wanted to better understand their point of view. Soon enough they were talking straight about their perspectives, as midwesterners tend to do.

I learned that their opposition was based on three beliefs: Nuclear energy was too costly, waste disposal was unmanageable, and the additional 2,360 megawatts of baseload generation capacity wasn't needed. I disagreed with some of their positions, but I listened. The nuclear power they opposed would have replaced old coal plants with serious carbon dioxide emissions, but that issue hadn't yet surfaced. Today some of them are rethinking their stance on alternative sources of power as they confront climate change.

Stake in the Ground

I tried to create a collaborative environment internally as well as externally. I strongly believed that we needed a culture respectful of divergent views, in which problems could be identified early and unconventional solutions could be found.

The 100 days gave me time to learn the business and the personal dynamics. Then I prioritized my tasks. Near the top of my list was one that had arisen in a meeting with a state senator who chaired the environmental committee: PSI needed to integrate environmental risks into its decision making. Failure to do so had nearly caused the company to break down.

Prior management hadn't seen the risks from environmental opposition as legitimate until it was too late.

I proposed that we study the corporate environmental charters of other utilities and then create one for PSI. To my surprise, we found not one utility with a board-adopted public statement about environmental considerations in its decision making. We decided to write a charter by convening our diverse stakeholders: customers, investors, state government officials, consumer advocates, employees, and environmentalists. Some members of my team worried that dialogue would further empower groups that opposed us and would evolve into a negotiation. They were right—but that was part of the reason for doing it. We wanted a charter that established enough common ground that we would never again waste billions of dollars on half-constructing a plant.

We held meetings with about two dozen leaders from different stakeholder groups. Each meeting began with an acknowledgment of our objective: to provide clean, affordable, and reliable electricity to our 575,000 customers 24 hours a day, 365 days a year. Everyone agreed with this mission, but environmentalists focused on "clean," consumer advocates stressed "affordable," and factory owners put a premium on "reliable." Nevertheless, the framework gave everyone in the room insight into the practical trade-offs involved in providing universal access to electricity. Using that framework, we negotiated a 10-point corporate charter.

Our board ratified the charter in 1990. We printed it in our annual report, and I hung a copy above my desk. We had planted a stake. Now we needed to follow our words with actions.

The First Cap and Trade

Acid rain became more prominent in the public debate in 1989, after the findings of a 10-year federal government study on the effects of sulfur dioxide emissions were released. I spent two months consulting various experts on the issue, and met with members of Congress in Washington. I concluded that legislation to curb SO_2 emissions was inevitable. The practical questions were: What would that legislation look like? What impact would it have on customers in Indiana and the 22 other states that generated more than 50% of their electricity from coal?

President George H.W. Bush soon began championing an innovative market-based solution called cap and trade. Instead of the Environmental Protection Agency's traditional command-and-control approach, Bush—in collaboration with the Environmental Defense Fund and other groups—proposed a declining cap on SO_2 emissions. The cap would be combined with an emissions-trading mechanism and a declining allocation of free allowances to spur innovation and create a market for new low-cost solutions.

Cap and trade was a smart and creative compromise. It departed from uniform regulations that failed to consider the generating portfolios and geography of individual utilities. It generously allocated allowances to utilities in coal-dependent states in the early years and provided incentives to open low-sulfur coal mines. Most important, it enabled utilities to modernize their plants and meet aggressive emissions targets without sending electricity prices skyrocketing.

I assumed that my industry peers took a similar view of this idea. However, most executives at the 1989 annual meeting of our trade association, the Edison Electric Institute, were opposed to government action. The CEOs of the largest utilities took the hardest line. They disputed the science. They argued that the health hazards hadn't been proved and that the technology to reduce emissions was too expensive. Most of them were dismissive when I spoke up to ask, "Isn't there a way we can support this to our benefit? The technology is evolving, and it seems like we could do this."

These power brokers saw PSI as a small player without influence and me as a young guy not yet aware of how the industry worked. But my belief deepened that some form of cap and trade would come about and that our stakeholders would benefit if we took a stand in front of the issue. After all, as a regulated utility, we earned a return on all our capital expenditures, including those for environmental compliance.

In the spring of 1990 I testified before Congress in support of market-based cap and trade. Some of my industry peers were upset by my action, but others began to acknowledge that the world was changing, and having a seat at the table could be helpful. It was certainly helpful for PSI. The Clean Air Act Amendments established cap and trade that year, and PSI and other coal-dependent utilities were allocated a relatively high number of allowances, which gave us time to make a deliberate and sustainable transition to cleaner generation.

The results spoke for themselves. From 1990 to 1993 our market capitalization increased by more than 65%, from $900 million to $1.5 billion. Significantly, this increase in shareholder value did not come at the expense of our customers. In fact, we lowered our real price of electricity in Indiana from 6.2 cents to 5.87 cents per kilowatt hour. Our rates were among the most affordable in the country. By 1995 we had also reduced our SO_2 emissions by 30%.

Our ties to local communities strengthened as PSI developed more of a national reputation. That helped us grow and attract new talent to the company. In 1994 we merged with Cincinnati Gas & Electric, effectively doubling our size and extending our service territory into Ohio and Kentucky. Among my first actions as CEO of Cinergy—the new company—was to create an updated environmental charter, which was adopted at the first meeting of the board.

Fast-forward a decade to the issue of global climate change. Here, too, we were early advocates for action. As we investigated the science connecting carbon emissions to the rise of the earth's temperature, I remembered the days of the acid rain debates. I heard similar voices of resistance and denial among my peers at industry meetings. But this time we were a major player in the room. In 2006 Cinergy merged with Duke Energy, headquartered in Charlotte, North Carolina, and I was named chairman, president, and CEO.

The Tide of a Low-Carbon Future

"There is a tide in the affairs of men," Shakespeare wrote. After a deeper investigation into climate change, it became clear to me that the science was sound: Burning fossil fuels contributes to global warming. As an industry, we needed to figure out how to operate in a carbon-constrained world. As a company, we needed to understand the issue, stay ahead of it, and help shape a sustainable solution. And, just as when I was the new CEO of PSI, we needed to build a diverse coalition of stakeholders who could collaborate, negotiate, and proactively face the challenge.

In July 2006, thanks in large part to the leadership of General Electric and the World Resources Institute, a first-of-its-kind coalition of 22 companies (16 of them on the *Fortune* 500) and five leading environmental organizations created the U.S. Climate Action Partnership. The purpose of USCAP was to urge the federal government to enact strong legislation to reduce greenhouse gas emissions. As soon as USCAP was launched, critics tried to discredit it. A few people even called on me to resign as chairman of the Edison Electric Institute.

Those reactions weren't surprising. We knew we were taking a risk, and we had anticipated resistance. A key moment occurred at an EEI board meeting in January 2007, shortly before USCAP issued its first public call to action. I proposed that we go around the room and let each CEO express his or her views. Some of those from small and midsize utilities spoke forcefully about our need as an industry to deal with the realities of carbon emissions. Surprisingly, no one openly disagreed. Even the most skeptical CEOs acknowledged that if we didn't have a seat at the table, we would be on the menu. We left that important meeting with an industry consensus: The way we produced and consumed electricity was not sustainable, and we needed a set of principles to guide our support for legislation establishing a price on carbon.

Cap and Trade, the Sequel?

Over the past four years USCAP and EEI have advocated for a comprehensive cap and trade policy for carbon. They have helped give the business community a voice in the discussion about how to responsibly transition to a low-carbon future. Recently, however, our efforts have suffered a setback owing to political gridlock and misunderstandings. This is unfortunate, because the longer we wait as a nation, the more difficult it will be for the U.S. to remain competitive in the new energy economy. We need bipartisan solutions, because regulatory uncertainty complicates business decision making. This is especially true for utilities, whose investment decisions are based on time horizons of 20 to 60 years.

Regardless of what happens in Washington, the fact is that we have been living on borrowed time in the U.S. electricity markets. The real price of electricity remained flat for more than five decades in much of the country, largely because we didn't replace our aging power plants. Many of them were built in the 1950s, 1960s, and 1970s; as they are retired and replaced, the price of electricity will increase substantially.

Absent a constructive national energy policy, we must continue to innovate and integrate new technology that will help us generate cleaner, more sustainable electricity. Once again, we find ourselves collaborating with groups that some may consider controversial. For example, we've formed partnerships with a number of leading energy companies in China to share best practices and learn from the Chinese as they bring new energy technologies to scale. My bet is that technology developed from unique collaborations will bring us to a low-carbon future faster than national or worldwide policy can. But we still need smart government action. We still need a road map, for the sake of business, society, and the environment.

So when I'm on the road these days speaking about our vision, and I'm asked that question: "How can you advocate for a low-carbon future ...?" my answer begins with four words: "How can we not?"

Originally published in May 2011. R1105A

GROWING AROUND THE WORLD

OVER THE PAST SEVERAL DECADES, MANAGERS OF ESTABLISHED companies have faced one of the biggest opportunities in the history of business: The chance to dramatically grow revenues by expanding globally.

It's a set of opportunities that comes with its own set of challenges. Different governments play by dramatically different rules—as the CEO of Amway learned when China outlawed direct sales, the marketing model his firm had been using for decades. Managing a global workforce adds complexity—which is why one CEO describes how he abandoned traditional notions of "expatriates" and "locals" and instead created an executive corps that's evolved beyond having a "home" market. Some of the challenges are cultural: In a memorable scene, the CEO of Heinz describes how his Chinese hosts liked to play "Hail to the Chief" when he entered the room at a banquet—a compliment that sent his wife into unstoppable spasms of laughter.

These leaders make their views on globalization clear: Despite risk and inconvenience, language barriers and jet lag, the hard work of breaking into new markets is well worth the toil.

Burberry's CEO on Turning an Aging British Icon into a Global Luxury Brand

by Angela Ahrendts

Angela Ahrendts is the CEO of Burberry.

The Idea

Before Angela Ahrendts became Burberry's CEO, licensing threatened to destroy the brand's unique strengths. The answer? Centralize design and focus on innovating core heritage products.

When I became the CEO of Burberry, in July 2006, luxury was one of the fastest-growing sectors in the world. With its rich history, centered on trench coats that were recognized around the world, the Burberry brand should have had many advantages. But as I watched my top managers arrive for our first strategic planning meeting, something struck me right away. They had flown in from around the world to classic British weather, gray and damp, but not one of these more than 60 people was wearing a Burberry trench coat. I doubt that many of them even owned one. If our top people weren't buying our products, despite the great discount they could get, how could we expect customers to pay full price for them?

It was a sign of the challenges we faced. Even in a burgeoning global market, Burberry was growing at only 2% a year. The company had an excellent foundation, but it had lost its focus in the process of global expansion. We had 23 licensees around the world, each doing something different. We were selling products such as dog cover-ups and leashes. One of our highest-profile stores, on Bond Street in London, had a whole section of kilts. There's nothing wrong with any of those products individually, but together they added up to just a lot of stuff—something for everybody, but not much of it exclusive or compelling.

In luxury, ubiquity will kill you—it means you're not really luxury anymore. And we were becoming ubiquitous. Burberry needed to be more than a beloved old British company. It had to develop into a great global luxury brand while competing against much larger rivals. Among luxury players, Louis Vuitton Moët Hennessy (LVMH) had almost 12 times—and Pinault-Printemps-Redoute (PPR) more than 16 times—Burberry's revenue. We wanted a share of the disposable income of the world's most elite buyers—and to win it, we'd have to fight for prime real estate in the world's most rapidly growing consumer markets. In many ways, it felt like a David-and-Goliath battle.

One "Brand Czar"

On the surface, I might have seemed an unlikely CEO for a company that was considered quintessentially British. I was raised in a small town in Indiana and educated at Ball State University. I was a classic midwesterner—something the *Financial Times* had fun mocking when I first took the job. But I'd been fortunate enough to work with and learn from some of the most inspirational leaders in the fashion industry, from Paul Charron to Donna Karan. And I had 25 years of experience on my side.

I also clearly had one attribute that made me a good fit: I admire and respect great brands and helped to build some over the years. From Apple to Starbucks, I love the consistency—knowing that anywhere in the world you can depend on having the same experience in the store or being served a latte with the same taste and in the same cup. That's great branding.

Unfortunately, Burberry didn't have a lot of that. An experience in any given Burberry store in the world might be very different from the customer's previous one. As part of my transition, I spent six months working closely with my predecessor, hitting the road to get a sense of Burberry worldwide. In Hong Kong, I was introduced to a design director and her team, who proudly showed me the line they were creating for that market: polo shirts and woven shirts and everything with the famous Burberry check, but not a single coat.

Then we went to America, where I was introduced to another design director and design team. This team was creating outerwear, but at half the price point of that in the UK. Furthermore, the coats were being manufactured in New Jersey. So we were making classic Burberry raincoats that said "Made in the U.S.A." I later learned that we had outerwear licensees in Italy and Germany making trench coats that were even cheaper than those in the United States.

Great global brands don't have people all over the world designing and producing all kinds of stuff. It became quite clear that if Burberry was going to be a great, pure, global luxury brand, we had to have one global design director. We had an incredible young designer named Christopher Bailey, with whom I'd worked at Donna Karan and who I knew was a sensational talent. So I introduced him early on as the "brand czar." I told the team, "Anything that the consumer sees—anywhere in the world—will go through his office. No exceptions."

Within a year we had let the entire Hong Kong design team go and had brought some of the U.S. outerwear team to the UK, where we centralized all our design under Christopher. We closed the New Jersey factory—along with one in Wales that was making polo shirts—and began investing in our Castleford facility in Yorkshire, which makes our heritage rainwear. Closing the Welsh factory caused a political firestorm—I was even called to testify before Parliament alongside Burberry's highly respected chairman—but we stood behind our decision. As a company, we always do what's best for the brand, because our job is to protect it and keep it powerful and relevant. If we do that, even if it involves closing a factory with 300 employees, many more jobs will be created in time. We've doubled the head count at Castleford since then and almost tripled our global workforce to nearly 10,000, adding more than 1,000 jobs in the UK over the past two years alone.

Sticking to the Core

Burberry is 156 years old; its coats were worn in the trenches of World War I by British soldiers, and for decades thereafter they were so much a part of British culture that the company earned a royal warrant, making it an official supplier to the royal family. Sir Ernest Shackleton wore a Burberry during his Antarctic expedition. Movie legends wore them on the silver screen. For more than a century the Burberry trench coat was cool. But when I became CEO, outerwear represented only about 20% of our global brand business. Fashion apparel and check accessories were leading our strategy. The more we examined the situation, the clearer it became that this wasn't consistent with our luxury vision.

It's not unusual for a luxury company to be born from a single product and then diversify. Louis Vuitton began with luggage, and Gucci with leather goods. But even as they diversified, each continued to earn the majority of its revenue from its original core products. Surveying the industry, we realized that Burberry was the only iconic luxury company that wasn't capitalizing on its historical core. We weren't proud of it. We weren't innovating around it.

Furthermore, we were almost ignoring some of our strongest assets. Our weaving facility in Yorkshire produced the exclusive waterproof gabardine on which the company was founded. Thomas Burberry had created this fabric and the trench coat design for those early military and exploration commissions. The weaving facility was near the Castleford trench coat factory, in the north of England—fortunately, we hadn't resorted to outsourcing in faraway places. What could be better than an authentic heritage brand with a great vertical supply chain? But we weren't investing in it. We weren't optimizing it.

After brainstorming and formalizing our instincts, we commissioned a consulting firm to provide us with competitor benchmarking. Our instincts confirmed, we clearly saw the way forward: We would reinforce our heritage, our Britishness, by emphasizing and growing our core luxury products, innovating them and keeping them at the heart of everything we did. I have to admit that some managers were cynical. A lot of them had been at Burberry for a really long time. I'm sure they left saying, "Focusing on trench coats—that's our strategy?" But most of us were confident that it was the right plan.

The Ethos of the Trench

The decision to focus on our heritage opened up a wealth of creativity. Christopher and the designers and marketers all started dreaming up ways to reinforce the idea that everything we did—from our runway shows to our stores—should start with the ethos of the trench.

At the same time, we had to shift Burberry's historical corporate structure to reflect this new, purer point of view. We had great people, but we were organized like a department store. We had a person over each men's category and a person over each women's category. They made decisions that worked for their departments but might not make sense for the whole business. We needed to change, to focus on the big picture: the brand. In addition to putting Christopher in charge of all design, we had to hire functional expertise—a head of corporate resources, a head of planning, and a chief supply chain officer. It was all pretty basic, but necessary if we were to reach our goals.

To strengthen our retail operation, we decided to focus on markets where our competitors already had a presence, signaling the right kind of consumers to support a luxury brand. As our first blueprint for expansion, we identified every market in the world where two of our peers had stores and we had none. In the past six years we've opened 132 new stores, and we've refocused our retailing staff on outerwear. Trench coats are among the most expensive items we sell (many of them are priced over $1,000), but the staff was least equipped to sell them. Our salespeople had become accustomed to selling what was easy—relatively inexpensive items such as polo shirts. On commission, they'd be better off selling one trench coat than 10 polo shirts. They understood the math, but they needed tools to fully appreciate and communicate why the trench was the best investment for their customers. We established strong sales and service programs to put product education front and center. We created videos to demonstrate Burberry craftsmanship: All the collars are hand-rolled and hand-stitched. We equipped our sales associates with iPads and our stores with audiovisual technology to show these videos to best effect. We knew that beautiful, compelling content would connect customers to the brand and our iconic trench.

We also began to shift our marketing efforts from targeting everyone, everywhere, to focusing on the luxury customers of the future: millennials. We believed that these customers were being ignored by our competitors. This was our white space.

The decision was not without controversy; we were choosing to aim squarely at a generation that had no current knowledge of Burberry's core product. The effort had to be led by design—we needed to create outerwear that was innovative, cool, and so inviting that people would become repeat customers. Burberry used to have just a few basic styles of trench coats: Almost all were beige with the signature check lining, and the differences between them were minor. Now we have more than 300 SKUs, from capes and cropped jackets to the classic Burberry trench in a range of vibrant colors and styles, with everything from mink collars and alligator epaulets to studded leather sleeves. We had to infuse the new lines with our heritage. We also had to rethink our entire marketing approach for these customers—to make it digital. When we began, we had a few regional websites, so we consolidated them and redesigned everything on one platform. It showcases every facet of the brand. It has become the hub of all our marketing and branding, and a trench coat is always one of the first things you see when you go online. The site is designed to speak to that millennial consumer through emotive brand content: music, movies, heritage, storytelling. And we understand how critical it is. More people visit our platform every week than walk into all our stores combined. And the majority of our employees at corporate headquarters in London are under 30. They understand who we are trying to reach.

Now every major new initiative has the trench coat front and center. In 2009 it was the inspiration for our first social media platform, artofthetrench.com. Celebrating the iconic trench and the people who wear it, the site has had more than 2.5 million visitors to date. Last year, when we took our first step into customization, it was never in question that we would launch with the iconic trench. Burberry Bespoke went live on burberry.com offering some 12 million possible styles, and we are now introducing it in our physical stores in London and Chicago. And as we take direct control of our fragrance and beauty business next year, we will fully leverage the trench—as we did so successfully in the launch of Burberry Body perfume.

Rewards of the Transformation

In a way, we're right back to our roots. I always remind employees that we didn't found the company, Thomas Burberry did—at the age of 21. He was young. He was innovative. We say that his spirit lives on, and that it's this generation's job to keep his legacy going.

The company transformation paid off. Today 60% of our business is apparel, and outerwear makes up more than half of that. At the end of fiscal 2012, Burberry's revenues and operating income had doubled over the previous five years, to $3 billion and $600 million, respectively.

That's not to say it has all been smooth sailing. Getting Burberry back on track took years of hard work, and we're still navigating tricky waters in a cyclical global luxury market. In September 2012 we took the unusual step of issuing a sales update ahead of our quarterly earnings report: We were seeing a slowdown in traffic globally. A few weeks later, with better insight into the numbers, we were able to report that although traffic was down, the *quality* of our sales was actually improving: We were realizing higher transaction values, better conversion rates, and greater demand for our more elevated Prorsum and London lines. So although the aspirational customers at entry price points are behaving more cautiously, the brand is resonating ever more strongly with our core luxury audience.

We've always said we're not immune to the ebb and flow of the macroeconomy, but that doesn't change our vision. We have absolute clarity about—and commitment to—our proven strategies, which gives us confidence for the long term. That's how we run our business and how a great global brand is created. In 2011 Burberry was named the fourth fastest-growing brand globally by both Interbrand (behind Apple, Google, and Amazon) and WPP/BrandZ (behind Facebook, Baidu, and Wells Fargo). In 2012 it was the fastest-growing luxury brand on Interbrand's index. That's beyond what we imagined was possible back in that strategy meeting in 2006.

Today it's taken for granted inside the company that the trench coat must remain our most exciting, most iconic product. It guides all our decisions. Our sales associates understand it. This product is who we are. That is evident when I observe what our employees wear to work. If you ask a Burberry senior executive how many trench coats he or she owns, the answer is likely to be eight or nine. Everyone has a packable version. Everyone has a white one. Everyone has an evening one. We have all different lengths.

As for me, I don't have an exact count, but I can safely confess to owning a dozen. They're not just raincoats anymore. They are the foundation of a great brand and a great company.

Originally published in January–February 2013. R1301A

Reckitt Benckiser's CEO on Building a Company Without Borders

by Bart Becht

Bart Becht is the CEO of Reckitt Benckiser, headquartered in Slough, England.

The Idea

You may never have heard of Reckitt Benckiser, but in the past few years the company has out-performed its rivals P&G, Unilever, and Colgate in growth—even during the downturn. Here's how.

They say you can't go home again. If you work for Reckitt Benckiser, you *can* go home—but you may not want to, and you certainly won't have to. Many companies, when they describe themselves as global, mean they have operations around the world, they work virtually and in all time zones, and their key people are developed through stints in other markets. Our version is more comprehensive. Most of our top managers haven't held jobs in their countries of origin for years and view themselves as global citizens rather than as citizens of any given nation. We have operations in more than 60 countries. Our top 400 managers represent 53 different nationalities.

We've spent the past 10 years building this culture of global mobility because we think it's one of the best ways to generate new ideas and create global entrepreneurs.

And it has paid off. Products launched in the past three years—all the result of global cross-fertilization—account for 35% to 40% of our net revenue. For example, Finish, an all-in-one dishwasher tablet you drop into your machine, is now the leader in its market category. Recently we successfully introduced QuantuMatic—an automatic dispenser of dishwasher detergent that doesn't need to be refilled for up to a month. With constant innovation like this we've enjoyed steady, profitable growth, even during the downturn. Since 2005 we've outpaced all our big competitors. During the recession we've invested more than ever in marketing, and we grew at a rate of 8% (at constant exchange rates) in 2009.

A Company Without a Country

Reckitt Benckiser resulted from a merger in 1999 of Reckitt & Colman—a British purveyor of household cleaning products with a great stable of brands—and the Dutch-listed Benckiser, a much smaller but better-performing consumer goods company. But we don't want to be known as an Anglo-Dutch enterprise, or by any other label based on our operations or history. We're not any country's company—we're a truly multicountry company.

That is by design. Postmerger we mixed the national cultures quickly in every corner of our operations. Premerger many of the local businesses had been running themselves more or less independent of the rest of the world and without regard to overall corporate priorities. We transferred people who embodied RB's values into key positions in new markets. Managers from one side of the merger were purposely moved to another territory, and then moved again. Now in every country we have people of many nationalities as well as local citizens. Today an Italian is running the UK business, and an American is running the German business. A Dutchman is running the U.S. business, an Indian the Chinese business, a Belgian the Brazilian business, and a Frenchman the Russian business. It's not that you can't advance at RB in your local company. You can. But we also offer unique global mobility and experience to people who want to grow their careers on a world stage.

To facilitate this mobility, we established compensation rules that apply equally to our top 400 managers in all markets, making international transfers easy. We have just one employment contract, and our salary ranges were developed with global benchmarking. Our annual cash bonus structure and long-term incentive plans are the same for everyone, as are our pensions, medical plans, and other benefits. We have no expatriates in the traditional sense, no tax equalization or guarantee of a job back in one's home country. When employees take jobs in other countries, they're transferred as "local hires." We've built in standard protocols to make it easier for people with families to move. For example, we fund whatever school the employee chooses for his or her children because we understand how important that is to a family's adjustment. That way, we can instantly accomplish a transfer—we don't have to negotiate a lot of convoluted contractual nonsense. We have moved people to new countries in as little as two days.

We also do something pretty rare with graduates. In some markets we help foreign students to get work permits in the countries where they've been studying. The very fact that they have traveled to study means they are internationally minded and thus likely to be keen to work in other countries as well. At a lot of companies it's assumed that employees, having "seen the world," will sooner or later return to their home countries to continue their careers. Our idea is that you focus primarily on the best job possible for you, regardless of country.

That kind of life isn't for everyone, and not everyone has to follow that path. But those who love it really love it. It's exciting, and it gives pace, challenge, learning, and a buzz to people's careers—along with the satisfaction of being able to be entrepreneurial and innovative.

We try to put our high potentials in stretching situations around the globe. For example, we had one excellent employee who wanted to be moved to an international marketing job. We had an opening in India, but that would have been a poor choice for him—he's Indian. Our previous three marketing people in India were German, French, and British. If this employee wanted to grow, he needed to acquire different experiences and learning, so a better development opportunity would be for him to work in Brazil or Mexico. Our high potentials have to find their footing very quickly, and most of them grow tremendously when we take them out of their familiar zone.

Even their failures in new markets are important learning experiences for our high potentials. One of our top managers, who is Dutch, still talks about the hard lesson he learned when we transferred him to Turkey. In The Netherlands, where he had worked before, billing and receivables were predictable and orderly. In Turkey the currency suddenly collapsed by 70%— while he was focusing on market share rather than on delinquent receivables. As he puts it, there's nothing like a currency failure to change your views on tight financial management.

Conflict Is Good

With so many different native languages in our company, it was necessary to make English the official language for all meetings. I'm Dutch, but I don't speak Dutch with any of my Dutch colleagues, because if others are around, it excludes them. We are one team with one language. English isn't most people's native language, and often our English isn't pretty. But the way we see it, it doesn't matter as long as you give a view. If you don't express your opinion, you don't have an opinion, and that's a fatal weakness for people who want to do well at Reckitt Benckiser. You have to stand for something, no matter how bluntly you communicate it.

That means our meetings are a bit chaotic. Everybody wants to be heard, so it's more like an Italian family dinner than a nicely organized board meeting. What takes over in our meetings is an intensity and a feeling that we have to fight for better ideas. Conflict is good. We don't care about consensus. Not having it doesn't slow us down and doesn't mean that people aren't aligned. We make decisions fast and then all stand behind them.

What isn't tolerated is conflict that simply slows down decision making or is for political or personal gain. Almost every key decision is made in the meeting at which it's first discussed. We expect people to come armed with facts, be prepared to argue their point of view, and be willing to live with the decision we ultimately make. Get 80% alignment and 100% agreement to implement. And move quickly.

But I also don't believe in crushing minority views. If we have 10 people in a room, eight of them agreeing on one thing and two passionately believing something else, we don't try to resolve it to everyone's satisfaction. We allow those two to experiment with their ideas—even if everyone else thinks they're wrong. At the end of the day, what counts is not what the 10 people in that room think, it's what the consumer thinks. So we let them run maverick small-scale experiments to get consumer feedback. Sometimes our biggest ideas come that way.

About six years ago we had a huge internal debate about a product called Air Wick Freshmatic, which automatically releases freshener into the air on a schedule. It originated when one of our brand managers in Korea observed a new kind of automatic scent dispenser in stores there. In his opinion it was not a well-designed product, but he thought the idea was intriguing, so he brought it to a group meeting at our headquarters. Vigorous debate ensued.

A couple of our managers believed it should be a consumer product in Europe, but a lot more thought that made no sense—it might work in Korea on a very small scale, but it would never work in Western markets. For one thing, it would have to be priced well above the standard air freshener, and it wasn't clear that the market would support that. Also, this would be our first foray into something electronic, with wires, batteries, interval switches—a complex technology combination. The product would require new manufacturing facilities if it went to any scale. But two people saw the potential and were willing to fight for the chance to prove it.

If somebody wants to stand up under stress and say, "No, I passionately believe in this. You guys are all wrong! We've got to do this," then I'm willing to take a chance. So in this case I said fine, here's the money—go figure it out, but do it on a small scale. And that's what they did.

In January 2004, initial testing of the idea with consumers in the UK produced extraordinary results. By the end of the year the product was in more than 30 other countries, and we'd overseen the building of a new factory in China to make it—which meant we had to source materials we had no prior experience with.

Today Air Wick Freshmatic is sold in 85 countries, with a wide range of options for consumers. It generates well in excess of £200 million annually. That product had the most successful launch in our history.

Of course, things don't always work out that well. We've launched some beautifully thought-out products that we were passionate about—but consumers weren't. A few years ago we introduced a wonderful product to clean your microwave: You put a little sachet into the oven and start it. While the oven is heating, the sachet pops and spreads cleaner around. When it's finished, the sachet has become a cloth to wipe your cleaner away. It was a beautifully designed product. But it turns out that people don't actually want to clean their microwaves all that often, so we pulled it from the market. If we are going to fail, we want to fail small and quickly.

Failure is actually a huge incentive for the kind of people who fit well with our company, because they're so personally competitive that they'll work even faster for the next success. Everyone wants to do something to get on the map.

I just moved one manager from Chile to Turkey. He earned that move because he had done something very challenging in his market—he'd launched one of our "powerbrands," the sanitizer Dettol, in Latin America. It wasn't the biggest success we've ever had, but the point is that he did it. He was the guy who brought Dettol to Chile and created a platform for its growth. That's his mark on the business.

That kind of thing earns you a promotion in this company, and the promotion will probably take you to another part of the world. Some people look at us and think they'd have to be nuts to work here. We're looking for people with a certain level of maturity, intensity, and competitiveness. If you bring all of that to Reckitt Benckiser, it will be rewarded.

As the CEO who has guided the company for more than a decade, I'd like to take credit for having a brilliant strategy or unique insights into the global marketplace. But in reality the "vision" slide we use today is the exact same one we've used since the merger. We have a very simple approach to the business: Focus on 17 powerbrands in fast-growing categories, innovate and invest behind them—and do so in every market.

At the end of the day, what is most distinct about Reckitt Benckiser is its people and culture. I can tell in three minutes if someone would be a good fit for our company. We'd rather have a position open for a long time, if necessary, than put the wrong person in place. It's that important.

Originally published in April 2010. R1004K

Aramex's CEO on Turning a Failed Sale into a Huge Opportunity

by Fadi Ghandour

Fadi Ghandour is the founder and CEO of Aramex International and was a founding partner of Maktoob .com, the world's largest Arab online community.

The Idea

Fadi Ghandour has built one of the most successful entrepreneurial enterprises to emerge from the Arab world, Aramex International, overcoming rejections, cash-flow crises, and naysayers in every country where he tried to do business.

In 1984, two years into building the express delivery company Aramex, I was preparing for the most important meeting I'd ever had. My partner, Bill Kingson, and I were hoping to persuade the Seattle-based Airborne Express to buy 50% of Aramex for $100,000.

At the time, out of a modest office in Amman, Jordan, we had launched several other small offices in the Middle East, hoping to become the first courier company based in that region. Our operations were tiny (we hadn't yet exceeded $1 million in revenue), I was personally playing a range of roles from chief salesman to occasional delivery guy, and the cash flow was uncomfortably tight. We were what I would describe as a guerrilla setup—a scrappy, hand-to-mouth business.

The Middle East was not yet seen as a growth opportunity for global courier companies: Skirting civil wars and complex political relationships was an enormous logistical and bureaucratic challenge. In addition, in some countries the business market wasn't yet demanding courier services; in others those services were monopolized by companies or the postal authorities. We thought that such an investment from Airborne, along with the explicit endorsement of one of the world's most respected logistics companies, could seal the future of our start-up.

Bill and I did get in to meet with both the CEO and the COO of Airborne Express, but they swiftly turned us down. Airborne was just starting to explore expansion outside the U.S. and wasn't ready to invest in a small market like the Middle East, let alone in a start-up. That was a huge disappointment to Bill and me. But we left the meeting with a valuable consolation prize: the promise of some business. At that time Airborne was occasionally asked to courier packages to various Arab countries; it would use either a competitor or some small London-based company to deliver in the region. Because the Middle East was such an insignificant part of Airborne's business, there would be little risk in giving those packages to Aramex. But to us it meant the largest and most important account for a long time. Our pitch had been that we could reliably handle whatever business Airborne acquired in the region—so it wouldn't have to turn to a competitor. We could be a neutral partner, acting on its behalf.

I realized immediately that Airborne's offer would give us an opportunity to learn from one of the world's most successful courier companies—and, more crucial, to take advantage of its technology and global reach. Instead of getting a 50% owner, we would get a master class on how to grow our own business. That partnership would make the difference to our survival—and provide us with the rapid learning curve to set our own ambitions high. Nineteen years later, when Airborne was sold to its former archrival, DHL, not only had we learned everything we could from it, but we were ready to be a global leader in our own right.

"We Are Airborne Express...and Federal Express...and..."

Business from Airborne gave us enough credibility to knock on other doors. I realized that the prime competitors in the logistics and courier business feared one another more than they would fear us. So we sold our services as being provided by safe, neutral hands. We would call clients and say, "We are Airborne Express," or "We are Emery"—whatever company we were representing. We wore many hats and customized our services to suit whoever gave us business. If you looked back at the global offices of some of the major package-delivery companies in the 1980s and 1990s, you'd find some recurring addresses. Those were actually Aramex offices.

After knocking on the door at Federal Express time and time again, we finally gained it as a client in 1987. Aramex thus acquired its single largest account to date, because FedEx had more packages going into the Middle East than all its competitors combined, giving us a healthy monthly infusion of cash.

But our first serious relationship was to be our most significant. Airborne Express started to build a global alliance of regional courier companies like Aramex in order to offer customers service in every corner of the world without having to run or acquire all those operations itself. We were among the first of what would eventually be roughly 40 companies in the alliance—which was called Overseas Express Carriers (OEC)—whose responsibilities included establishing common operating procedures, rates, and quality assurance. Because Airborne provided its package-tracking technology to all its OEC partners, we had an enormous competitive advantage at a very low cost. (We also acquired e-mail early on, achieving a quantum leap in management efficiency.) Previously Aramex had relied on faxes and telex machines for tracking and tracing; we didn't have the resources or the expertise to create our own system. Suddenly we were part of a sophisticated global operation. We'd been given access to similar systems from FedEx and Emery, but without permission to use them for our own Middle Eastern customers. Airborne's system elevated us to a whole new level of service.

Nevertheless, building a regional Middle East company in those days was a huge challenge. As I said, wars, invasions, and post office monopolies were often nearly insurmountable barriers to service delivery. Sometimes we had to operate under a freight-forwarding umbrella while we waited for a courier company license, or risk having our operations shut down by local officials. In Egypt that license would cost $80,000 a year—a hefty amount for a start-up. I was kept busy traveling around the region looking for partners that would do a joint venture with us, agree to represent us, or "sponsor" us. Our goal then was simply an office address, a couple of cars, and a phone; we outsourced customs clearance to agents and found other small courier companies to deliver whatever packages we had. The first five years of the company's life were spent making sure we had an office in each country so that we could perform the services our global clients required.

Adding Business Bit by Bit

But by 1994, with relative peace in the region, our business had reached $38 million in revenue and we could see enormous growth potential. Unfortunately, so could some of our biggest customers. Federal Express began cutting back on countries it wanted us to handle and setting up its own operations across the region. By then we already had an established brand and an indigenous customer base in the Middle East. Our strategy was to be cautious and stealthy. We started by focusing on small and midsize companies that were sensitive to cost. Our salespeople targeted clients that would give us direct business worth maybe $200 to $1,000 a month. We found that something as simple as a 10% discount over the competition—with our Airborne-granted ability to offer reliable tracking—was enough to win them over. It was grassroots sales: a shipment here, a shipment there, slowly building our revenue and number of clients.

At the same time, the global logistics industry was consolidating: FedEx and UPS had acquired companies such as Gelco and IML in Europe and Asia; Emery and Purolator had merged. FedEx bought Flying Tigers—an all-freight airline. In addition to expanding our presence geographically, we diversified our revenue stream by becoming a one-stop shop for freight forwarding; shipping by air, sea, and land; and a variety of logistics services across the region.

We also focused on making the most of our participation in Airborne's OEC alliance. We stayed heavily involved in its governance for strategic reasons—we wanted to continue to develop our business relationship with Airborne and our alliance colleagues. We did joint sales calls with them. We pushed Airborne to bring us U.S. business in the Middle East. We seized every opportunity to learn what clients required and differentiated ourselves by offering customized services. We tried to align ourselves as closely as possible with Airborne; it may have looked to the outside world as if Airborne owned us.

By 1996 it did—at least a part of us. A little over a decade after we had offered 50% of our small company for $100,000, Airborne bought 9% for $2 million. It saw Aramex as a potential platform for going global without having to build its own Middle East operations from scratch.

The First Good Night's Sleep

Having a toehold in the Middle East was good for Airborne's serious global ambitions. For us, the deal was catalytic. Though by that point we had revenue of $52 million, our operating income was only $2.4 million. Worse, as is true for many entrepreneurs, our monthly cash flow was consistently precarious. With that $2 million in the bank, I had the first good night's sleep in 14 years. Up to that point my life had revolved around daily meetings about accounts payable, how much money we had in banks across the world, and how we could scrape and scrimp and pay. We had a somewhat justified reputation for being a late payer.

We immediately communicated to all our strategic suppliers that we were ready to better manage our payables with them. Until we got that $2 million, I hadn't actually been sure we could survive. Suddenly, instead of a hand-to-mouth start-up, we were a start-up that could pay its bills on time—and that already had hefty revenues. It put us in a great place to stabilize and grow the business.

After Airborne's investment, we tried to raise additional capital for expansion, thinking that we could attract regional investors interested in our growth story. But we failed, mostly because they could not understand our non-asset-based business model or grasp that a small company from the region could actually compete with the giants of the industry.

In July 1996 Bill said we should go public on the NASDAQ. My reaction was "You must be kidding!" But in January 1997, after some tough months of preparing to adhere to SEC requirements, we became the first company from the Arab world ever to go public on the NASDAQ. Our IPO was for only $7 million, but Airborne's name made a huge difference for us. In all our road shows we would talk about the partnership, and we could see that it gave U.S. institutional investors confidence in us. All of a sudden regional investors, too, were interested. We followed up with secondary offerings and ultimately raised a total of about $14 million.

Though we were still active in Airborne's alliance, that influx of capital allowed us to ramp up our own growth, and we didn't waste a minute. We were confident enough to start pushing the boundaries. We began moving into territories outside the Middle East, including India, Sri Lanka, Bangladesh, and Hong Kong. This aggressive expansion was a constant point of disagreement between us and Airborne as we became much more independent and less reliant on OEC partners in our operations.

We did fear losing access to Airborne's tracking system, which had carried us for more than 10 years. So I made building our own system the leading priority for the company. By 2000 we had recruited a good IT team that was busy creating the system internally and with outside vendors. The team got a boost when a senior Airborne employee in Europe, who had considerable global operations experience and intimate knowledge of the technology needed for tracking and tracing systems, decided to resign. That allowed us to recruit him, despite Airborne's discomfort. His job from day one was to focus exclusively on building the system with our technology team in Jordan, which took about two years.

Our Place in the Sun

In 2003 our preparedness plan paid off when, as we had long feared, Airborne announced that it was to be acquired by DHL. Airborne gave us nine months' notice that it would be withdrawing all its support and business from us. By then we had operations or skeleton operations in key markets and were only six months away from having a fully independent system for package tracking and tracing. Immediately after the announcement about Airborne's acquisition we called a meeting of the OEC partners in London. I stood up and said, "Listen, Airborne is going, but by the time it switches off, Aramex will be able to provide you with a tracking system that will maintain the alliance." We were ready to replace or take over every operation that Airborne was going to exit.

When Airborne actually switched off its systems, in March 2004, we said, "Thank you very much" and switched ours on. It was almost a nonevent. In that moment Aramex went from hat-in-hand hopeful to global leader. It was a fantastic feeling. We had learned and developed with our partners along the way, and now we were ready to lead.

In some ways it was a sad end to our relationship with Airborne, but within Aramex we were celebrating. We were truly an entrepreneurial company, and the partnership had prevented us from realizing our full potential. So we were finally going to take our place in the sun.

In January 2002 I had taken the company private again through a leveraged buyout in partnership with the newly formed private equity firm Abraaj Capital. This deal was the first of its kind in the Middle East and set the stage for a booming private equity industry in the region. In 2005 Abraaj exited the investment through an IPO on the Dubai Financial Market that was dramatically successful: We had wanted to raise $270 million, and we were oversubscribed by a factor of 64.

At year's end our 2010 global revenue was estimated at $600 million and our operating income at $60 million. Our market capitalization is now $900 million. What felt like a big disappointment in 1984 didn't work out so badly after all.

Originally published in March 2011. R1103A

Genpact's CEO on Building an Industry in India from Scratch

by Pramod Bhasin

Pramod Bhasin is the chief executive officer of Genpact.

The Idea

As the head of GE Capital in India, Bhasin found its growth hamstrung by government bureaucracy. Then he had a vision—he could offer back-office services across GE Capital. It was the beginning of Genpact—and of an entire industry.

For several months in the late 1990s, I was inundated with phone calls from competitors and other companies that wanted to visit the offices of GE Capital in India. Taking competitors on tours of the facilities isn't among the responsibilities of most top executives—indeed, it isn't done at all. But I agreed because I viewed the requests from such companies as Standard Chartered Bank, Bank of America, and Accenture as a sign that we were on the cusp of something incredible.

And we were. Today my company, Genpact, handles business process management and employs 43,000 people around the world. It also indirectly contributes, we believe, to the employment of another million people, who work in businesses that support us and our employees. We are in 13 countries and we operate 39 facilities serving 400 other companies. Genpact spun off from its parent company, GE Capital, in 2005 and is now a $1.26 billion publicly traded company.

But 13 years ago it was little more than a small division of GE Capital. Then the head of GE Capital in India, I was trying to find ways to grow the business. At that time the division was the first 100% foreign-owned financial services company that had been allowed into India. In our effort to create a local market, we were providing back-office services such as processing car loans and credit card transactions. India had just begun to open its borders—we were, in effect, an experiment by the government. But I could see how vulnerable the business was to changes in government policy and philosophy. We were hamstrung by regulations and red tape. When Indian banks faced a liquidity crisis, the government asked them not to lend to us, because it assumed that our borrowing from them was contributing to the liquidity problem. I recognized that a single regulatory stroke could change the dynamics of our organization completely. And it was hard to build a sustainable business that was so dependent on regulations under the government's control.

At the same time, I could see on a daily basis that an eager, ambitious talent pool existed both within the company and across India. Why not take advantage of it to build our business? We could expand our back-office support services to GE Capital all over the world.

I remember asking a handful of people I trusted if this idea was feasible. All of them said, unequivocally, no. What I was talking about would require building a large-scale facility unlike anything that existed in the region; hiring huge numbers of people and training them to Six Sigma standards on products they knew nothing about; persuading regional and national governments and telecommunications companies to set up and ensure service and infrastructure at a level unheard of in India; and creating an entire business ecosystem.

The concerns that were expressed ranged from the extreme (a terrorist attack would take us out) to the thoughtful—some of which I'd anticipated, such as that mission-critical processes might fail in our hands, or that if we messed things up, we might destroy the whole company's supply chain. Some people within GE worried that we'd be stripping out a critical layer of judgment—middle management. We would lose crucial records. They also had simple concerns that were easily dismissed, such as whether we would be able to set up modern offices and hire people who spoke English. But many concerns were valid and would require extremely careful planning on my part.

Completely Uncharted Territory

It was a nearly unimaginable undertaking. Many things could go wrong. So, I thought, we would need a foolproof plan. We'd have to think defensively—to get ahead of any real concerns.

I didn't do any business plan modeling or studies to prove that an opportunity existed. To me, it was obvious. I knew that if we could get sophisticated technology to support us—a very big if in India at the time—we had the raw talent to offer our services at a small fraction of the cost elsewhere. So in 1997 I approached Gary Wendt, who then headed GE Capital, for money to launch a pilot project. He gave me the princely sum of $2 million to make it work.

In hindsight, getting the initial investment was the easy part. (We eventually spent closer to $5 million on the start-up costs.) We had virtually nothing in place to make such a global operation work. We couldn't just sit down and do the proper analysis to plan it, because this was completely uncharted territory. We did draw up a business plan, but there was so much finger-in-the-air stuff that I don't think it had much credibility. We didn't even know at the start how big the venture could be. We just said, "Let's light a fire and see what happens." We did know, however, that given the low costs of highly educated labor in India, we could probably build an operation that would save GE Capital 30% to 50% of what it was then spending on similar services. That was really the essence of our business plan. It was also pretty much all we knew.

Having a few people trained to provide minor back-office support for a nascent Indian market was a far cry from handling a large volume of work and calls from all over the world at any time of day. We needed to conceive the entire operation from scratch. We decided that we had to become very good, very quickly, at four key elements: hiring the right people, training them, building a tool kit to replicate our learning in other parts of the world and to move processes from one location to another, and embedding Six Sigma quality controls in our operation from day one. We would be a beta site with the potential for huge growth at GE Capital—if we got it right.

We had no expertise in recruiting and training the people we'd need for the work. And the products they'd be supporting, such as mortgages and credit cards, were completely foreign to most of our potential employees; training would have to begin at an extremely basic level. Even more challenging, we'd first have to train our trainers. No Indian trainers knew about mortgages and the other sophisticated financial products GE Capital offered the public. They didn't even have the knowledge of such products that we take for granted in America—how credit cards work, who pays the money and when, how a plastic card leads to someone's bank account. We had to teach them everything. The gulf between what they knew and what they were going to be employed to do was enormous. One of the best things I did right up front was recruit Raman Roy from American Express.

He had already built a small back office for AmEx and knew what would be required. He led our efforts during the early years with great creativity and problem-solving skills.

But what I was most afraid of was that the head office wouldn't consider our operation to be of sufficient quality. So we set out to avoid failure at all costs. Every scrap of work had double or triple checks before it went out the door.

We had to literally build the infrastructure around us. We started on the floor of our existing office building in Gurgaon, which was about 8,000 square feet. There were many other hurdles—some enormous, some basic. One of the biggest was creating a reliable telecom system in a country that was far from modernized. We set up multiple phone lines to make sure we had backups in case of any possible problems. To ensure service, we installed the first satellite dish on a commercial building in India. We had to figure out how to sufficiently soundproof the cubicles for workers who would constantly be on the phone. We began by asking people to bring curtains and saris from home. In hindsight, it was pretty funny. But we were trying to be creative with our limited resources.

"Trespassers Will Be Recruited!"

Considering the intensity of the buildup, the day we went live with our staff, in late 1998, was fairly mundane. We weren't doing anything on the phones. We were handling what's known as white mail—paper that comes to credit card operations about things like changes of address. Before we set up our operation, these very simple tasks would have been handled in much higher-cost locations in the U.S. It didn't take long for our project to gain momentum. We'd had 8,000 applications for our first 20 jobs; 5,000 of the applicants were clearly eligible. By the following year we had 300 employees. Raman Roy actually put up a sign outside our building that said "Trespassers will be recruited!" We began to handle increasingly complex back-office support, such as mortgage applications, auto loan approvals, disbursals, and accounting transactions.

With people coming on staff so quickly, we needed all kinds of attendant services that we hadn't originally anticipated. We had to have vans and SUVs to transport employees to and from work at all hours—requiring a level of organization then unknown in India. (To this day we offer transportation to 15,000 workers.) We had to provide food for a 24-hour rotating staff of what would become 4,000 people on any given shift—working in an undeveloped suburb that offered no facilities and constructing business continuity plans from scratch. And we had to demonstrate to customers and recruits (and their families, who had concerns about their children's involvement in the operation) that this would really work.

That's what led to our willingness to give tours of what we were building. Every time people walked through our facilities, they were impressed by the size and sophistication of our operation. We learned how to tell our story very well—not only to the GE brass and competitors (we eventually stopped allowing the latter into our facility) but also to the people we would be relying on to create support services like that round-the-clock transportation. We actually created "prospective parents' days" so that the parents of the young, single women we were frequently hiring could see their daughters' workplace.

How Do You Spell That?

We knew we had a tiger by the tail, because demand surged—not just from GE businesses but from other companies that had heard about what we were doing. It was the beginning of an entirely new industry in India. In 1998 we had 20 people doing this work. By 2001 we had 12,000. We were trying to hire and train a thousand people a month, and the pressure on us was very high. Our work was increasingly mission-critical for GE, and I feared that at the pace we were growing, quality would decline. It did.

We started providing new services for different GE divisions, but at some point our breakneck expansion was just too much. Often we weren't at our best on calls handling products and services that were new to our group. Once, the vice chairman of GE had a problem with his computer and was put through to our help desk in India. The customer support person asked him where he was calling from, and when he said Fairfield, Connecticut—well-known as GE's headquarters—our guy asked him how to spell it. Believe me, I heard about that. It seemed as if we were not on top of our game—and we weren't. Looking back, I sometimes find these stories hilarious, but then I knew we had to slam on the brakes and get this stuff right.

With that fast-paced growth, attrition also began to soar, reaching 50%. Our hiring engine wasn't good enough to replace that many employees every year, never mind train them to Six Sigma standards. So we had to pull back. We deliberately stopped growing for a full year, from 2001 to 2002, in order to get a handle on quality again. It was obvious that we had some issues, because our clients were talking about them. That year, when the world's markets were skittish after 9/11, we stopped all hiring, redoubled our training of managers, and rethought our training processes until we felt we had achieved better quality control.

That was a useful pause in our exponential growth, because it enabled me to develop a vision of where the business should go in the future. It was clear to me that the potential lay in expanding our services beyond just one customer. By 2002 we were back in growth mode. We now have operations all over the world, including Dalian, which is considered the outsourcing hub for China.

Back in the beginning, I knew we were on to something incredibly exciting, but even I am surprised at how enormous and game-changing our growth turned out to be. We helped spawn an entire industry of business process outsourcing in India—though we are still the leader in terms of revenue. As I look around at the physical transformation of the towns in which we operate, I'm proud of what those early-stage ideas turned into. When we first started building in Gurgaon, you couldn't buy a decent coffee or tea or sandwich. It's now a thriving community five times the size of Hoboken. And all that has been built on the shoulders of those initial 20 hires we made in 1997. I don't know how many people get an opportunity to lead that kind of transformation in their lifetimes.

Originally published in June 2011. R1106A

Heinz's CEO on Powering Growth in Emerging Markets

by Bill Johnson

Bill Johnson has been the president and CEO of the H.J. Heinz Company since 1998 and its chairman since 2000.

The Idea

This year more than 20% of Heinz's revenues will come from emerging markets such as China, India, Indonesia, Russia, and Brazil, versus less than 5% a few years ago. Longtime CEO Bill Johnson describes his strategy for growing sales in developing economies.

When I assumed the leadership of Heinz's Asia/Pacific business, in 1993, the company's revenues from that part of the world were hardly a blip—and I'd never visited most of the countries in the region. I made my first trip there soon after I took the job, and it really opened my eyes.

I went to visit a small baby-food factory we operated in China. There were no finished roads to get there, so I took a train. It was an old British train from the 1930s, and passengers were cooking on hibachis at the backs of the cars. I remember being amazed by the number of bicycles I saw. I went to markets where live poultry was being sold. And, of course, I saw food that was foreign to me. At one dinner the host pulled me aside beforehand and said,

"You're probably going to be exposed to a lot of foods you're not familiar with, so if you don't want to eat it, just move it around on your plate and smile a lot." Sure enough, during the meal I was presented with an entire fish with the head intact. Its eyes seemed to be staring at me. I wasn't sure exactly what to do with it, so I offered it to my host, who acted as if it was a great honor.

China, India, Russia, and Indonesia are very different from the Western European and North American markets where Heinz was focused at the time, but I could tell even during my first visits that they represented the future of the business. The middle class was clearly starting to emerge. The people in those countries had motivations and desires similar to those of Americans—they were going to want the same kind of variety and conveniences.

Back then most of our emerging market businesses were very small—they were more about sticking our toes in the water. But it was obvious that growth in the developed economies was going to slow down, and that these emerging markets were where the new growth would be. Although we still refer to these countries as "emerging markets," I don't think the label is accurate anymore. Clearly they're not fully developed economies, but they are building infrastructure—roads, airports—that is world-class. And for consumer-oriented businesses like ours, they're a primary focus.

Soon after I became CEO, we developed our first long-term emerging market strategy, with an emphasis on what we call the Three A's. We even put it on the cover of our annual report one year.

The first A is "applicability": You have to make sure the product suits the local culture. We do sell some ketchup in China, but the dominant condiment there is soy sauce; if we're to compete in sauces, that's what we need to offer. You also have to be aware that your notion of how a product might be applicable will differ from that of the people you're selling to. In Korea they put ketchup on pizza, which was anathema to me. The first time I visited the Philippines and tasted the ketchup, I found that it was very different from American ketchup. It turned out that it was made from bananas. It didn't suit me, but it's what Filipino consumers want, so it's applicable.

The second A is "availability": You have to make sure you sell in channels that are relevant to the local population. In the United States we're used to modern grocery stores and super-centers; if a company gets shelf space in Safeway and Kroger and Walmart, its products are available to virtually 100% of the population. But that's not true in emerging markets. In Indonesia less than one-third of the people buy food in modern grocery stores—they still shop in tiny corner stores or open-air markets. In China chain grocers have a 50% share; in Russia they have around 40%; in India it's less than 15%.

The third A is "affordability": You have to remember that Westerners are wealthy compared with people in the rest of the world and that the things we take for granted—such as a giant bottle of soy sauce—may be unaffordable luxuries to them. You can't price yourself out of the market. We try to address this issue by offering different package sizes or recipes. For instance, in Indonesia we sell small packets of soy sauce—the size a Westerner might get with take-out sushi—for three cents apiece. That wouldn't make sense in a developed market, but in Indonesia we sell billions of those packets because they're affordable, and besides, people don't necessarily have refrigerators or pantries to hold larger sizes for months at a time.

A few years after we unveiled the Three A's strategy, I added a fourth—"affinity." That means you want local employees and local customers to feel close to your brand, and you need to understand how they live. That's a large part of why we rely on local managers for our emerging markets businesses.

I believe they bring a deep understanding of local consumers and employees. Typically we have only one or two expat managers in any market. When we need to improve skills such as marketing or finance, or to implement our particular ways of doing business, we send in our Emerging Markets Capability Team—a group of senior people from Western businesses who travel around and coach local managers.

In some cases we take the Heinz brand into a market and try to establish it organically. We did that in China with baby food—we started there in the mid-1980s, and today Heinz is China's leading brand of baby food. But more often we "buy and build." For instance, over the past year Heinz acquired Quero in Brazil and Foodstar in China to accelerate our growth. Under our strategy, we look for solid brands with good local management that will get us into the right channels, and we buy local infrastructure as well. Then we can start selling other brands—including Heinz—through the same channels.

Our approach to evaluating acquisitions in emerging markets is very different from our approach in developed economies. Some of the due diligence is the same: We look at the operating metrics of the business. Is it growing? Are there synergies? Can we manage it? Does it fit with our core business? Does it add scale or scope? This business-focused due diligence is often complicated by the premiums we pay for an emerging market acquisition—you want to be really sure the growth is going to be there, so you have to look at per capita consumption trends, the macro environment, and the overall state of the category.

Then there's a whole second set of due diligence issues, which also differ from what we do in developed economies. We look at how the company goes to market, the tax system, the regulatory environment, currency trends, and the political climate, comparing them with what exists in the United States. We take these things for granted in developed economies, but they're a big consideration in emerging markets, where governments are often much more active. This process may take a lot of time, and the companies we're considering as acquisitions are sometimes frustrated by that. But these issues are very important. We've walked away from deals in Ukraine, Vietnam, and other markets because our due diligence told us there were considerable risks involved in trying to generate acceptable returns on the businesses.

For managers, probably the most important factor in growing a business in an emerging market is understanding the risks. We've tried to manage that by diversifying: Over the years, we've invested pretty equally in all the BRIC countries plus Indonesia and Venezuela. We've begun investing in South Africa and Mexico. Diversifying helps mitigate not only the political risks but also the currency risks, which require really adept financial management. I sometimes say that Heinz used to be a dollar-pound-euro company, but there's no doubt that in the future it will be dominated by the five R's: the Brazilian real, the Chinese renminbi, the Indian rupee, the Indonesian rupiah, and the Russian ruble. Those currencies are volatile, but they're going to be the strongest currencies in the world going forward, because their economies are the strongest. If you spread your risks across markets and across currencies, you won't panic or run away the first time you have a blowup.

However, you also have to know when the risk outweighs the potential reward. For example, we created a really good business in Zimbabwe during the 1990s. But by the early 2000s the government was too unstable, the currency had devalued, and we couldn't plan or get resources. So we walked away from the market. We also pulled out of some cities in Russia after the ruble devalued in the 1990s.

But generally we focus on the long term. We have learned that to succeed in emerging markets, you need to be risk aware but not risk averse. Indonesia provides a great example of that. We bought a big business there in 1999. The country was just starting to democratize and have elections; it wasn't especially stable. Frankly, some people wondered if it was a good place for an American company. Today that's a $400 million business for us, versus $80 million when we bought it. ABC is one of the world's largest soy sauce brands, and it's very profitable.

Another key to growing in emerging markets is to tailor products to local tastes. I try to sample many of the products we bring to market. I'm curious, and local managers and employees really appreciate it when I try something unfamiliar. Some of the foods don't agree with me—like the Philippines banana ketchup. We sell a chili sauce in Indonesia. Every time I go, they ask me to taste it. It's so hot that I have to drink a gallon of water afterward, but the local population loves it. Sardines are popular in Indonesia, and meat pies are popular in South Africa—I'm not a big fan of either. In India we acquired Complan, a high-protein nutritional beverage for children. We recently introduced a new variety that tastes like almonds. Personally, I'm not crazy about the taste; fortunately, Indian consumers have a different opinion. This year we expect Complan to generate more than $200 million in sales, and it's our best-selling product in India. You have to be mindful of the "rule of the golden tongue"— just because you don't like something doesn't mean the local population won't like it.

Also, I'm always looking to see if some of these products can be sold in developed economies. Every year, I ask our managers in those markets to look at emerging market innovations that might work there. Consumers all over the world are looking for bargains, so a lot of ideas for lower-priced products are becoming relevant in Western markets. I don't like the phrase "mature brands," and we still manage to grow sales of products like ketchup, even in soft Western economies. But it takes hard work and innovation. We've had a lot of success with new packaging—such as squeeze bottles—and now we're manufacturing more-sustainable bottles that use up to 30% renewable plant-based material and innovative technology developed by our partner, the Coca-Cola Company. Innovation can still drive growth in developed markets—just look at Apple. But it's definitely more difficult. In emerging markets Heinz is also increasingly focused on connecting with consumers through social media to glean valuable insights and drive awareness of our new products and innovations in markets like Indonesia and India.

We expect more than 20% of our revenues (over $2 billion) to come from emerging markets this year—and more than 30% by 2015. Our U.S. business is around 33%, so that's really significant. Our company is ahead of U.S. competitors in this area—they're rushing to catch up. Many of them have made mistakes in emerging markets. They've become too dependent on one or two markets, instead of diversifying. They've relied on expats to manage their local businesses. They've rushed in with Western brands, Western package sizes, Western pricing, without understanding the nuances of the markets. Many of them have also been too impatient. They're ready to walk away too quickly. Those markets require patience. Our Indian business took seven or eight years to get right. You have to be patient, flexible, and open to ideas from local management. At the same time, Heinz is leveraging the strength of our global brand. For instance, we are growing our ketchup and condiment sales globally by partnering with quick-serve restaurant chains that are expanding rapidly in emerging markets.

Being successful in those markets also requires that every manager—including the CEO—work hard to build relationships. I have attended a lot of banquets in Asia. They're an important way to make friends, especially with government officials, but they can be exhausting. When I travel there today, I'm usually happy to have a dinner at the hotel. Still, the cultural differences can be amusing. A few years ago the Chinese government presented me with the Marco Polo Award, which they give to the company that does the most to improve U.S.–China relations. They had a big dinner with a lot of government officials and a lot of ceremony. When I entered the room, they played "Hail to the Chief." My wife couldn't stop laughing.

Despite the cultural differences, we've found that customers everywhere are similar in some ways: They all want convenient, high-quality products at good prices. Heinz is a 142-year-old company that's had only five chairmen, and in many of those cultures that kind of longevity is appreciated. Ultimately, it's all about courage. Are you prepared to stick it out? Emerging markets are the future—but they're not for the faint of heart.

Originally published in October 2011. R1110A

Amway's President on Reinventing the Business to Succeed in China

by Doug DeVos

Doug DeVos is the president and co-CEO of Amway.

The Idea

After the Chinese government outlawed direct selling, Amway repeatedly revised its business model to build a reputation as an honorable corporate citizen. In 2006 it received a new license, and China is now its largest market.

When the Chinese government outlawed direct selling, in 1998, Amway was already well established in China and had built a large-scale factory there. The company faced a big decision: Should we pull up stakes, or could we find a new way to sell?

We chose the latter course, and in the decade that followed, Amway China revised its sales model five times to meet changing regulations. Today China is our biggest market, accounting for more than a third of Amway's sales.

To understand Amway's business in China and the lessons we've learned by operating there, it's helpful to know some of our history. My dad, Richard DeVos, and his longtime friend and business partner, Jay Van Andel, founded Amway in 1959. The company was started with the idea of providing entrepreneurial opportunity for anyone who wanted to own and run a business. Amway doesn't discriminate. We welcome everyone, regardless of age, race, religion, gender, or geography. In some parts of the world this has been a breakthrough concept.

Dad and Jay were adventurers and liked to travel. Thirty-eight years ago they were visiting places like Hong Kong, mainland China, and the Middle East and asking themselves, "What would it take to bring Amway here? What would the business look like? How would it fit with this culture?"

Patience and Cooperation

That last question has been especially important. One of the biggest lessons we've learned as we've grown around the world is that a true understanding of the marketplace, including the culture, the economics, the politics, and the people, is essential. Our strongest resource is always our local leadership team. That's the first lesson we applied to our business in China.

Amway first entered Asia in 1974, with the opening of our Hong Kong affiliate, and then went into Malaysia in 1976. In 1979 we began operations in Japan, which quickly became one of our top markets and remains so today. By the late 1980s more than half of Amway's revenues were coming from outside the United States. So when we began operations in the People's Republic of China, in 1995, we'd already been doing business in that part of the world for more than 20 years. I was running Amway's Asia Pacific business at the time, and by 1998 China was a $200 million operation and growing fast.

Then we heard rumors that the Chinese government was becoming unhappy with the actions of some direct sellers—or, more accurately, scammers disguised as direct sellers. These unscrupulous companies damaged the reputation of the fledgling industry and of legitimate direct sellers like Amway, Avon, and Mary Kay. Issues related to product quality, reliability, and trust were rampant. Chinese officials needed to protect consumers and to put a stop to unethical practices. But the action the government pursued was extreme: outlawing direct selling and punishing legitimate as well as unethical sellers.

The idea that direct selling could be outlawed was incomprehensible to us. This method of marketing was the foundation of Amway's business—it had been tested and proved over time and across borders. And now it appeared that we could be put out of business, despite our commitment to and investment in our China operation.

When Eva Cheng, who ran Amway China at that time, called me in the middle of the night to report that the ban was likely, she advised that we not lose sight of an opportunity: We could cooperate with the government to help it understand the problems and find solutions to them. Working with the Chinese to create good direct-selling legislation would be the right thing to do for consumers, our industry, and our business.

A Chinese proverb, loosely translated, says, "If you are patient in one moment of anger, you will escape a hundred days of sorrow." Eva was right. We could be patient. We could be cooperative. We could seek solutions to strengthen our industry and protect consumers. And we could partner with the Chinese government and our competitors to create reforms that would set the stage for our industry to grow and flourish in China.

A day or two later we had a board meeting. My family and the Van Andel family, who remain Amway's primary shareholders, were all present. Eva reported on what we were facing. My father stood up after the presentation and said that he approved of her recommendation to work with the government and that he wanted to stay the course. Everyone else agreed.

A Nearly Complete Overhaul

That was the second major lesson in our China experience: It was essential that we remain true to our mission and our core purpose. We had to remember that Amway isn't simply about the products or the sales channel; it's about opportunity.

The regulatory changes China required forced us to ask some hard questions about our business model. The government wanted Amway and other foreign direct sellers to establish stores in China's conventional wholesale-retail channels. But if we shifted from a network selling model to traditional retail stores, would we still be Amway? The more we considered this, the more we realized that the essence of the company—providing a business opportunity based on core values of partnership, integrity, and personal responsibility—would never change. But even as we preserved those essentials, we could change our operations to accommodate China's new regulations.

We chose not to go to Beijing to complain. Instead we asserted that Amway and the Chinese government were in the same boat, that we fully understood the problems that unethical direct-selling companies were creating, and that we supported the government's need to create tough new measures. We let government officials know that Amway wanted to help find a solution that would demonstrate to the world that China cared about the interests of consumers and legitimate foreign investors alike.

There was almost an art to addressing these challenges. We would have to create physical stores—something we'd never done before. That meant selling products to people who came in off the street—again, not our usual way of doing business.

Typically, when we enter a new country, we import products from the United States. But for China we would manufacture goods there. We had to change our entire distributor compensation system. And because we couldn't rely on the word-of-mouth marketing that drives direct sales, we chose to do brand advertising—something else we'd never done up to that point. In short, we had to overhaul nearly everything we did.

Honorable Corporate Citizenship

Trust was vital, both internally and externally, and this was an important third lesson. Trusting relationships would allow us to move quickly to adapt to changes. With our own distributors we sometimes had to say, "Trust us on this." There wasn't always time to walk everybody through every detail.

During and after the regulatory transition, we worked closely with the Chinese government. We felt we needed to prove ourselves to its officials. We wanted them to know that we operated an honest business that was creating economic opportunities for Chinese families. We believed in direct selling, and we believed in our business model, but we knew we needed to demonstrate that Amway would be a long-term honorable corporate citizen in China. I give the government officials a lot of credit: They listened earnestly and they recognized that we wanted to create a mutually beneficial opportunity. They also judged us on the actions we took, not just the words we spoke.

As all this was going on, however, it was clear that China was becoming more and more interested in establishing closer ties with other economic powers. Its leaders were talking about joining the World Trade Organization. People in our industry believed that the government would relax the prohibitions on direct selling as part of that process. And, in fact, in late 2005 legislation was passed that would allow Amway to return to a direct sales business model. We received our new license to do business in China in 2006.

We Stayed the Course

Looking back, I see how important it is to build a business by taking the long-term view—the fourth lesson we learned. We're in this business for generations. That applies not just in China but in all our markets. As my dad suggested, we stayed the course. We did what was necessary, even if it sometimes felt like taking a step backward. We were humble without becoming weak. And we kept working hard, because providing opportunity to people all over the world, from all walks of life, is the right thing to do.

The rules in China are still unique. The way we operate our business and compensate our sales force there is very different from what we do in other parts of the world. But we've learned a lot, and our revised business model is working. It has established our industry as a respectable part of the Chinese economy. And today China is our largest market, with more than $4 billion in annual sales.

Although the changes we made to remain in China seemed like a big leap at the time, we've since exported some of those ideas to other Amway markets. For example, physical locations are now a strategic initiative for us in many regions. Although we don't have traditional stores in the United States or Latin America, we do have what we call "mobile brand experiences" in those markets, in which we showcase the Artistry (skin care) and Nutrilite (vitamins and dietary supplements) brands with customized tour buses on display at various events. In Europe we have Amway brand and training centers. Being forced to change our model in China helped us realize that we need to regularly adapt to succeed in different markets.

By understanding the market; staying true to our mission; building strong, trusting relationships; and taking a long-term view, Amway weathered the storm of a direct–selling ban and emerged as the market leader. My father and Jay saw that potential, and we're very glad they did.

Originally published in April 2013. R1304A

Celtel's Founder on Building a Business on the World's Poorest Continent

by Mo Ibrahim

Mo Ibrahim, the founder of Celtel, is the chairman of Satya Capital and of the Mo Ibrahim Foundation, which focuses on the governance of African countries.

The Idea

Frustrated by Western ignorance about Africa, Ibrahim decided to take advantage of the continent's enormous telecom opportunity himself. Among the challenges he faced was creating an infrastructure from scratch.

As a native of Sudan who has spent most of my adult life in the West, I've always been aware of just how ignorant Westerners can be about Africa. But every so often someone says something that manages to surprise me. One such conversation took place in 1998. I was running MSI, a software and consulting company in the UK, and I regularly worked with the world's biggest telecom companies. To me it was obvious that huge opportunities existed for those companies to develop mobile communications in Africa, a continent that had been largely ignored by the telecom industry. I began asking all my clients,

"Why aren't you going to Africa? You're paying millions of dollars to get licenses in other countries that you could get free in some African countries." One day I pulled aside a senior telecom executive and urged him to apply for a license in Uganda, which was seeking assistance. He said, "Mo, I thought you were smarter than that! You want me to go to my board and say I want to start a business in a country run by this crazy guy Idi Amin?" I was stunned. I said, "Idi Amin left Uganda years ago!"

At the time, I didn't consider myself an expert at sizing up business opportunities. I'd spent my adult life first as an academic, then as the technical director for British Telecom's early foray into cellular communications, and ultimately running my own consulting company. I was a techie engineer. My hero was Albert Einstein. I never dreamed of being a regular businessman.

But even I could see that developing mobile communications in sub-Saharan Africa—where most people had never *used* a phone, let alone owned one—was an opportunity too big to pass up. I realized that in many Westerners' minds, Africa connoted uprisings, dictators, deserts, AIDS, and poverty—and it still does, even now. But the story is far more complex. The African continent includes more than 50 countries and has a total population of about one billion spread over 11.7 million square miles. Africa ranges from the bazaars of Morocco to the big business complexes of Johannesburg. In the late 1990s it was also the most underserved telecommunications market in the world. In all of the Democratic Republic of Congo (DRC), for instance, which had a population of roughly 55 million, there were only 3,000 phones in 1998. The possibilities were enormous.

The huge gap between supply and demand wasn't the only attractive aspect of taking mobile phones to Africa. Unlike the developed world, Africa had no fixed-line phone networks, so mobile phones would face no competition. In the West people are used to having many communication channels—letters, e-mail, social media—and as vital as mobile phones have become, they're still just one more way to be in touch with other people. Africa is a different world. If you live far away from the village where your mother lives and you want to talk to her, you might have to make a seven-day journey. If you could just pick up a device and speak to her instantly, what would be the value of that? How much money would you save? How much time? To me it was obvious that cell phones would be a huge success.

My clients refused to see it that way: Africa was too unknown and too risky. So I decided I had to do it myself. Despite the size of the opportunity, I would face huge challenges. I had no support from established telecom players. I had no experience building this kind of company on my own. I knew I'd face hurdles—but I had no idea how significant they would be.

Establishing Credibility

In 1998, when I decided to launch a project to explore setting up mobile communications in Africa (which later became the company Celtel), the consulting firm I was running had 800 employees. We had few problems. We billed our clients, and revenue came in. Celtel started out with just five employees. Although the consulting firm provided our initial investment, I spent a significant amount of time raising capital: $16 million in the first year, to acquire licenses and begin building infrastructure, and ultimately more than $415 million during our first five years. With funding established, we had to design, build, and operate phone systems in countries with antiquated or nonexistent infrastructure.

The first challenge was to establish our credibility. We had great technical people and a good track record in network design, but we had not run our own network before. So we had to build our competence and convince the regulators and telecom ministries that we could deliver. Fortunately, we had virtually no competitors, and I had managed to recruit an experienced board, which included Sir Gerry Whent, Vodafone's first CEO; Sir Alan Rudge, a former deputy chief executive of British Telecom; and Salim Ahmed Salim, a former prime minister of Tanzania. Our board members not only gave us credibility but also helped us recruit the talent we needed to grow.

One reason major telecom players were afraid of Africa was its reputation for corruption. From the beginning we needed a plan to deal with that. We insisted on accepting only licenses we had won in an open bidding process; we would never accept them if they were offered under the table or after dining out with some prime minister. (We declined to pursue opportunities in Guinea and Angola for related reasons.) To make sure that no one in the company tried to take matters into his own hands, we instituted a rule that the full board had to sign off on any expense over $30,000. It wasn't easy to hold this line, but in the end it was very helpful, because it enabled us to build a company that was completely transparent. Board members helped prevent corruption, too. For example, Salim, the secretary general of the Organization of African Unity (now the African Union) for 12 years, is so well respected across the continent that if an official hinted at a bribe, he could call the right government person and frame the situation as an embarrassment to Africa. That was usually enough to stop it. Our directors' connections created a protective layer around our company.

We focused first on a handful of countries that had inexpensive or free network licenses available, including Uganda, Malawi, the two Congos, Gabon, and Sierra Leone. The pent-up demand was almost overwhelming; we couldn't move fast enough. When we set up operations in Gabon, for example, customers actually knocked down the door of one of our offices trying to get in. That's how badly people wanted to make phone calls.

In the West, mobile phones started out as products for the affluent, and a decade passed before they were widely available to the middle class. In Africa we needed to make them available right away to very poor consumers. Our customers wouldn't have access to the kind of money that Westerners paid for monthly mobile contracts. So we created better options for each market, such as prepaid cards (or "scratch" cards) that for just a few dollars' worth of the local currency could be used to buy cellular service. That eliminated the prospect of unpaid bills and ensured that our cash flow in each country would be smooth.

At first Celtel was a sideline for MSI. But it quickly became apparent that the challenge and excitement of building such an ambitious operation was enough to merit my focused attention. So in 2000 I sold MSI to Marconi for more than $900 million, and over the next few years I put all my energy into building a cellular communications company that would defy the naysayers about Africa.

Building the Network

Each country where we set up operations offered unique challenges. Doing business in a place like the DRC was a nightmare, because it had no good roads—and sometimes not even any bad roads. We had to use helicopters to move our base stations and take heavy equipment up a hill or into the middle of nowhere. We also had to figure out how to get power to those spots. Building anything in sub-Saharan Africa is a really tough task. We had to supply our own electricity and our own water. We had to refill our generators and replenish our batteries every day.

Building a mobile company in Europe requires doing deals with existing telecom companies, filling out forms, and making calls. In Africa we had to literally build the network, tower by tower. And there were political challenges. The capitals of the two Congos, for example, are near each other, separated by a river. When we first set up in those countries, a wireless call across the border had to be routed via satellite through Europe, at a cost of more than $3 a minute—a prohibitive expense for local customers. The Congos were so protective of their borders that they didn't like such transmissions anyway. They were fine with our creating traffic within one country, and they were fine with residents' calling other parts of the world, such as Europe. But telecom traffic across government boundaries in Africa? We had to negotiate with both governments for two years before we were allowed to invest in a microwave link across the border, which eventually enabled us to charge just 28 cents a minute. Traffic between the two countries rose 700% the first week we offered that rate.

In Sierra Leone, of course, we were in a region at war. We had to make it crystal clear that we were a neutral company with no allegiances. When the capital fell to rebels, we had to pull our staff members out of the country. They returned later with UK members of the UN peacekeeping mission, whom we provided with phones and service. Because both sides in the war needed to communicate, no one sabotaged our towers. We quickly became the market leader in that country.

Cultural challenges were actually less of a problem than I had anticipated. When you start to meet with people at the village level, you find that Africans are very easygoing and hospitable. We always had great relationships with local communities. Because we didn't deal in bribes, we looked for other ways to help the impoverished areas in which we were setting up operations. We built schools and clinics where we could. We looked after our local employees. We instituted management training and technical training—providing people who'd been denied an education with completely new skills. That training was always a big item in our budget, but it was a great investment in our company's future. It helped attract back to Africa some highly qualified people who had sought (as I had) a career in Europe because they lacked exciting options at home. Not only did we pay them the same salaries they would have commanded outside Africa, but they could feel they were giving something back to the homeland.

We also extended health insurance to the families of our workers, which is a really big deal in Africa. Some companies provide no coverage at all, never mind to extended families. In the United States, when you think about providing an employee with health insurance, you assume you'll be covering four or five people at most. In Africa that number can be much, much higher. This benefit helped us become a truly African company. By 2004—six years after we'd launched—99% of our 5,000 employees were native Africans.

Finding the Money

That year we had 5.2 million managed customers and operations in 13 countries, with revenue of $614 million and a $147 million net profit. Celtel was a strong, rapidly growing business. But raising money may have been my biggest challenge. We had to do round after round of fundraising, usually for short-term funds, just to keep the business afloat. It got frustrating. Financial institutions simply didn't see Africa the way they saw, for example, India and other emerging market economies. They thought Africa was riskier as a market; they all but discounted the consumer populations as simply too poor to be good customers; and they didn't trust local governments to support honest business growth.

Around that time we sought a loan. The banks required us to offer the assets of the whole company as security—to obtain just a few million dollars at draconian rates and terms. We eventually accepted the terms because we needed the loan, but clearly we had to find a better long-term source of capital. So we decided to do an IPO on a reputable stock exchange, such as London's. When word got out that we were considering an IPO, we received unsolicited offers to buy the whole company. Ultimately, we agreed to one of those offers and sold Celtel for $3.4 billion to the Kuwait-based Mobile Telecommunications Company (now Zain). Ironically, the same banks that had insisted on our entire assets as collateral a few months before now agreed to finance that enormous transaction for MTC secured only—surprise, surprise—by those very assets. Despite all we had built, they considered an African company less valuable than a company in almost any other part of the world.

Do I ever feel sad that such an exciting adventure ended so quickly for me? Well, I look at what we left behind, and it's very good. We created a large company, but we created an even larger economy that grew up to support the business, from the subcontractors who built the network to the people who supplied diesel fuel for our generators to the retailers who sold the scratch cards that gave consumers their airtime. You cannot believe how many workers in Africa benefited from one company's setting up shop there. At the time of the sale, Celtel was operating in 13 African countries under licenses that covered more than a third of the continent's population. We'd invested more than $750 million in Africa and helped to bring the benefits of mobile communications to millions of its people. Every now and then I think, "Wow, it was wonderful, and now it's over." But I'm OK with that.

Originally published in October 2012. R1210A

DOING SMART DEALS

IN THE LIFE OF BOTH A COMPANY AND ITS TOP MANAGERS, there are few decisions with higher stakes than whether or not to do a deal.

In the case of young firms, the deal in question is typically an initial public offering—a process that can make the founders rich but also subject the company to a disorienting set of new demands from regulators and shareholders.

For more established firms, IPOs are replaced by M&A—the decision to buy or sell a business.

The essays that follow offer the corner-office view of each of these kinds of transactions. Google CEO Eric Schmidt describes the unconventional Dutch auction its founders decided to utilize for its IPO—and how the entire process almost went off the rails due to an ill-timed interview with *Playboy* magazine. Rohm and Haas's former CEO describes how the carefully planned sale of his company nearly came undone when the 2008 financial crisis hit—and how teams from both companies struggled to save the deal. And the leader of family-owned Enterprise relates how his car rental company purchased key rivals Alamo and National and how, instead of imposing its values as in a traditional "takeover," Enterprise sought to learn from its new brands.

One striking element of the essays that follow is that, compared with most management tales, there's a lot of suspense: Hearing these CEOs describe the twists and turns, you can't help but wonder how the story is going to end. Students of business know that many mergers end poorly for shareholders, which is one reason why it's useful to learn all we can from leaders who've made these difficult choices.

Google's CEO on the Enduring Lessons of a Quirky IPO

by Eric Schmidt

Eric Schmidt is the chairman and CEO of Google.

The Idea

When Google announced its intention to go public, in 2004, all eyes were on its unorthodox strategy. Here's how it played out.

It happened six years ago, but I still remember every detail of our journey to becoming a public company. It was a uniquely "Googley" experience that to this day says a lot about who we are.

An IPO can change a company. Many in the media seemed certain that if we went public, the Google ethos wouldn't survive. A public offering would be "one of the worst things that could happen to Google," said Danny Sullivan, editor of the *Search Engine Watch* newsletter and a well-regarded industry commentator. People predicted that we would suddenly be divided into haves and have-nots on the basis of how many shares of Google stock each of us held. The talent would cash out and quit. A new focus on pleasing Wall Street would cause us to lose our prized objectivity and independence. Developing the infrastructure to become a public company would dull our edge. Ultimately, people feared that as Google transitioned from a bright young start-up to a mature public company, it would lose the quirky spirit that had made it so innovative.

None of that happened. And I firmly believe that at our core we are the same company we were then—just a lot bigger. Although it is dangerous to read too much into a single event, I think one of the reasons we have held on to our values is that we chose an unconventional path to going public. Larry Page and Sergey Brin, Google's founders, began their "Letter from the Founders," which was included in our IPO prospectus, by saying, "Google is not a conventional company. We do not intend to become one." They went on to warn potential investors that we would invest in risky projects that might result in home runs—or might never pay off. Choosing a new path to follow doesn't always produce the best results, and the road can be bumpy. Google's road to that IPO was anything but smooth.

The company was founded back in 1998. I came on board three years later. Although we were growing rapidly, in both employees and revenues, we were in no hurry to go public. But given our size—and, more particularly, the fact that we wanted our employees to have equity in our growing enterprise—in early 2004 we found ourselves in the position of having to release our financial results to comply with U.S. securities laws. At the time, those laws required Google to become a publicly reporting company once it had 500 shareholders, and to file the associated financial statements within 120 days of the end of the year in which we crossed that mark.

We had until late April 2004 to file the necessary registration statement with the Securities and Exchange Commission. But the securities laws did not require us to have an IPO in the traditional sense. In fact, we could have simply become a publicly reporting company without selling any shares to the public.

We faced three choices: We could restructure to get back below 500 shareholders (meaning, essentially, find a way to buy back shares from our employees); we could continue to be a private company but at the same time live with having to report our financial results like any public company; or we could go public. Not surprisingly, we explored some unconventional alternatives, such as trying to develop an internal market for our employees' Google shares. In the end we opted to take the usual path for a venture-backed technology company and make an initial public offering of our common stock. However, we wanted to structure our IPO in a way that was anything but usual.

The Dutch Auction

We pride ourselves on trying to do things right, and we viewed this process of going public as a giant IQ test. How should we sell shares? At what price? Whom should we bring in to help us? What was the proper way—the Google way—to do this?

In debating those questions, we reviewed as much data about prior IPOs as we could get our hands on and agreed on a few things we did not like about the typical process. We didn't like the "pop" often experienced by successful technology companies when they went public. The difference between the IPO price and the price of a company's stock at the end of the first day or week of trading seemed to us to be money that should properly be in the hands of the company. But ordinarily, large institutions with connections to the underwriting syndicate are the only group allowed to buy those shares at the IPO price, and they flip them a few days later for a healthy profit. Somehow that didn't feel right for Google. We wanted something much more transparent and open—and we wanted our users to have a chance to take part.

As we were reviewing our alternatives, we were drawn to an approach championed by WR Hambrecht, an investment bank based in San Francisco, which argued that auctions were a better way to raise capital than the traditional underwritten IPO. In what is known as a Dutch auction, a company would collect bids from all interested investors and then group them by how much each investor was willing to pay. The company (and its bankers) would then move down from the top bid until it reached the highest price at which it could sell all the shares it wanted to offer. The company could choose that price (or, for a variety of reasons, a lower one) and then sell all the shares that were bid on at the chosen price or higher as soon as the stock was traded on its exchange.

We liked this approach. It was consistent with the auction-based business model we used to sell our ads, so we felt we understood the underlying dynamics, and it had a strong intuitive appeal for us. We also liked the idea of opening up our auction to everyone—retail investors as well as traditional institutional buyers. We hoped that an auction would do a better job than the traditional approach of setting a price for our shares—and would allow our share price to remain stable after we went public.

I know this may sound like baloney, but we settled decisively on the Dutch auction after we got a letter from a little old lady— or at least someone who claimed to be a little old lady. She wrote something along the lines of "I don't understand why I can't make money from your IPO the way the stockbrokers will."

We thought she had a point about the basic fairness of the system. So we decided to go with our version of the Hambrecht model, even though it would add considerable complexity to our IPO. No company the size of Google had ever done such a thing. Our auction would be on a significantly larger scale than other auction-based IPOs. We would have to build systems to support that increased scale. And those systems would need to be reviewed by the SEC. Wall Street viewed our decision as arrogant.

The analyst Henry Blodget wrote in *Slate*, "Participating in the Google IPO auction is gambling, not investing, and the most likely outcome is a waste of money and time."

Undaunted, we worked through how to structure our IPO, and we stopped communicating with the press. The SEC's "quiet period" requirements prevented us from talking about our business in the run-up to a possible initial public offering. Under those rules, companies are encouraged to make sure that in all material respects, only the prospectus speaks for the company. Because Google was in the media spotlight during this period, people came out in droves to criticize our business, our management, our culture, our IPO—almost every aspect of who we were. And because we had to remain silent, we weren't able to defend ourselves, correct misinformation, or try to reassure the public.

"Don't bother to bid on this shot-in-the-dark IPO," a *Business-Week* columnist concluded—a not-uncommon sentiment. But there wasn't much we could do about it. Yet as we kept silent, we realized that people didn't really know what Google had become. There was a gap between what was written about us and reality. Ultimately, we published our financials, but until then many people thought of us as a bunch of idiots with lava lamps (and perhaps they still do). The fact is, we had really started to take off.

A Sort of Limbo

As the filing deadline approached, we were still scrambling to get things in order. Just a week before the due date, for example, we realized that we were three board members short of the number of independent directors required to meet the listing standards of either the Nasdaq or the New York Stock Exchange. So we quickly added three heavy hitters. We also drew criticism because of the way we opted to structure our dual-class common stock.

The world had figured out our expected filing date, so the media focus on Google in late April was intense. Constant news stories, TV-station vans on the campus, unrelenting calls to our muzzled communications team, rampant employee speculation—it was quite a time. We were legally required to present our financials by 2:00 PM on April 29. But we pulled a fast one: We announced to the world at 11:00 AM that we were going public. It caught everyone by surprise.

The IPO process and our business then entered a sort of limbo as we waited for, and then responded to, the SEC's comments on our registration statement. This is a standard part of the process, although it took longer for us than for most other companies because the SEC also had to get comfortable with how we had designed our auction. In the end our legal and management teams worked from May through early August to address the SEC's concerns. Our decision to include a letter from our founders in the prospectus didn't exactly help us from a timing perspective. Larry and Sergey's letter described the values by which we planned to run our business. The job of the SEC is to evaluate the completeness and accuracy of qualitative and quantitative statements made in a prospectus. It really isn't in a good position to evaluate and comment on values. The commission made it clear that it wanted us to remove the letter from the prospectus, out of concern that it would confuse potential investors. We held our ground. I encourage anyone to go back and read that letter. I am struck by the fact that most of the values it set forth are, six years later, still the values that drive our company.

By this point the press coverage had become so negative that we stopped reading it—although I still have all the clippings. "Google is putting a nail in the coffin for technology IPOs," one analyst concluded. I've always thought that the bad press actually helped our business, because it raised awareness.

Our revenue depends on traffic, and our traffic exploded during this period. I feel certain there's a correlation.

We were now on track to go public in August. We'd known for months that August is a bad time to go public—Wall Street is essentially on vacation then—but it seemed that all our delays were inevitably leading to a late-August IPO. And given that more time seemed to beget more problems, we didn't want to delay until September. So we kept moving and finally started to get everything lined up.

Until...the September issue of *Playboy* hit the newsstands. It turned out that Larry and Sergey had given a long interview to the magazine back in April, and it was published in this issue. It was a very generic interview (without any pictures, I might add), but it almost derailed the whole IPO.

All Hell Broke Loose

The problem was that the interview, which of course touched on business issues, may have violated the "quiet period" rules I mentioned earlier. All hell broke loose, and the SEC considered forcing us to postpone the entire process. A month earlier the commission had delayed Salesforce.com's IPO because Salesforce had been featured in a lengthy profile in the *New York Times* during its quiet period. (Interestingly, it was headlined "It's not Google. It's that other big I.P.O.") That article, along with the subsequent publicity, prompted the SEC to push Salesforce to put a hold on its offering. We were worried that we faced a similar fate.

I sat down with Larry and Sergey to make it clear that it wasn't their fault—that I knew they hadn't realized they were doing anything technically wrong. We had a lot of work to do, but first I wanted to make sure that the two of them felt OK about everything. Then, working with the regulators at the commission, we came up with a solution: We included the *Playboy* interview in our official SEC filing as an appendix—meaning it would be available to any potential investor.

In mid-August the bidding began, based on our published expected IPO price range of $106 to $135 a share. It was a tough environment: Several tech companies had decided the market wasn't right and had pulled IPO plans of their own. In fact, the bidding for our shares didn't go particularly well. We seemed to be in a perfect storm of bad news: The *Playboy* article had been the joy of pundits and talk-show hosts everywhere; we had endured months of media criticism; we were dealing with an SEC investigation into our employee option program; and our financial performance in Q2 was experiencing a modest seasonal "flattening," which led analysts to question whether we could maintain our growth rates. (They soon reaccelerated.)

In addition, Wall Street was angry with us. In keeping with our auction model, we had wanted the information we communicated to our retail investors to be largely consistent with what we communicated to more-sophisticated institutional investors. Institutional investors are used to getting deep under the hood of a potential tech IPO when they meet with executives. They were not happy with the few extra details we were willing to share with them beyond our standard management presentation, which we had made available online to both retail and institutional investors. It didn't help that we had created an admittedly very amateurish video (shot by handheld camera) to introduce our executive team. One meeting in particular, with mutual-fund and hedge-fund investors at New York's Waldorf-Astoria Hotel the day after our pricing announcement, was roundly criticized as not serious enough and thin on details. (That was fair—on both points.)

There weren't a lot of orders, and to be frank, we wondered if we'd made a mistake in choosing an auction-based approach.

The offers that did come in were at or below the low end of the range we'd anticipated. When the bidding period ended, it was clear that we weren't going to be able to sell all the shares we had planned to sell in the price range we wanted. I met with the board to discuss whether we should delay our IPO and hope to get a higher price later. Our underwriters believed that we could close the IPO with a price around $80 to $90 a share if we reduced the number of shares for sale—a disappointing outcome. In the end we decided to close the IPO for a number of reasons, the most important being that it was time to put this chapter behind us and get back to running our business. So on August 18 we agreed to price it at $85 a share.

After the Countdown

We flew overnight to New York to watch our shares start trading on the Nasdaq on Thursday, August 19. We showed up in the morning, bleary-eyed. That day the *Wall Street Journal* had run a front-page piece with the headline "How Miscalculation and Hubris Hobbled Celebrated Google IPO," and CNBC commentators were talking us down all morning. I remember thinking as we headed down to the Nasdaq trading floor, *We're screwed*.

Just before the trading started, there was a countdown on the floor: 5-4-3-2-1. We watched the first trade, but it wasn't at $85—it was at $100, an 18% increase over our IPO price. Someone was making fast money. Despite our efforts, people were buying and flipping within an hour, taking a quick $15-a-share gain. The volume was huge.

All day long the stock price never went down. It closed at $100.30.

We were now public. Thrilled and exhausted, we flew home to California. By the following Monday our stock was trading at $105 to $110. Now there was an unbelievable amount of excitement in the press. Even the *New York Times* had weighed in on its editorial page: "Google still exudes that unabashed Silicon Valley anti-establishment attitude.... Nowhere was that more apparent than in the way it sought to dictate to Wall Street the terms of its own sale, as opposed to the other way around. This is a commendable impulse—I.P.O.'s have generally been structured to benefit insiders."

The IPO had consumed so much of our time and focus that I decided we needed closure before we could get back to business. The Olympic Games were taking place in Athens then, so they were on our minds. I asked Omid Kordestani, a senior executive at Google who has a wonderful voice, to say something appropriately Olympian to our management team to conclude our ordeal. He stood up in the boardroom we use for our executive management meetings and declared: "We now pronounce the end of the Google IPO."

I told everyone to get back to work. As a management team, we haven't talked about the IPO since.

So what had we done right? What had we done wrong? The right is easy to point to: Going public is a massive undertaking, and our finance, legal, and management teams had risen to the task, tackling the many obstacles in their path with tenacity, intelligence, and patience. In the end we made it, even if we did stumble somewhat coming out of the gate. As for the wrong: To this day I can't fully explain why our stock price opened so high—causing the pop we had tried to avoid. A lot of complicated factors played a role.

For a CEO, outcomes are what matter most. Although personally I would prefer to run a private company (it's easier), we made the decision to go public, and Google ended up succeeding beyond our most optimistic dreams.

And the naysayers were wrong. We didn't change. Basically, the same people are still running Google, in accordance with the same values we had as a private company. If you have the right people and the right values, and if you stick to your goals, you can go through a process like this and remain coherent as a company.

Crazy as the whole process was, I wouldn't change a thing—except maybe that *Playboy* interview.

Originally published in May 2010. R1005J

Rohm and Haas's Former CEO on Pulling Off a Sweet Deal in a Down Market

by Raj Gupta

Raj Gupta, the retired chairman and CEO of Rohm and Haas, serves on the boards of Hewlett-Packard, The Vanguard Group, Tyco International, and Delphi Automotive. He is a senior adviser to New Mountain Capital.

THE IDEA

The sale of Rohm and Haas to the giant Dow Chemical was forged at a premium price in July 2008. The transaction was unconditional. But then the financial markets crashed. Here's how Rohm and Haas's CEO kept the deal alive.

Shortly before Christmas 2008, I left my office at the specialty chemicals company Rohm and Haas for what I thought would be the last time. I had spent much of the year leading up to my long-planned retirement orchestrating the sale of the company—a deal with its former rival Dow Chemical had been forged in July 2008—and there was little left to do but hand over the reins. I had succeeded at one of the hardest goals I'd ever been set: quietly negotiating a friendly sale for $18 billion. All we still needed was the Federal Trade Commission approval that, per our agreement, would trigger the close of the deal within

48 hours. As I drove away from the office on December 18, a colleague called to say that, as planned, my office had been essentially demolished in preparation for its new occupant. My assistant had been reassigned to work with our COO. My work with Rohm and Haas was finished.

But it nagged at me that I hadn't heard recently from Andrew Liveris, Dow's chairman and CEO. Market conditions had worsened globally, and the equity and credit markets were in turmoil. Dow had been expecting a large cash influx of $9.5 billion from a proposed joint venture with Kuwait Petroleum. On December 29 Kuwait canceled the venture. But our deal with Dow was unconditional. And then I got the call.

"Raj, you and I need to sit down and go over where we are," Liveris said. Because I didn't even have an office at Rohm and Haas anymore, I had to arrange for temporary space at our Philadelphia headquarters—and a temporary assistant. When we met, I learned that Dow saw no way to get the cash it needed elsewhere, given the state of the financial markets and its own deteriorating financial performance.

I organized an emergency conference call to brief the directors on the situation. We believed that our contract with Dow was airtight. Our shareholders had approved the transaction in October by an overwhelming majority. The board and I had a fiduciary responsibility to complete the deal.

I had led the process from the beginning, and the board was very clear that it was my role to see it to an end—one way or another. My personal credibility was on the line.

An Unexpected Request

In November 2007, representatives of the Haas family trusts, which collectively owned 32% of outstanding shares, had asked me to explore disposing of all or most of their holdings at a "full and fair" price within 12 to 18 months. The timing and nature of the request were surprising. Until then the trusts had appeared to be very happy with the level of their ownership and the performance of the company. The board and I, perhaps naively, believed that as long as John C. Haas, the 89-year-old son of the founder, was alive, no such request would be made. We clearly did not read the tea leaves.

Rohm and Haas had been a quiet but steady business since its founding, in 1909. Our performance had been strong, with an average annual return to shareholders of 13.5% since 1949. For the past 30 years we had increased our dividends by an average of 10% a year. The majority of shares were held by the family trusts, several large institutional shareholders, and employees. I was only the sixth CEO in the company's history. In my 10 years as CEO, the board hadn't faced any big, difficult decisions until now.

I took my leadership in the sale very personally, and I was determined to keep the company whole and operating smoothly during this extended period of uncertainty. I spent months exploring options and strategies with the board and our outside advisers. In hindsight, the timing couldn't have been worse. The economy was starting to weaken, and the request that we sell for all cash at a premium price, though entirely reasonable, limited our options. We identified just three companies as strategic buyers—on the basis of their interest, their ability to finance a transaction of this size, and the likely business synergies: BASF, with headquarters in Germany; Dow, based in Michigan; and DuPont, based in Delaware.

I had layers of concern: What if potential buyers didn't show up? What if our discreet outreach to potential buyers was inconclusive, just as the economy was rapidly deteriorating? The worst possible outcome, I thought, would be an aborted process; our key stakeholders would doubt our strategy and future at a time when we needed steady support and performance.

Rohm and Haas's success rested on building relations for the medium to long term. Our position was downstream in the industry value chain; our customers relied on the performance embedded in our science and our commitment to ongoing technology support. Confidence in our future was essential. A mishandled disclosure or rumormongering would cause chaos among our employees and customers and risk destroying the foundations of the enterprise.

I had invested a great deal of time and effort in forming personal relationships with many of my peers—in particular the CEOs of BASF, Dow, and DuPont. The burden was on me to deliver a buyer, so I arranged individual face-to-face meetings with them to plant the seed. I told them we recognized that financial conditions were not as favorable as they could be, but our board supported my outreach. If they wanted to explore this opportunity, they'd have to get back to me swiftly.

The Brewing Deal

Within a week Andrew Liveris called to say he was ready to talk. He came to Philadelphia with an all-cash bid of $74 a share—in the range of value our advisers had suggested. At that time our stock was trading at $52 a share, and the highest it had ever gone was $62. His offer was good for only 48 hours.

The board concluded that it was our fiduciary duty to get in touch with BASF and DuPont to see if they wanted to make an offer. BASF's CEO, Jürgen Hambrecht, returned my call within 15 minutes. "Raj," he said, "I was hoping you were calling me to say that this whole process is off, given what's going on in the world." But he promised to get back to me quickly, and he did—with an offer of $70 a share, all cash, no conditions except regulatory approval. DuPont, however, let us know that its interest was restricted to only part of our portfolio.

The brewing deal was so secret that I virtually lived a double life for months. Only the board, six people within the company, and a few of our outside advisers knew about it. I was the focal point for all information and decisions. All our meetings were held offsite and during off hours, including many weekends.

We announced the deal with Dow on July 10—at a final price of $78 a share—and I'm sure that every Rohm and Haas employee in the world was in absolute shock. The shareholders were delighted, however, and the industry press called it the "deal of the century." From July into the fall, the stress of seeing the deal through took its toll on me. We worked hard to keep employees, shareholders, and customers well informed and comfortable about the company's future. But I was getting e-mails at midnight: "Are you awake?" The answer was always yes, I'm awake. There were 22 board meetings and dozens of phone calls with the directors from the time we first explored the idea of selling the company until the deal closed. I knew it was crucial that I present a calm face to my staff, but I was constantly worried.

In August, totally unexpectedly, I learned that I had prostate cancer, which added a new dimension to my stress. A low point came when I passed out on a flight to Germany and had to be admitted for emergency care. I withdrew from day-to-day operations to focus on my health and had surgery a few months later. My sole responsibility to the company remained seeing the deal through.

When Liveris and I met in January 2009, it was with just one key adviser each. He laid out all his concerns and issues and what he was trying to resolve. I could see that he had a herculean task on his hands. "Andrew," I said, "I understand what you're dealing with, but you have to put yourself in my situation. I need something to take to my board. I'd like to tell them that you fully intend to close the deal but you need more time. Give me a deadline, and we can go public with an announcement that this is the situation." I offered to assist with the Haas family trusts to get some kind of bridge financing. Liveris didn't want to pursue that. Ultimately, he offered to let us know by June whether Dow could do the deal or not.

On January 23 we got FTC approval for the deal. According to the contract, Dow had just two working days to close the transaction. That was simply not going to happen. Dow's backup financing lines would expire in June, but I believed that the company had enough resources, given time, to complete the deal under the original terms. Nevertheless, we had to protect our shareholders. With the board's approval, we filed suit in Delaware, asking the court for an expedited hearing to enforce our contract. Everyone was well aware of the significance of that lawsuit: We were essentially asking the court to decide whether Dow—and implicitly any other company—should be held to the terms of a deal regardless of external conditions. Our court date was set for March 9, and we knew the world would be watching.

Our board sent a letter, which we made public, to Dow's board, urging it to take control of the situation and honor the contract. Speculation in the financial press was intense: Would the transaction close? If it didn't, would our share price fall dramatically? Would Dow be forced into bankruptcy or have to sell valuable assets to close the deal?

I spent this period explaining to Rohm and Haas employees why we had to take this drastic action and why it was in their best interests and our customers' that the deal go through. My energy went into urging employees to stay calm, keeping the board informed, and communicating with key customers, the Haas family trusts, and our large hedge fund shareholders.

On Wednesday, March 4, less than a week before we were set to square off in court, I received an e-mail from Andrew Liveris. "Raj," he wrote, "should we give this one last try?" We agreed to meet in New York the next day, along with our respective advisers. We also decided that each of us would bring one highly respected board member to help facilitate the process. Our discussion focused on two key points: how to obtain bridge equity sufficient to reduce the debt financing required and how to keep Dow's credit rating from being downgraded to junk status by Standard & Poor's and Moody's.

Dow came up with some creative solutions, including working out arrangements with two of Rohm and Haas's largest shareholders, the Haas family trusts and Paulson & Co., to obtain the equity financing. And we participated in calls with S&P and Moody's to persuade them that Dow's situation warranted "investment grade" status. This was all hastily done in the days before our Monday court appointment. At 8 PM on Sunday, Andrew called me and said, "Raj, we're making progress. We don't have all the answers yet, but can you go to the judge and tell him that we are working on it?" In court the next morning we asked the judge for more time, and he said, "You can have all the time you want." I think he was relieved.

By 4 PM that day Dow had arranged its financing and we had an agreement, which we asked the judge to read into the record. The same day—one of the lowest points of the year for the stock market—Dow's directors signed off on the deal. Up until then I hadn't been certain it would really happen. Our stock had been trading down, and at one point it went under $50 a share. But in the end we got the $18 billion.

On March 31, I finally left Rohm and Haas for the last time. The deal closed the following day. I hadn't allowed myself to breathe a sigh of relief until that moment. It was a bittersweet victory for me, because I had invested so much of my time and energy in building the organization and managing for the long term that it was hard to let it go. I took solace in the fact that most of the family trusts' proceeds from the sale were invested in charities right away. There's a sense, though, that the company doesn't exist anymore, which is sad for me.

But I concluded that I could move on with my life—the retirement I had long planned. I'm not certain I could lucidly recite that day's events. Certainly I can't offer profound reflections on them. At the time, I was focused on the misfortune of having had to deal with this problem at the end of my career. Now, with the benefit of more than a year's hindsight, I recognize that we had a strong dose of good fortune, too, which allowed us to achieve this nearly impossible outcome.

Originally published in November 2010. R1011A

DuPont's CEO on Executing a Complex Cross-Border Acquisition

by Ellen Kullman

Ellen Kullman is the chair and CEO of DuPont.

The Idea

Executives at DuPont worked for six months on the $7 billion acquisition of Denmark's Danisco. Ellen Kullman details the challenges and opportunities that arose—and offers lessons for others involved in M&A.

Two days before Thanksgiving 2010, my phone rang. Tom Knutzen, the CEO of Danisco, was on the line. His company, a Danish leader in industrial biotechnology and nutritional ingredients, was in play, and a European chemical group had offered to buy it. His question to me: Was DuPont still interested in acquiring Danisco?

A few months earlier Danisco had altered its rules governing shareholder votes to make a potential acquisition less onerous for a buyer. Just after that change I'd met Tom for dinner in Copenhagen. He'd confirmed that if he were ready for a possible deal, he would call DuPont.

Danisco was already on our M&A radar. It was a joint venture partner, and its two core science-based businesses were potential growth opportunities for DuPont. At the time, Corporate Plans, our strategy group, had a list of 10 to 12 possible acquisition targets, and I was watching three or four closely, including Danisco.

In the fall of 2010 many companies might have put M&A far lower on the priority list, as we all navigated the economic recession. Fortunately, DuPont had emerged from the downturn with a strong balance sheet, and thanks to the prep work we'd done on Danisco through the years, we were ready to value the company. Time, however, was a challenge: Danisco wanted offers from all bidders by January 7. Another company had already made an offer, so the race was under way as we reached the starting line.

I hung up with Tom and called my CFO, Nick Fanandakis. We immediately pulled together a small team to size up the opportunity. What we needed was the speed and agility to gather and analyze a lot of information and, if it was in our best interest, to act quickly. The team prepared a two-sentence expression of interest, and then all the members went home for Thanksgiving dinner, knowing full well it might be the last meal they would enjoy with their families for a long time.

On Monday I met with my seven-person executive team, and we agreed that DuPont should consider acquiring Danisco. We secured approval from the board later that week. For the next 30 days the due diligence group—eventually about 25 people—worked in two cross-functional teams. One studied the issues and opportunities presented by Danisco's biotech business, and the other focused on its nutrition and health division. Members of both teams met regularly with the executive team for guidance. The people in those due diligence groups were experts in their fields, so although we tested their theories, we trusted them to do their jobs.

On Friday, January 7, after hearing from the teams, we agreed on a final binding offer within the range our board had authorized. After a weekend of back-and-forth negotiations, Danisco's board chairman accepted our offer late in the day on January 9. We executed the legal documents, and in the morning we announced the news: DuPont would buy Danisco for 665 kroner per share, the equivalent of about $6.3 billion and a 25% premium on the company's January 7, 2011, share price of 530 kroner.

Everyone was thrilled. We had executed on our plans to acquire Danisco at a record pace. But I wasn't ready to celebrate yet. It's a long road from an accepted offer to a completed transaction—especially in a complex cross-border acquisition between publicly traded companies. Foreign regulatory regimes, governance procedures, and even local customs often delay or obstruct such deals. This can create windows of time that speculative investors can use to drive stock prices up or down, further complicating negotiations. We thought we might be able to get our deal done by March. As it turned out, the process would take longer than we had expected.

The Evolution of a Science Company

Most people think of DuPont as a chemical company that's been around for more than 200 years—the one that brought the world Kevlar, Tyvek, Teflon, and Corian. But we have shifted our strategy to embrace biosciences as well. Thanks to recent advances such as DNA mapping, nanoscale imaging, and the emergence of computer analytics for scientific data, it's now possible to make high-performance, sustainable ingredients and materials that traditional chemistry can't. We see this as a huge growth area, and we are changing our portfolio accordingly to use the integration of biology, applied materials, and chemistry to create innovations in food, alternative energy, and advanced protection materials and services.

In 1998 Chad Holliday, my predecessor as DuPont's CEO, made our new intentions clear. He announced plans to divest Conoco, our oil and gas subsidiary. A year later DuPont purchased Pioneer Hi-Bred, an agricultural seed company. Around the same time, Chad asked a small team to investigate an expansion into industrial biosciences. I was tasked with leading that group, and our first big success was a joint development agreement with Genencor, which later became a division of Danisco, and the development of an ingredient to make renewable plastics for home goods, automotive parts, and apparel.

Even as we focused on organic growth in the mid-2000s, we considered further acquisitions, particularly in the industrial biotech space. Genencor had been one option, but when Danisco bought it outright, in 2005, that target disappeared. We also continued to pursue joint ventures—we produced a soy protein with the agribusiness company Bunge, and we brought second-generation cellulosic biofuels to market with the merged Genencor and Danisco.

When I was told I would become CEO, just days before the collapse of Lehman Brothers, in 2008, I had to put my game plan for growth in the drawer and instead deal with a global recession. Some parts of our business stayed healthy through 2009, but others were struggling. So my first initiatives involved cutting costs and streamlining our company from 23 business units to 13. Finally, in 2010, things started to improve, and my confidence grew. By July we had started to talk to the board about strategic growth again. Plan A was to do it organically, but we also had a Plan B: acquisitions. Our directors agreed with that flexible approach, and since you can't predict when those opportunities will arise, I asked Corporate Plans for a deep dive on our most promising targets. Thus Danisco was on our short list. Our methodical approach allowed DuPont to catch up with the other companies interested in the acquisition.

Don't Fall in Love with a Deal

The decision to bid for Danisco wasn't automatic. Of course we liked its Genencor business. We had liked it when it was up for sale in 2005, and its portfolio was even stronger in 2010. We also liked Danisco's focus on science, application development, and customers. The questions were, What value would we put on the whole portfolio? What were its segments, market positions, and models for competing? We had a lot to learn in a very short time.

Between Thanksgiving and the January 7 bid deadline, our due diligence teams performed heroically. It was a war-room approach: People ate and slept at the office and canceled holidays, without being able to tell friends, families, and colleagues why. One executive even participated in a three-hour conference call from the Vatican while watching his daughter's high school band perform for the pope. Everyone pushed tirelessly to understand Danisco's businesses, how they would fit strategically with ours, and how we should value them. We also considered who else might be bidding and what their financial positions might be.

People dropped everything to work on this deal. Focusing that hard on anything can lead to an emotional attachment, but that's a pitfall one must avoid. You can't fall in love with a deal; you have to fall in love with what it does for your company. And even then it has to be at the right price. That's why we let our team members do their own critical thinking, hash out their various opinions, and give us their recommendations. They'd been debating the valuation for weeks, and I'd been asking questions and listening closely. Twenty minutes before the final bids were due, we got one last briefing from all key parties—our bank and legal advisers, Corporate Plans, the M&A organization, and people in the relevant business units. We absorbed everyone's insights, made sure no information or opinions had been held back, settled on our offer, and conveyed it. Although it seemed to take ages, the response time was not long. The Danisco board accepted.

Preparing for the Long Haul

We had not reached the finish line yet. In fact, the longer process had just begun. Owing to the size and scope of Danisco's operations and ours, we had to secure regulatory approvals from more than 10 countries, including the United States, members of the European Commission, and China. We had gone through the U.S. and EU processes routinely for other transactions, but China was new and the timeline uncertain. It took just over four months to complete all regulatory approvals. Again, the deal team showed extreme grit.

Then there were the shareholders. In the U.S., tenders from only 51% are necessary to acquire and control a public company. In Denmark, 80% is required to control and 90% to absorb and delist from the Copenhagen Stock Exchange. That rule, combined with the extended regulatory delays, gave hedge funds, which owned 20% of Danisco's stock, an opportunity. They started driving up the stock price in the hope that we would be forced to increase our offer. By April 15, when we finally had the regulators' blessing, Danisco's stock was trading at 668 kroner a share and only 48% of shareholders had agreed to the deal. I was disappointed. At our annual meeting the following week, I told the board that we needed to reevaluate our offer.

That didn't mean automatically raising it. One option was to simply hold firm and then walk away if we didn't get support from the shareholders. But it was important for us to consider whether anything had changed since January. Danisco had been posting good financial results. Was there more value in the company than we'd thought? And was there something that we didn't fully understand about the shareholders—not just the hedge funds, but the institutional investors in Denmark who were balking at what we considered to be a fair offer? Nick and I flew to Copenhagen to find out.

Over a couple of days of back-to-back meetings with the Danish investment community, we got a clearer picture and made some key judgments about our path forward. These face-to-face conversations were critical for the actions we took next and, ultimately, for the successful outcome of the deal.

We asked our team in Copenhagen to map out the scenarios. We wanted to segment the shareholders and figure out which groups were likely to tender if we raised our bid to various levels within the board-authorized range. We needed to have real numbers, not theories. After looking at the team's projections, Nick and I discussed and agreed where we should be. I told the team, "If we hold, we'll lose." On April 29 we increased our offer by 5% to 700 kroner a share, or $7 billion, and declared that this was a full, fair, and final offer. If we didn't get 80% of the shareholders, we would walk away. Nick and I flew back to our Wilmington headquarters.

Now we had to wait and see how many shareholders would tender their shares before the deadline, which was May 13. At first I was anxious. I just wanted the deal to be done. Many others felt the same way. There was a lot invested here, not just financially.

After a few days, however, I found myself growing more relaxed. I realized, and emphasized to everyone else, that we had done everything we could. The bid was right. And we would be fine with or without Danisco. We still had Plan A.

Ready to Roll

Nick and I rarely go out for lunch, but we did on the day the tenders were due. We figured we would get 80% to 90% shareholder approval—a reasonable outcome, because it meant the deal would go through, but not ideal, because we might still have to win over an additional 10% from among the holdouts in order to delist and fully integrate Danisco. We were walking back to the office when our Copenhagen contact called Nick. We'd gotten 92% of shares tendered. The bank advisers had counted twice. I was thrilled and proud of our efforts. I will never forget the day.

On May 19 we completed the acquisition. This was a big, bold strategy. The space was interesting, but we needed to figure out how we were going to play in it. We did our homework. We worked on improving the value of our existing nutrition and health business, and we focused on creating broader value for the company. Danisco was a very complementary fit, a culture we knew and people we knew; we could get it at a price at which shareholders would see value for it in a very short time. But it wasn't enough to just get the deal done. If we didn't execute and integrate well, and if we didn't get synergies quickly, it wouldn't be a victory.

We were ready to act. I knew who should lead the new groups, and I made the appointments immediately. In our first postdeal call with the Danisco leadership team, we took great pains to talk about our shared core values and how we might blend our respective cultures. Just four days later we held Welcome Week, during which senior executives visited all the DuPont and Danisco locations affected by the merger, explaining our strategy and our commitment to redeploying redundant employees where we could. The presentations were consistent, but each was also customized to local concerns.

During that week senior executives spoke directly to more than 10,000 employees. We followed this with regular pulse surveys—one of the first best practices we learned and adopted from Danisco—that created a heat map of potential geographic locations where there might be confusion or miscommunication. Within a week those issues were addressed as transparently as possible. By the end of August we had integration projects defined, scoped, and resourced—everything from renegotiating trucking contracts to merging our HR and finance groups.

Our initial target of $130 million in cost savings will be achieved a year ahead of schedule. The pieces are fitting together faster than we expected. The integration of Danisco is a big win for DuPont and its shareholders. Yes, the deal process was long, complicated, and frustrating at times. But the people of DuPont powered through it because we knew this acquisition would enhance our biosciences capability and accelerate the company's readiness for its next 100 years of growth.

The right strategic acquisition, at the right price, is worth the wait.

Originally published in July–August 2012. R1207A

Enterprise's Leader on How Integrating an Acquisition Transformed His Business

by Andrew C. Taylor

Andrew C. Taylor is the executive chairman of Enterprise Holdings.

The Idea

When the car rental company acquired Alamo and National, rather than execute a "takeover," it moved slowly and sought to learn from its new brands.

I n 2007 Enterprise Rent-A-Car was marking its 50th anniversary. We had much to celebrate. With more than $9 billion in global revenue, we were the largest car rental company in the world and one of the largest family-owned and -operated companies in the United States. As the industry leader, we had been approached from time to time about acquisition opportunities—especially after several of our competitors merged or changed owners in the mid-1990s. However, while our major rivals had always focused on renting cars at airport locations, Enterprise had concentrated on "home city" rentals, with much of our business coming from people who needed a car while their own was being repaired. So we had never really been tempted. We were growing steadily and organically, in local neighborhoods and at airports. We believed in our strong, do-it-yourself culture. And we had little interest in altering what was working so well.

But all that changed on Valentine's Day in 2007. That morning the *New York Times* reported that two of our biggest airport rivals, Vanguard (which owned National and Alamo) and the Dollar Thrifty Automotive Group, were close to an agreement on a $3 billion merger. We saw right away that this deal would be bad news for Enterprise. To continue our growth, we needed to increase our share of airport rentals; if four rival brands were combined into one competitor, our climb would become that much harder. We quickly started the debate: Should we make a bid for Vanguard?

Such a deal had obvious attractions. Both National and Alamo were already well established at airports across the country, while we were still battling to obtain decent space at some major facilities. Our brands also seemed to complement one another: Although Enterprise was known for its "everyday low price," Alamo's discounts appealed to price-sensitive shoppers, and National competed for premium business travelers. What's more, neither Alamo nor National was a major contender in nonairport rentals, which meant that we had virtually no overlap with Vanguard's facilities, technology, and personnel.

But our company had never done a deal anywhere near this size. I knew it might be unpopular with our executive team. Some would question why we should acquire these rivals when we were already gaining ground on them. There would also be big operational and cultural differences. Most Enterprise branches were neighborhood locations where a small team of employees serviced about 100 cars; National's and Alamo's airport branches were much bigger. Enterprise's culture focused on customer satisfaction and "promote from within" policies as paths to business success, whereas Vanguard's culture stressed operational efficiency. Enterprise owned 100% of its branches; Vanguard had both corporate-owned locations and independent franchises. For its branches, Enterprise hired only college graduates looking to move up in the company; Vanguard's branch personnel included many employees who expected to spend their careers at a single location.

Big differences, no question. But the more we discussed the potential deal, the clearer it became that we should proceed. All our independent directors were in favor of it. So we made a phone call to Vanguard's owner, the private equity firm Cerberus. It was clear that the firm would welcome our all-cash bid and the prospect of a speedy close, so we quickly settled on a price of approximately $3 billion of invested capital. Over the next few months we did our due diligence and worked to win antitrust approval.

Integrating an acquisition like this is a tough job. A lot of companies fail at it, and even when an integration succeeds, the acquired company sometimes feels that it has been swallowed up or "conquered." With Vanguard, however, we worked hard from the start to execute a thoughtful and respectful integration. We wanted to learn all we could from the company's brands, not impose our systems and methods at every turn. On the surface the deal was about boosting Enterprise's presence at airports, and that did happen. But in the process we also learned a lot about ourselves and changed our company in ways that have equipped us for faster growth on a global scale.

Meshing Cultures and Values

When the deal closed, in the summer of 2007, we began what can best be described as a deliberate integration. It was far more important to do it right than to do it quickly. We could afford a thoughtful approach, not only because our private ownership shielded us from short-term financial pressures, but also because we got Vanguard at an affordable price. I knew there was no significant financial risk to Enterprise, even if the deal did not work out. Although we lacked experience in major acquisitions, we moved forward in what turned out to be the right way.

First we focused on the two companies' cultures, using a simple message and a few powerful symbols. On August 1, after I signed the papers that closed the deal, my family and members of our executive team flew to Tulsa, Oklahoma, for an evening meeting at Vanguard headquarters. I introduced myself and my family, stressing our commitment to making this combination work over the long term. I was convinced that the same business philosophy that had propelled our growth would drive Enterprise and Vanguard together. "Employees on both sides of the transaction," I said, "are now part of a company that is dedicated to three things: listening to and satisfying our customers, creating opportunities for our employees, and achieving long-term, sustainable growth." The message seemed to resonate with the audience. I emphasized that as a family-owned organization, we aimed to bring stability and continuity to Vanguard. This was welcome news at a company where a series of ownership and management upheavals over the previous decade had left employees feeling a bit unsettled and disenfranchised. I also announced that as part of our measured and steady integration process, Vanguard would operate as an autonomous subsidiary for at least a year.

We had already made it clear to Vanguard employees that there would be no "invasion of the white shirts" from our St. Louis headquarters—a reference to Enterprise's well-known conservative dress code. Greg Stubblefield, one of our strongest field executives, whom we'd appointed as the president of

Vanguard, took just two Enterprise executives with him to work in Tulsa. Greg's job was to help the two companies learn from each other. When a new direction was chosen, it would reflect the best elements of both cultures and operating approaches. Vanguard clearly had a lot to teach us about airport operations. At Orlando, LAX, and other big airports, National and Alamo managers presided over thousands of rental transactions every day. Their systems and processes operated on a much bigger scale than ours. At the same time, they had a quality assurance process that was specifically designed to head off potential problems. We eventually adopted this program at Enterprise airport locations—an illustration of how we took ideas from Vanguard when they complemented (or were better than) our own.

Meanwhile, we used the first year not only to listen and learn but also to share our values and practices. From the beginning it was understood that we had a lot to teach about achieving consistently high customer satisfaction. During the 1990s we had developed the Enterprise Service Quality index (ESQi) for measuring and managing it. The index confirmed that customers who were fully satisfied with our service were three times as likely to rent from us again. Managers' ESQi scores were an important factor in their compensation and advancement. Vanguard immediately adopted the index for both Alamo and National, although it informally tracked results for six months before fully implementing it.

Three Distinct Characters

During this get-acquainted period, our St. Louis-based integration committee analyzed many issues, including the brand portfolio, the general management structure, and the question of franchises. One key question was whether we would maintain all three brands or combine Enterprise and Alamo. When we'd first considered the deal, the answer was far from clear. But as we studied Vanguard's marketing and operations, we came to see that each of the brands was distinctly positioned to serve a well-defined segment.

National appealed to business travelers; we referred to them as "rental experts" because they wanted to get in and out of their vehicles as fast as possible, without stopping to fill out forms or deal with customer representatives. And they were willing to pay a premium for those benefits. National's loyalty program, the Emerald Club, was a major driver of reservations and repeat business. Alamo, on the other hand, was a destination brand for vacationers, often from outside the United States, who were headed to places like Las Vegas and Disney World. Its customers generally looked for bargains on the internet. Meanwhile, Enterprise's strong track record of affordable pricing in home-city markets attracted customers to its airport locations as well. Each brand had significant value and offered its customers what was most important to them. So we worked to reinforce the distinct character of each.

Our back-office operations, though, were a different story. We were very interested in finding operational ways to leverage our joint ownership. Because Alamo and National facilities were generally colocated at airports, we tried to position Enterprise as close to them as possible, and we removed brand identification from vehicles so that the operations could share cars when necessary. (National and Alamo had pioneered this approach, allocating vehicles to National's business customers during the workweek and to Alamo's leisure customers on weekends.) This fleet management approach increased flexibility and lowered costs.

Next we had to decide on an organizational structure. Enterprise is highly decentralized: It operates through regional subsidiaries in which branch managers have significant P&L responsibility and ultimately report to general managers, who also enjoy plenty of autonomy. For Vanguard, virtually all management decisions were centralized in Tulsa. We debated about the best way to run a multibrand airport operation, and the more we looked at it, the more we saw the advantages of adapting our regional structure. This meant, however, that many Enterprise general managers would have to oversee big, factorylike operations at airports, manage discrete market segments, and strike the right balance in promoting all three brands. At the same time, most Vanguard employees would need a better understanding of the home-city market.

This is where we realized yet another advantage of moving carefully on the integration. We had time to equip our general managers for a much bigger job and to identify and prepare Vanguard managers who could thrive under the new structure. In many cases, Enterprise personnel wound up holding the general manager positions, but we also put Vanguard managers into those critically important slots in markets such as California and Hawaii.

Meanwhile, about a year into the integration process, and just as the country was sliding into one of the worst economic downturns in history, Enterprise relocated 80 employees from Tulsa to our St. Louis headquarters. Along with some attrition and a small number of job cuts, that left approximately 400 people to staff a "shared services" center at the former Vanguard headquarters building. Today the Tulsa team, now more than 500 strong, provides sales support, oversees accounts payable and accounts receivable, manages vehicle administration (such as tags, titles, and citations), and coordinates damage recovery responsibilities.

We also launched a new corporate identity—Enterprise Holdings—so that we could speak with a unified voice across our portfolio of three car rental brands. That last major step in our two-year integration process built on the Enterprise name and heritage and reassured all our stakeholders that our founding values were still front and center.

A Change for the Better

It has now been more than six years since we found that Valentine's Day gift in the *New York Times*. Without question, the deal we made has worked out very well. In fact, it paid for itself in less than three years. Total revenue for all three brands now surpasses $15 billion—that's pretty healthy growth in a tough economy, especially for the travel industry. Meanwhile, from 2007 to 2013, the combined market share at airports for all three brands climbed from about 28% to more than 33%. And for the first time, our brands captured the top three rankings in the J.D. Power and Associates 2012 North America Rental Car Satisfaction Study.

National's performance is a particularly good story. The brand had suffered under leadership turmoil and a lack of investment from 1997 to 2007, but National is now competing as a top-tier brand at airports. It even outperforms Enterprise on our companywide service quality index. That is fine with us—it gets Enterprise's competitive juices flowing.

We have also learned to work with Vanguard's franchises. As independent businesses, they manage their own affairs, have their own distinctive cultures, and are free to use the National and Alamo brands to compete with Enterprise. We have been open to acquiring franchised territories whenever they are available, and at this point we have absorbed the majority of U.S. locations and a significant number of Canadian ones. But where franchisees remain in control, goodwill and cooperation obtain on both sides.

An unexpected benefit of learning to work with franchisees—not only in the United States and Canada but also in the Caribbean, Latin America, and Europe—is that it has helped us better understand partnerships in other contexts, including foreign markets, as we continue to expand our global footprint.

Our biggest lesson from the Vanguard integration is that our company can execute a major acquisition without risk to our fundamental values and culture. But we have learned other lessons, too. We have learned that the most important factor in deciding whether to do a deal is a clear understanding of what is to be gained. We have learned—as we suspected from the outset—that in integrating a merger you should work deliberately, because you get only one chance to do it well. And we have learned that symbolism matters. It was important that Enterprise not send a whole cadre of executives to Tulsa to execute a "takeover."

Today Enterprise Holdings is stronger than ever. Our values have not changed, and they never will. But the Vanguard deal did help our company change—for the better.

Originally published in September 2013. R1309A

FINDING
A STRATEGY
THAT WORKS

MANY OF THE BEST-SELLING ARTICLES IN THE HISTORY OF
Harvard Business Review have focused on strategy, for good
reason: Figuring out what businesses to compete in and how to
gain—and retain—an advantage over rivals is exceedingly tricky,
particularly in a fast-changing global economy.

In the essays that follow, CEOs describe how they've made
difficult strategic choices as the world changes—whether it's
figuring out a way to keep a manufacturing business in the United
States, deciding to kill off a 244-year-old eponymous product, or
struggling (and ultimately failing) to save a movie rental business in
an industry moving toward digital.

The opening essays in this book played off of Jim Collins's
simple dictate: "First *who*, then *what*." The essays In this section
make clear that that sequence doesn't necessarily speak to the
magnitude of complexity. To put it another way: Getting the "what"
right can be extraordinarily challenging, too.

It's also clear that these days the "right" path isn't likely to stay right for long. Lately, the most common buzzwords from academics who study strategy include such terms as "transient advantage" or "adaptive strategy." Learning how other leaders navigate shifts is crucial in a world in which managers must be constantly attentive to strategy.

General Electric's CEO on Sparking an American Manufacturing Renewal

by Jeffrey R. Immelt

Jeffrey R. Immelt, the chairman and CEO of GE, heads President Obama's Council on Jobs and Competitiveness.

The Idea

Labor costs caused many U.S. companies to outsource manufacturing. A broader set of metrics has led GE to reverse course and invest heavily in renewing American manufacturing operations.

More than 50 years ago, at Appliance Park, in Louisville, Kentucky, GE invested $1.2 million in a UNIVAC, the first computer deployed commercially in the United States. The UNIVAC was the size of a small garage, weighed almost 30,000 pounds, and took an entire workday to complete its calculations. Yet it was a game changer. In fact, in 1954 Roddy F. Osborn predicted in this magazine that GE's use of the UNIVAC for business data processing would lead to a new age of industry: "The management planning behind the acquisition of the first UNIVAC to be used in business may eventually be recorded by historians as the foundation of the second industrial revolution; just as Jacquard's automatic loom in 1801 or Taylor's studies of the principles of scientific management a hundred years later marked turning points in business history."

Today, again at Appliance Park, another investment is breaking new IT ground. This past summer we opened a cutting-edge data center in one of the original buildings in the complex. It is among the few data centers to have received Platinum LEED certification, and it is filled with refrigerator-size racks of servers, each of them with computing power millions of times greater than the UNIVAC's. The facility carries 350 watts (versus the usual 70 watts) per square foot, significantly improving power and cooling efficiency. It has raised GE's uninterruptible power supply (UPS) efficiency to 99%.

The $40 million data center and a multiyear IT project to replace more than 330 systems across the business with integrated software are just part of a larger $800 million investment in Louisville (and a total $1 billion investment in GE Appliances). We will create some 1,000 jobs in the United States by 2014.

Although IT is really the backbone of the business—critical to our success, job creation, and growth—the data center alone won't usher in another industrial revolution. But the role it will play in helping to drive efficiency, productivity, and quality is symbolic of the transformation of Appliance Park, where we are redesigning all our product lines and the way in which we manufacture them. In some cases we are totally rehabbing factories that haven't been used in 15 years. What GE is doing at Appliance Park, and what GE's employees are doing in research labs and on factory floors across the United States, says something about how we make decisions concerning where to manufacture our products. It shows that when we invest in our people and our technologies and create new business models, we can bring manufacturing back to the United States and be profitable.

This doesn't mean that we are simply reversing what we have done and retreating from performing R&D and manufacturing outside the U.S. The fact is that we are—forevermore—going to play in a global economy, where competition is tougher, customers are more demanding, and the pace of change is faster. To win, we must play and we must improve everywhere we do business. Thus we must find the place where we can develop and produce the best products and services at the lowest cost, wherever that may be. So we will continue to source commodities and manufacture products abroad and to invest in our R&D centers around the world to obtain the lowest costs, access talent, and be near customers. This isn't bad for America. The fact of the matter is that thousands and thousands of U.S. jobs exist because of our ability to compete globally.

Still, today at GE we are outsourcing less and producing more in the U.S. We created more than 7,000 American manufacturing jobs in 2010 and 2011. Our success on the factory floor rests on human innovation and technical innovation—the keys to leading an American manufacturing renewal. When we are deciding where to manufacture, we ask, "Will our people and technology in the U.S. provide us with a competitive advantage?" Increasingly, the answer is yes.

Human Innovation at Appliance Park

About 30 years ago, as the business became less profitable, GE began moving manufacturing out of Appliance Park to low-cost countries in a combination of joint ventures and outsourcing. The decision was relatively simple. We had strong brand recognition and customer loyalty—two things we believed would continue whether our products said "made in Kentucky" or "made in Korea." We reasoned that if we could lower our costs enough, we would quickly reverse the slide in profitability. We weren't alone: Many other businesses saw outsourcing in emerging markets as a solution.

But for our appliances business, emerging markets eventually offered something else: competition from former suppliers of whole products, particularly in Asia. As these competitors improved their lines and lowered their prices, even customers who had grown up with and knew only GE refrigerators and dryers began to explore alternatives. Other forces were at play as well. Shipping and materials costs were rising; wages were increasing in China and elsewhere; and we didn't have control of the supply chain. The currencies of emerging markets added complexity. Finally, core competency was an issue. Engineering and manufacturing are hands-on and iterative, and our most innovative appliance-design work is done in the United States. At a time when speed to market is everything, separating design and development from manufacturing didn't make sense.

Complex trade-offs have always been involved in location decisions, but as these trade-offs shifted, around 2008, we came to the conclusion that outsourcing was quickly becoming mostly outdated as a business model for GE Appliances. In fact, I would say that we had a do-or-die moment. We considered selling the business but decided instead to develop the new products we would need to compete and win. To do that, we'd have to change swiftly and dramatically. The question was where and how to invest. In today's economy, you can't just compete on cost in a lot of businesses and ask "Where is the market? What is our superior customer-value proposition?" Regaining our competitiveness, delivering value to our customers, and generating shareholder return would require not just investment but an entirely new approach—one centered on ensuring not only that we had the best people but also that we empowered them to execute. Our business strategy could no longer rely on having employees literally hand off what they were best at doing. But we could change the environment in which they worked, engaging the entire workforce from design to development to assembly. That is human innovation.

Human innovation has three key elements. The first is building in-house innovation capability. In Louisville that has meant hiring more than 300 industrial designers, engineers, and other salaried team members with new skills and expertise in areas such as wireless technology and advanced manufacturing; investing in research to better predict and identify consumer trends; and building IT infrastructure like that state-of-the-art data center.

The second element is lean manufacturing. At Appliance Park we have torn down functional silos and replaced them with a "one team" mentality. Designers, engineers, and assembly-line workers together determine the best way to meet their goals; they own the metrics. For instance, we know that one key to success is driving down manufacturing hours per unit. The team decides just how to do that. Managers post their action items and deliverables for all to see, and employees have a strong sense of accountability. If they conceive an idea for redesigning an appliance that weighs less and has fewer components and lower material costs, they can build it. They take pride in this ownership, and the results speak for themselves: For example, in some factories it takes nine hours to build a refrigerator. Our employees in Louisville are working to cut that by more than half. By revamping what was a 25-year-old dishwasher line, the Appliance Park team has reduced the time to produce by 68% and the space required by more than 80%. While the focus remains on creating the best designs and the highest quality, everything leads to the intended cost-cutting by-product of reducing waste.

The third element in human innovation is a new model for labor relations, most evident in the competitive wage agreement between our union workers and management. It wasn't easy for them to find common ground. Both sides had to face new realities, make tough choices, and accept concessions. The union accepted a lower starting wage for new hires; we pledged to create new jobs in Louisville and promised that if the new processes and automation that go along with advanced manufacturing led to redundancy, we would redeploy workers, not let them go. Last fall the appliances business announced about 450 new factory jobs at the negotiated competitive wage. We received 6,000 applications in less than an hour. Labor-management relations that are based on honesty, mutual respect, and the recognition that both sides have an interest in the success of the enterprise can lead to competitive advantage.

One result of our new approach to manufacturing was that in 2009 we announced that GE would make the GeoSpring hybrid water heater at Appliance Park—the first new product line we had brought to Louisville in 50 years. Six months later we announced a new washer and a new dryer. In October 2010 we announced that we would create four U.S. Centers of Excellence for the design and manufacture of refrigerators. When they are completed, GE will offer the highest percentage of U.S.-made refrigerators among full-line appliance makers. Between now and 2013 we will completely redesign all our appliance product lines. We will put thousands of Americans back to work, mostly at Appliance Park. And, most important, we will win in the market by not only investing in U.S. manufacturing but also transforming it with human innovation.

Technical Innovation at GE Aviation

We will continue to invest in products throughout our businesses, because technical innovation—more specifically, advanced manufacturing and materials processes—is the other key to America's manufacturing revival. A great example sits about 600 miles south of Appliance Park, in Ellisville, Mississippi. That is where, in 2013, we will start production at a new manufacturing facility to meet accelerating global demand for GE Aviation's jet engines. We plan to invest about $60 million and create 250 jobs in a new 300,000-square-foot facility to manufacture advanced composite components for our jet engines.

Why Ellisville? Why has GE Aviation invested hundreds of millions of dollars in more than 30 other U.S. sites? And why, this past fall, did we announce plans for another advanced manufacturing plant in Auburn, Alabama, that will produce precision machined parts for commercial and military engines?

The answer is technology and sophistication—in advanced manufacturing, computer modeling, and material sciences and composites. For example, the use of different qualities of carbon fiber and resins enabled us to create unique, impact-resistant fan blades, fan cases, and components that sharply reduce engine weight and offer more durability than the traditional all-metal versions. I'm biased, of course, but I believe that this level of sophistication is simply unmatched anywhere else in the world. That didn't happen in a vacuum. Rather, it is the product of a decade of R&D investment—$12 billion, beginning when the entire aviation industry was reeling—that is now paying off. Today, with 50,000 commercial and military engines in service, we are the world's largest producer of jet engines, and they're the biggest, most powerful, and most efficient ones in the world.

If the GE Appliances story is about manufacturing teams taking ownership and working together with unions, the GE Aviation story is about the technical innovation and expertise that makes building our engines in the United States the only choice. Just as in our other businesses, when we decide where to manufacture, or where to open an aviation R&D center, a lot of complex factors are at work. With aviation we take into account the need to protect our proprietary technology. We consider that GE Aviation's technical innovation is dual sourced, supporting both commercial and military engines. Finally, we look at where we can partner with the intellectual capability of American universities.

The decision to open a plant in Ellisville was based on our success in Batesville, a town in northern Mississippi, where we opened a facility three years ago. By partnering with Mississippi State University, we have developed a highly sophisticated proprietary process for manufacturing components made of carbon-fiber composites. We hope to replicate that relationship and its results in Ellisville, working with the University of Southern Mississippi. We are also opening an R&D avionics center on the campus of the University of Dayton, in Ohio. To spread risk and gain market access, we will continue to use some international suppliers. And our domestic facilities can't become complacent. They need to remain competitive. But these partnerships—and, quite frankly, the battle among states to land them—are vital not only for designing and producing the materials, systems, and processes that will come to define air travel but also for developing tomorrow's engineers, who are critical to America's competitiveness.

Of course, the ultimate test at both Appliance Park and GE Aviation will be whether we can sustain what we have started. It is critically important that we drive down manufacturing costs. But that won't be worth much unless we can offer reliable, efficient products at competitive prices. Two things are clear: First, outsourcing that is based only on labor costs is yesterday's model. Second, GE employees will deliver—because of their ability, because of their attitude, and because they expect to. Every GE employee in the United States, from the factory floor to the boardroom, knows we can win. And we will win only if we're not afraid to compete.

As a country, if we want to revive U.S. manufacturing and regain our competitive edge, we have to execute. But we also need confidence and the mind-set that we can outperform anyone. We should start by making a serious commitment to manufacturing and exports.

People talk about the Darwinian nature of markets. They say that America has undergone a natural evolution from farming to manufacturing to services, as have other mature economies. But nothing is predestined or inevitable about the industrial decline of the United States. China is growing fast because it is investing in technology and has zero intention of letting up on manufacturing. We shouldn't be afraid of that; we should be inspired by the competition.

To meet that competition, we'll need a strong core of innovation and a stable financial system built around helping small and medium-size businesses and industrial companies to succeed. We'll need an updated infrastructure to support manufacturing, which the private sector can help fund—better roads and airports, broadband capability, and a bigger and smarter electricity grid. Finally, we'll need well-trained teams. Like the Appliance Park employees building hybrid water heaters; the GE scientists developing composite materials for safer, cleaner, more-efficient jet engines; and the software engineers working on the industrial internet at GE's newly announced center in Silicon Valley, only the best-trained workforce will make America faster, better, and more competitive over the long term.

The nation's consumers cannot lead this recovery. Business investment and exports must.

That is the imperative. But before an imperative comes an impetus for action. We can't do any of this if we're afraid to get in the game. We need to believe that we can design, develop, and produce here in the United States; that we can do it cost-effectively and efficiently; and that we can win. Then we need to find ways to collaborate and make the necessary investments. If we do, our workers will prove America's potential.

Originally published in March 2012. R1203A

Prada's CEO on Staying Independent in a Consolidating Industry

by Patrizio Bertelli

Patrizio Bertelli is the CEO of Prada.

The Idea

While rival fashion houses have struggled and been acquired by conglomerates, Prada has prospered. Its CEO says that has a lot to do with the company's culture.

At Prada we have had to cope with our fair share of the unpredictable and the unexpected. Originally we planned to go public in Milan in late September 2001, but the 9/11 tragedy, followed by the second Gulf War, the outbreak of SARS, and a global credit crisis, upset our plans. We reacted to these events in a timely and innovative way, seizing new opportunities, and launched our IPO in Hong Kong in June 2011. In the 1990s we believed that our future depended on our ability to gain market share through acquisitions in Western Europe and the United States. But now we are focused mostly on our core brands, Prada and Miu Miu, and the emerging markets—such as China, which supplies 22% of our revenue.

Despite the events of the past decade, Prada has prospered even as many other fashion houses have struggled. Perhaps more remarkable, we have retained our independence in an industry increasingly dominated by luxury conglomerates. The difference, I think, derives from our organizational culture. Although we have often had to change our plans, the way we manage the company has remained constant. The values that guide our decisions, the way we organize ourselves, how we communicate with one another and with our stakeholders—these have changed hardly at all. Therefore, if a key to Prada's success exists, it is related to these principles. In my view, they are universal and can be successfully applied by anyone.

Control Through Transparency

At Prada we have no secrets. At many companies managers in charge of a particular function—whether design or merchandising—dislike it when people in their department talk to colleagues in other departments. They want to maintain control, and they often do so by hoarding knowledge and restricting communication.

Naturally, you must let people have control over what they do. Good designers should be the masters of their designs, or their ideas may be spoiled. Good managers shouldn't be second-guessed, or no one will want to make decisions. But control must not become obstruction. A designer or a manager should be able to exercise it without limiting access to information.

In fact, a culture that values transparency gives managers more control than one that values control. Transparency between functions enables Prada to respond to changing market tastes very quickly. We don't design for the sake of designing; our creative energy is integrated with our commercial ambitions. We're not unique in this respect. In the 1970s Yves

Saint Laurent, Chanel, Gucci, and Giorgio Armani were also good at blending the creative and the commercial. To a great extent they, like Prada, owe their integration skills to a partnership at the top—in our case, between Miuccia Prada and me. People working closely with Miuccia in design will talk often to people working closely with me on the commercial side. This enables us to be fast. Any department store will tell you that Prada delivers clothing and accessories very quickly after a design has been presented on the runway. It's difficult to overestimate the importance of this capability in the time-sensitive business of fashion.

Transparency also allowed us to easily adopt the reporting standards required of a publicly listed company. Family companies, especially in Italy, struggle with the very idea of disclosure, let alone its implementation. That's one reason many of them prefer to seek investment capital from large strategic partners. They feel that managing the relationship with a partner will be easier and they will retain control.

This is open to question, because partners are on your board. That's not a problem in itself. It is absolutely legitimate for a key financial partner to be involved in a company's strategic decision making. However, you never really know what the agendas and the true priorities of your partners are. They may harbor ambitions to take control, or try to pursue goals other than growth and margins objectives and results, in order to advance their own plans. Managing such cases is time-consuming, and very soon you find yourself negotiating all your decisions. By going public Prada has avoided this and can grow without compromising our core values or our design philosophy. It's easier, I have found, to be accountable to 10,000 shareholders than to manage one or two partners. Our willingness to be transparent to public shareholders has been fundamental to our remaining independent.

Go Where the Risk Is

A few decades ago, fashion houses didn't see Russia, India, the Gulf states, or China as an important market for luxury goods. Growth was all about markets in Europe, the United States, and Japan. We started our international expansion in 1983 with stores in New York and Madrid and followed up with stores in Paris, London, and Tokyo. In 1993 we opened a store in Beijing.

It's easy to say now that the future of fashion lies in big emerging countries such as China and Russia. But back in 1993 the world was a very different place. The memory of Tiananmen Square was still fresh. Hong Kong was gearing up for a communist takeover in 1997, and it was by no means clear whether China would tolerate the British territory's capitalist model. In 1991 Boris Yeltsin had faced down a coup attempt by communist hard-liners in Russia. The West looked like a much better bet: Europe was working toward a monetary union, which everyone was excited about; the U.S. was booming in the aftermath of financial liberalization; and the internet was taking off.

Of course, we weren't alone. Louis Vuitton, Armani, Gucci, and other French and Italian houses invested in China during that period. What was it that made us all so willing to take the risk? To some extent, the answer has to do with our Latin cultures. Anglo-Saxons have a different approach toward foreign markets: They tend to export their own cultures rather than adapt them to suit local ones. They're afraid, I think, that they'll be swindled, and they negotiate their deals accordingly. The problem with this attitude, of course, is that no one appreciates being treated with suspicion or with little trust and confidence.

The Italians and the French are much less afraid to trust people in, say, China. We've always demonstrated confidence in the Chinese financial and legal systems, and our business partners and the people in the government appreciate that and reciprocate. We also respect our partners' competence. Many foreign investors act as if they can do better than locals at making and managing things. But the Chinese are well educated and competent; they don't take kindly to being patronized.

In our business you cannot get anywhere without taking a leap into the dark. Every new design is a risk: You work hard and invest heavily in it, and it may all end in tears. But you can also win big. I'm starting to look now at Africa, which will be a huge market in 10 or 15 years. I think Africans will respond well to our approach to business, because they, too, are tired of being patronized. And does Africa really look any more challenging than Russia in the 1990s?

Give Respect to Get Performance

It sounds clichéd, but to get the best from your people, you have to show respect for them. This can result in surprising decisions. There was a time when some people regarded workers in England as lazy and careless, but I recognized that England has a very strong appreciation of craftsmanship and tradition, so we purchased a high-end footwear company, Church's shoes. People in Italy thought this was crazy.

Our first challenge was to decide what to do with the factories. Church's owned a plant in the middle of Northampton that employed 600 people, and the smart move appeared to be to relocate it out of town, which would give us more space at less cost. But when I visited the factory, I saw that people's lives were organized around its location. Most employees lived nearby and would go home for lunch. If we moved them out of town, we'd be robbing them of an hour at home and forcing them to bring sandwiches to work. Their quality of life would be compromised, and they wouldn't be getting anything in return. So we kept the factory in town.

That decision has paid dividends. We retained nearly all the company's very hardworking and talented people, who have rewarded us with increased productivity. And we've proved a larger point: English workers are both cheaper and more industrious than Continental workers.

You could say that work is about duties. People have a duty to work hard for me, but I have a duty to respect them as individuals. Another duty I have is to help them learn. That's a duty I owe to the company as well as to my employees, because a company whose managers take seriously the obligation to help their people improve will be a lot more competitive. Prada is rather good at developing talented employees. Many of our senior managers joined us as young people, and many of the people who have left us have gone on to launch successful businesses of their own.

Sell Only Your Own Designs

One principle we learned the hard way: Never buy a company where the founding designer is still working. Designers will sell a label only because they need the money. They will deeply resent what they see as a commercially focused interloper, and they will fiercely protect their rights over design. We made that mistake with the Jil Sander and Helmut Lang labels.

When we made those acquisitions, no one expected explosive growth in luxury products for the emerging economies. We believed that the best way to grow was to ally ourselves with U.S. and other European brands that shared our design sensibility and then apply our experience in bringing good designs to market. It was a reasonable belief, but if I had it all to do again, I would not make those acquisitions. It was challenging to even talk with those designers, let alone meet their marketing expectations. Had we devoted all our energy to developing Miu Miu and Prada, we would have become a lot bigger even sooner.

That said, we did avoid the mistake of trying to integrate our acquisitions. It's tempting to reduce costs by eliminating parts of the value chain that are duplicated across labels. But that's shortsighted when brands have strong identities. If you own a fashion label that someone else made, it's not just the designers of the acquired brand who may have concerns about brand integrity; it's also the customers. So we kept the acquisitions separate from our house brands, and although we struggled with them, our own labels were not compromised in the market.

Obsess over Details

In our business, people buy products not for their usefulness but for their own sake. Let me explain: In Prague and Milan, for example, the centers are paved with cobblestones. It's hard to walk on cobblestones in high heels, so you might think that our stores in Prague and Milan would sell mostly flat shoes. But in fact most of the ladies' shoes we sell there have high heels. Clearly, comfort is not the main selection criterion in luxury.

Because luxury is about the product itself rather than its function, small details—the touch, the exact look, the feeling it imparts—really matter. At Prada we expect everyone to appreciate this. We have to make sure that everything we do, from manufacturing to marketing, is done in just the right way. We sell thousands of products every year all around the world, which imposes terrific demands in terms of quality control. If the people making our products don't see our managers taking every detail seriously, how long will our reputation survive?

We're not alone in this. Steve Jobs famously got deeply involved in designing the look and feel of Apple's products and engaged personally in dealing with customer complaints. I, too, like to stay on top of the manufacturing and marketing of our products. So you won't find me in my office very often, because I'm always walking around looking at what people are doing.

A product-identity focus is also behind our preference for the own-store distribution that has driven Prada's growth. We want to set the context in which people decide to buy our products, and that, of course, is easiest if you own the stores in which purchases are made. So although we do distribute some of our products through the internet, we don't favor it as a distribution channel. It works well for mass-market products that compete on price, but perhaps less well for luxury products that engage touch and smell as well as sight. We're also concerned about compromising our image by using a channel where secondhand cars and books are sold. Of course, the internet is a powerful communication channel, and we are actively developing our ability to take advantage of that. But communication is very different from distribution.

Give Young Managers Real Responsibilities

I am a great fan of young people. We spend far too much time worrying about their having sex and smoking marijuana, and we lose sight of their energy and idealism, which can be hugely productive. For that reason, I don't believe in starting young managers off on the bottom rung. They won't learn a lot there, and I won't benefit from what they do know. When I hire young people, it's because they have something to offer. They must appreciate what other people in the company do, but I don't expect a young marketing hire to spend time stitching, because I need her to stay on top of what young customers are thinking. You also have to let the younger generation experience the world. That doesn't mean spending time in places like

New York, Paris, and Los Angeles. Prada needs young people who know something about Africa.

AS I LOOK to the future, I am sure that we will make more mistakes. But so long as we stick to our principles and continue to keep outward-looking young people at the top of the company, I feel confident that none of those mistakes will be fatal.

Originally published in September 2012. R1209A

Blockbuster's Former CEO on Sparring with an Activist Shareholder

by John Antioco

John Antioco was CEO of Blockbuster from 1997 to 2007.
Today he invests in retail franchise concepts.

The Idea

After losing a proxy fight to the activist investor Carl Icahn, Block-buster's then CEO faced a new obstacle: executing strategy in the face of boardroom opposition. He looks back on what he might have done differently.

W hen my assistant came into my office in early 2005 and told me that Carl Icahn was on the phone, it was a complete surprise. I knew, of course, that Icahn was an "activist shareholder," but I had no idea why he might be calling. Icahn told me he'd bought nearly 10 million shares of Blockbuster, where I'd served as CEO for eight years. I didn't know what kind of play he saw in Blockbuster—and I certainly didn't expect the new challenges his being our biggest shareholder would bring over the next couple of years.

Long before Carl Icahn arrived on the scene, Blockbuster faced its share of challenges. Indeed, expectations of failure were hovering over the company even before I joined in 1997.

Most outsiders were convinced that our bricks-and-mortar video retail business would be killed off by market shifts and technological advances. But I firmly believed we could keep the Blockbuster brand relevant, no matter how people decided to watch movies. Even though Blockbuster nearly doubled revenues to more than $6 billion from the time I joined the company, plenty of people were betting against us.

The atmosphere became even more difficult when a group of dissident directors were put into the board mix. CEOs need to be devising strategy, working with board members, energizing organizations, and dealing with shareholders, but most leaders are ill prepared to handle an activist shareholder who comes at the company with a proxy fight and wins seats on the board. This became readily apparent in 2005. When directors with preconceived notions are determined to serve as obstacles to management's plans, it's hard to find a formula for success. Three years after my departure as CEO, Blockbuster declared bankruptcy.

A Career Built on Turnarounds

In a way, it's ironic that Blockbuster is being featured in a special issue on failure, because I spent most of my career capitalizing on failure by fixing troubled businesses.

After graduating from New York Institute of Technology in 1970, I worked at 7-Eleven. Trainees like me restaffed and restocked failing stores and tried to keep them in business. I was assigned to Long Island—an area where the company had made mistakes in choosing both locations and operators. By the time I was 25, I was a district manager, running 35 stores in Suffolk County. Over time, we transformed the market into one of the company's most profitable. As a result I was promoted—first to northeast division manager, then to national marketing manager, and finally to senior vice president with worldwide responsibilities. In all, I spent 20 years at 7-Eleven. It was a rapidly expanding business with a lot of growing pains, which created many opportunities.

After leaving 7-Eleven, I spent a very short time as COO for Pearle Vision; then I became CEO of Circle K, a convenience store chain that was in bankruptcy. We took the company private, improved the business, and three years later sold it to Tosco, an oil company, earning our investors a more than quadrupled return on their money.

Next PepsiCo hired me as CEO of its struggling Taco Bell chain. There I learned an important lesson: Just because you're hired to lead a turnaround doesn't mean you have to throw out the existing strategy. On my fourth day at Taco Bell, its senior managers presented their business plan. Their analysis made sense. I saw no need to change it simply in order to put my fingerprints on it.

We executed the plan and turned three years of negative comparable store sales into positive growth. With that momentum, PepsiCo (which also owned KFC and Pizza Hut) spun off its restaurant group as Tricon. (Today it's Yum! Brands.) Around that time Sumner Redstone, the CEO of Viacom, called. He wanted to talk to me about running Blockbuster.

I met with Redstone for five hours in his bungalow at the Beverly Hills Hotel. It was a very good meeting except for one tense moment, when Sumner called the kitchen and personally reprimanded the chef for boiling his hot dog too long. I ended up working for Sumner for six years, and I never had a bad day with him. I found him to be a big-picture visionary and a very supportive leader.

I decided to join Blockbuster for a few reasons: I liked the brand. I saw a lot that could be fixed quickly. And I didn't believe that technology would threaten the company as fast as critics thought. Blockbuster was by far the biggest video rental company, but its market share was only 25%. To me, that was an opportunity.

A Challenging Model

A lot of what I learned about business came from my father, who was an independent milkman in Brooklyn. He believed that you need to focus on always giving customers what they want while still making money for the company. That's what I set out to do at Blockbuster.

Blockbuster's biggest problem stemmed from its business model. Movie studios sold VHS cassettes to rental companies for about $65 apiece, so a store had to rent out each tape about 30 times to make back the money. That's a big up-front investment for a product that most people want just during the few weeks after it first comes out. The whole industry was hurt by stores' never having enough copies of new releases.

We asked the movie studios to shift to a revenue-sharing system. We proposed that instead of buying the cassettes for $65 each, we would pay $1 a copy up front but give the studios 40% of rental revenues on their titles. Eventually they agreed. That allowed us to stock many more copies of hot titles and to advertise their availability. We rolled out an ad campaign about guaranteed availability that featured animated Blockbuster boxes singing the classic tune "I'll Be There." Comp store sales and market share grew strongly.

Even with this success, people continued to worry that video on demand was going to torpedo the rental business. It's ironic that we were hurt by a different technology shift: the advent of the DVD. Whereas VHS cassettes were mostly rented, DVDs were introduced by the studios as a retail product, and mass merchants like Walmart and Best Buy priced them below $20. The adoption rate soared.

DVDs also allowed Netflix to take hold, because they could easily be sent through the mail. Previously the video business had been driven by spontaneity: You didn't have any plans for the evening, so you decided to stay in and rent a movie. We weren't sure whether a model in which you managed your selections by means of a queue and got a movie in the mail a few days later would catch on. But in August 2004 we jumped into the online business in a big way. A few months later we made a dramatic change by eliminating late fees, which had always been a major customer irritant. Those moves put Blockbuster back into growth mode.

When we began these initiatives, Viacom still owned about 80% of us. We were planning to spend $200 million to launch Blockbuster Online and another $200 million to eliminate late fees. Viacom didn't think these investments made sense for its own strategy, so it sold its stake in Blockbuster, which became publicly held. Our stock was depressed by the $400 million planned investment—and that set the stage for the proxy fight.

A Fight We Were Doomed to Lose

Icahn got involved with Blockbuster in late 2004, when the company tried to buy Hollywood Video. Our goal was to orchestrate an orderly downsizing of its store-based business and take on its customers as our own while we also focused on developing alternative movie-delivery methods. Icahn bought positions in both companies as an arbitrage play. Ultimately the FTC declined to approve the deal, and another company—Movie Gallery—bought Hollywood Video. After acquiring his interest in Blockbuster, Icahn began giving interviews to the press and writing letters to shareholders (and to me) claiming that we'd botched the acquisition, that we'd spent too much money on our online business, that we shouldn't have ended late fees, and that the CEO (that would be me) was making too much money. By early 2005 he had decided to launch a proxy fight.

I was about as prepared for such a fight as I could be without ever having gone through one. You hire a bunch of lawyers and bankers, who give you their points of view. You hire a proxy solicitation firm. You write a letter to shareholders, and the opposing shareholder writes a letter. The reality is, we'd just been spun off from Viacom, and most of our stock was held by hedge funds. They were all in for a quick pop, and Icahn is well-known in that community. We were probably doomed from the start. I'm sure the hedge funds figured that having Icahn's guys in the boardroom could lead to a deal that would drive up the stock price. At our 2005 shareholder meeting, in a Dallas auditorium, the votes for Icahn's slate of directors were tallied up. The preliminary results showed that we'd lost. I felt like my guts had been ripped out. It was quite emotional. Most in the audience were Blockbuster employees, and quite a few tears were shed.

I went to the podium and basically said, "The results are the results, but as far as I'm concerned, our strategy is still our strategy. We're disappointed, but we'll work with Icahn and his designees to carry out the mission of the company."

Soon after that I went to New York and met Icahn in person for the first time. We ate at his favorite Italian restaurant, Il Tinello—they even have a dish named after him: Pasta alla "Icahn." In a social setting Carl is quite engaging. Having dinner with him was actually enjoyable. He has a lot of stories, from past deals to poker games. I came away thinking that maybe we could work this out, and that if Carl or any other directors had any good ideas, they should bring them on.

Carl and his two chosen directors were now on our board of eight. Even though he lacked a majority, sheer force of will gave him a lot of power. Since it could be a formidable task, after a while the other directors were disinclined to pick a fight with him. Then one of the sitting board members retired, and Carl and his directors kept vetoing choices for a replacement. The board settled on someone whom Carl would support for whatever reason. So within a few months he effectively controlled the board.

Carl never physically attended a board meeting at Blockbuster's corporate headquarters in Dallas—he called in. It's always hard when someone calls in to a board meeting, and with Carl it's even more difficult. He likes to make himself heard, and he can go on forever. He's not shy about interrupting, and he's not known for boardroom protocol. Frankly, it was a bit of a free-for-all. Eventually, to avoid having to deal with Carl on the phone, I began holding half the board meetings at his New York office. He was winning the power struggle bit by bit.

Having contentious directors was a nightmare; as management, we spent much of our time justifying everything we did. One of them had a bunch of ideas, such as putting greeting cards in the stores, carrying adult movies, and making a deal with Barnes & Noble to add a book section. Mostly, though, they questioned our strategy, which focused on growing an online business and finding new ways to satisfy customers, like getting rid of late fees. We presented data demonstrating that franchisees that had dropped late fees were outperforming those that retained them, but they remained unmoved. They wanted us to reinstate late fees, which would have been a disaster—as apparently it was when they were reinstated after my departure.

In December 2006 the situation finally came to a head over executive compensation. Blockbuster had a very good year, and management was due big bonuses. At the board meeting, when it came time to discuss bonuses, the board went into executive session, meaning I had to leave the room. When I came back in, they had decided that my bonus would be greatly reduced, despite my contract. I said I wouldn't take it and that I'd see them in arbitration. A few weeks later they cut me a check. I returned it.

Ditching the Existing Strategy

The compensation issue led to a long Friday-night phone discussion between Carl and me. We finally agreed that I'd leave the company in July 2007 and would be paid a negotiated bonus plus an exit package. I felt good. I felt it was time to leave. The board environment had become very frustrating and stressful, but instead of resigning and walking away with nothing, I had cut a deal giving me a major portion of the pay I was entitled to. After that phone call, I celebrated by having a margarita or two with my wife.

Although I was a lame-duck CEO for the next six months, I remained fully engaged, and the business was doing well. I firmly believe that if our online strategy had not been essentially abandoned, Blockbuster Online would have 10 million subscribers today, and we'd be rivaling Netflix for the leadership position in the internet downloading business.

For months the directors searched for a new CEO. After my departure they passed over an inside candidate I favored in order to hire Jim Keyes, with whom I'd worked years before at 7-Eleven. I didn't think he was the best person for the job, but obviously it wasn't my decision. I followed Blockbuster very closely for a few months after my departure, partly because I still held stock and options. Even though Blockbuster Online was growing incredibly fast and we had successfully slowed Netflix's momentum, Keyes made it very public that management planned to drastically change the strategy. The company announced a big price increase for online customers, cut way back on marketing, and decided to intensify the focus on the store-based business. Part of that was an ill-fated attempt to take over Circuit City, which went bankrupt soon afterward. All the members of the senior management team I'd worked with left the company. I sold my stock and bought a bunch of Netflix shares, which were then priced around $20. It wasn't an emotional investment. I could see that Netflix was going to have the whole DVD-by-mail market handed to it, along with a direct path to streaming movies into homes—which is exactly what Netflix has done. I thought I was a genius when I sold my shares at about $35. Today they're over $200.

I believe that Carl lost about $200 million of his original Blockbuster stock investment. I'd have been very happy if he had been able to figure out how to help the company succeed in a difficult environment for many reasons. Carl is very good at what he does—he can make investors rich. But my experiences with him at Blockbuster suggest that his expertise lies in areas other than helping to set a company's strategy while being a busy activist investor.

In hindsight, there are things that could have been done differently. It was probably a mistake to sell Viacom's 80% stake all at once—that's a lot of stock for a market that hasn't really been following the company. I probably should have met with Carl earlier, before the proxy fight, to lay out what we were doing and why. That might or might not have had an impact on his desire to hold on to the stock. And if I could turn back the clock, I might focus on the online business for a few more years and then drop late fees. Both were the right thing to do, but doing them simultaneously increased costs and made a bitter pill for investors.

I was home watching the morning news on September 23, 2010, when I saw that Blockbuster had filed for bankruptcy. I wasn't surprised—there'd been speculation that this day was coming—but I was sad and disappointed. I had spent roughly a quarter of my adult life leading that company, so I felt a sense of loss and some anger at the company's near demise. To be honest, my emotions about Blockbuster are still complicated.

The day the company's failure will hit me hardest is probably when my own neighborhood store closes. I went in there recently with my son, who's now eight. We have a deal where if he behaves well at church, I take him to Blockbuster and let him pick out a movie or a video game. On that visit we rented a couple of Wii games. As I looked around, realizing that this local institution probably wouldn't be there much longer, I felt an almost overwhelming sadness. My team and I had worked hard to create a future for this company. Unfortunately, turnarounds don't always stay turned around forever.

Originally published in April 2011. R1104A

EBay's Founder on Innovating the Business Model of Social Change

by Pierre Omidyar

Pierre Omidyar is the founder and chairman of eBay and a cofounder and chairman of Omidyar Network.

The Idea

Omidyar was inspired by eBay's social impact to create a hybrid model for his philanthropic Omidyar Network: a combination of non-profit and for-profit.

My journey as a philanthropist began in September 1998, on the day eBay went public. I'd spent two weeks helping with the pre-IPO road show, and we'd arrived at the New York office of Goldman Sachs. I was exhausted. The actual moment was pretty anticlimactic. We'd always assumed that when you go public, your stock starts trading the moment the market opens, but it doesn't work that way. You have to wait for the bankers to do their initial trades. So when the market opened, we just stood around on the trading floor with nothing to do. Nobody was really paying attention to us. There was an electronic ticker on the wall, and after about 45 minutes somebody gave us a heads-up that we should start looking for eBay. Sure enough, a few minutes later we saw our ticker symbol coming across from right to left. We cheered; we hugged; we high-fived.

We had priced the initial public offering at $18 a share, which made my stake worth a few hundred million dollars. During the course of the day the stock rose to nearly $54. My shares, like those of all the other insiders, would be locked up for six months, so at this point it was just paper wealth. But on paper my stake was more than $1 billion. It was shocking and completely unexpected.

Soon afterward I began having conversations with my fiancée, Pam—now my wife—about what we were going to do with all that wealth. It was clearly far more than we would ever need, and it had accumulated very quickly: EBay went public three years after I wrote the original software, so there wasn't a great sense of "Wow, we really deserve this—I've spent my whole life building up to it." We felt we had a responsibility to make sure those resources got put to good use.

Within a few months we'd created a nonprofit family foundation, which is what new philanthropists typically do. We took an informal approach. A friend of the family served as the executive director. We gave money to this charity or that charity. It was a responsive thing—we would read about something in the newspaper and it'd be "Let's give money." After a couple of years we realized we needed to professionalize the foundation and become strategically driven. We recruited some executives to help us think about how to take lessons from eBay and apply them to philanthropy.

Many people don't distinguish between charity and philanthropy, but to me there's a significant difference. When I use the word "charity," I think of what's needed to alleviate immediate suffering. It's just pure generosity driven by compassion, and it's important but never-ending work—there will always be more suffering. Charity is inherently not self-sustaining, but there are problems in the world, such as natural disasters, that require charity.

Philanthropy is much more. It comes from the Latin for "love of humanity." Philanthropy is a desire to improve the state of humanity and the world. It requires thinking about the root causes of issues so that we can prevent tomorrow's suffering. And if we want to make sustainable change, we have to put all the tools at our disposal to their best possible use.

By the early 2000s I'd realized what a profound social impact eBay was having as part of its business. It had about 100 million users, and it was teaching people that they could trust a complete stranger over the internet—at least, trust him or her enough to make a transaction. It was providing people with new careers and livelihoods. This was large-scale impact. I began to wonder: If I had created a nonprofit organization and set a 10-year goal to build a trusted network of 100 million people, with a start-up grant of $10,000 and no additional grants, would it have succeeded? Probably not. But somehow a business had been able to reach this level of social impact in less time, using less outside capital.

A Small Price to Pay

In thinking about philanthropy, I began looking for ways to harness the incredible power of business in order to make the world better. By 2003 I'd begun talking to my advisers about this issue. I was told that philanthropy consists entirely of nonprofits, and the tax system limits what you can do in that format. Specifically, it would be extremely difficult for employees of my nonprofit family foundation to look at proposals that might result in a for-profit equity stake instead of a grant. The complexity of the tax code—and the risks of running afoul of it—were high, so I began pressing at this point, asking my team to find a way for us to start investing in businesses philanthropically. Mike Mohr, my family adviser, said, "There's a way to do it, but you're going to lose a whole bunch of tax deductions." So I asked, "How much? Give me a figure." He went off to calculate it: If we stopped deducting the salary and overhead costs for the foundation, it would mean $1 million to $2 million a year in extra tax liability. My immediate reaction was that this was a no-brainer. In the context of spending $100 million a year, $1 million to $2 million seemed like a small price for getting the flexibility to use every possible tool to improve the world.

It was a challenge to structure this properly. We ended up creating a limited liability corporation called Omidyar Network, which employed all the staff members. That freed them to conduct due diligence without regard to whether the work turned into a nonprofit grant or a for-profit investment. The nonprofit entity remained a 501(c)(3), but it was in essence just a checkbook we used for making grants.

We were breaking new ground here—our attorneys had never seen a structure like this. We actually had to terminate all the foundation's employees and rehire them in the LLC. Today there's a name for people who make investments that can produce both impact and profit: impact investors. And the field is gaining a lot of attention and popularity. But at the time, there was no name for what we were trying to do.

Finding the right structure wasn't the biggest obstacle. We also faced a cultural challenge. The way a program officer does due diligence for a foundation is vastly different from the way an investment analyst does it for a venture capital firm. The main difference is that the two view risk in very different ways. Program officers are expected to be much more risk averse: If a foundation makes a grant to an organization that doesn't succeed, it's considered a big mistake. In contrast, the very best venture capitalists are happy if they get two out of 10 investments right, and they get incredible financial rewards when they judge risks correctly.

While we were making the structural shift, we needed to hire people with experience doing for-profit investing—people who understood how to evaluate a company's management, competitive landscape, and financial returns. This created even more challenges. How can you have nonprofit program officers and for-profit venture capitalists on the same team? How should you compensate them? We didn't get it right in the first few years—we weren't able to successfully blend the two cultures. It was difficult to incentivize the for-profit employees without disincentivizing the nonprofit staff. Some of the for-profit people we brought in didn't stay long, and the nonprofit employees may have felt they weren't valued. It took a lot of learning.

A Focus on Microfinance

Some of our first for-profit equity deals included companies like Ethos Water—which uses a share of proceeds to provide clean drinking water in India, East Africa, and elsewhere—and Meetup, which enables people with similar interests to create communities offline.

But soon we began investing heavily in microfinance—and it was then that we started to see the full value of the hybrid structure we'd created. During the 1980s and 1990s, most microfinance was conducted by grant-funded NGOs. That has changed: Today most of the biggest micro-lenders are for-profit, and we now had the ability to invest in them. These funds enabled the poorest of the poor to start enterprises and take advantage of educational opportunities. For instance, a family might borrow to buy a cow and sell dairy products, or to buy sewing equipment and sell clothing, and then use the profits to send their children to school. Since 2004 we've invested in 28 organizations—15 not-for-profits and 13 for-profits. We recognize that microfinance has come under increasing scrutiny because some organizations have paid insufficient attention to consumer protection and education. But it's critical to remember how much good microfinance has accomplished: It has given 150 million people, most of whom live on less than a dollar a day, the means to start businesses, generate income, and break the cycle of poverty.

In 2007 we made a big shift, restructuring Omidyar Network to get rid of the traditional hierarchical model and institute a partner style of leadership and governance. Simply put, we decided that because the organization was operating more like a venture capital firm, we should structure it more like one. We brought in our first-ever managing partner, Matt Bannick, who had built the international business at eBay and had led PayPal during its integration into eBay and its rapid international expansion. Over the past four years Matt has made a lot of changes and assembled a great team; right now we have more than 50 employees, of whom only one or two are from the early, purely nonprofit days. We've focused on figuring out how to use the levers of for-profit when necessary and the levers of nonprofit when necessary. To date Omidyar Network has committed a total of $442 million—$239 million in nonprofit grants and $203 million in for-profit investments. More than $100 million of that has been in microfinance.

Today our operation includes more than 10 employees in Mumbai, and that city has become a focus of our work. Obviously it has tremendous poverty, but it also has an incredible amount of intellectual capital. The juxtaposition of impoverished people and ambitious, educated entrepreneurs is extraordinary, and it's a juxtaposition that exists nowhere else in the world. In Mumbai wealthy bankers walk to work on the same sidewalks as beggars. The fundamental investment reason for our being in India is that the innovations created there over the next five to 10 years will dramatically improve the quality of life for people in extreme poverty worldwide. Many of those innovations will come from entrepreneurs and businesses. I'm excited to play a small part in that process.

For example, we've helped fund a company called d.light, which creates small, affordable solar-powered lamps. Most people don't realize that one in four families in the world lacks access to electric light. The main alternative is kerosene, but many people can't afford it—and it is harmful to both health and the environment. We've also helped fund a for-profit school initiative in Africa, and we're looking at health care applications there, too.

Use Every Tool

Initially we drew some criticism for our hybrid approach combining nonprofit with for-profit. The basic concern was "Here's a guy who was going to give most of his money to charity, but now he says he's giving some of it to for-profits, and he's probably just looking to make more money." Our critics believed it was going to be a net loss for the nonprofit community. Their concern was amplified by the fact that at the time, a lot of businesspeople were getting involved with nonprofits, which created a culture clash and some animosity. But there are deeper ideological issues at play. Businesspeople going into philanthropy or nonprofits typically have the idea that they need to "give back." This implies, of course, that when they worked in the business world, they were "taking away." I've tried to challenge that assumption.

A lot has changed since our early years, and many of the debates have calmed down considerably. Today there are numerous examples of social enterprises and businesses that try to provide services to the very poor and to do so in a responsible way. And people within the nonprofit sector understand that there's a role for business to play.

I'd like to think our work is just beginning. I'm now 44, and if I'm lucky I have another 50 years ahead of me. In the past few years we've learned that to have the biggest impact, you need the right capital structure and the right leaders. We have three full-time recruiters on our staff. That's really unusual for a philanthropic organization, but par for the course in venture capital. And like most venture capitalists, we take governance seriously. We have formal board memberships or advisory roles in roughly 50% of our portfolio organizations.

One of the biggest things I've learned in more than a decade of this work is that you really can make the world better in any sector—in nonprofits, in business, or in government. It's not a question of one sector's struggling against another, or of "giving back" versus "taking away." That's old thinking. A true philanthropist will use every tool he can to make an impact. Today business is a key part of the equation, and the sectors are learning to work together.

Originally published in September 2011. R1109A

Novartis's CEO on Growing After a Patent Cliff

by Joseph Jimenez

Joseph Jimenez is the CEO of Novartis AG.

The Idea

When blockbuster drugs give way to generics, pharmaceutical companies like Novartis must find new ways to grow.

For more than a decade, the top-selling Novartis product has been a drug called Diovan. It's an anti-hypertensive, which means that it treats high blood pressure, and patients who need it take the medicine every day. Scientists inside our company spent many years developing Diovan, and it has been tested on thousands of patients in clinical trials. Altogether Novartis spent well over a billion dollars on development and received a patent to sell Diovan exclusively for 14 years. When I joined Novartis, in 2007, our entire pharmaceuticals division had revenue of about $24 billion, and Diovan accounted for $5 billion of that.

But the company was looking ahead toward a big challenge: In the fall of 2011 the European patent on Diovan would expire, and a year later the U.S. patent would lapse as well. In the months leading up to those expirations, roughly a dozen companies around the globe would begin manufacturing generic versions of the drug. The instant the patents expired, those pills would show up in pharmacies—costing just a few pennies apiece.

For Novartis, that would mean an eventual annual revenue decline of about $4 billion a year (sales of Diovan would continue in countries where generic competition already existed). That's what we refer to in the pharmaceutical industry as a "patent cliff."

When I received a call about coming to Novartis, I'd worked in consumer packaged goods for more than 20 years. I went online and began doing basic research about the company. It didn't take long to identify the Diovan patent as its main challenge.

Patent cliffs are one of the biggest issues facing our industry. To put this in perspective, IMS Health, a health care information provider, predicts that by 2016 patent expirations will have caused a loss of $106 billion in sales from branded drugs over the previous five years, with the heaviest burden in 2012 and 2013. To cite the largest example, Pfizer's Lipitor, the best-selling prescription drug in history, went off patent in 2011, and analysts expect Lipitor sales to decline from about $11 billion in 2009 and 2010 to just above $3 billion in 2015. Most pharmaceutical companies are eventually confronted with a similar challenge. There's never been a good model for how a company in our industry can get through this transition. When I was appointed to lead the pharmaceuticals division, just six months after I arrived, I was determined to work with my team to change that at Novartis.

Early-Morning Tutorials

I started at Novartis as the head of consumer health, in charge of the over-the-counter business—drugs like Excedrin and Theraflu. I had much to learn. I had been an economics major at Stanford; I didn't have a science or medical background. The

OTC drug industry has some similarities to the consumer packaged goods businesses I'd run in the past—you're competing for shelf space against other branded products in grocery stores and pharmacies—so it seemed like a good fit. But in October 2007 Daniel Vasella, then the CEO and still the chairman of the board, called and said the board of directors wanted to make a change: They wanted the person who had been running the pharmaceuticals division to take over the OTC division, and they wanted me to lead the pharmaceuticals division, to bring fresh eyes to the issues we were confronting. Two Novartis drugs had recently been rejected by the FDA, and the board had concluded that the team would benefit from someone who had not grown up in the industry. I said, "You understand that I am not a scientist, and I'm not a physician." In my conversations with Vasella, he emphasized that there were a lot of brilliant scientists and physicians in the company, but he was looking for someone who could take a new look at how the external world was changing and determine how to reposition the pharmaceuticals division for success in the years ahead.

Even so, I needed to get up to speed on the science. I found a Novartis employee who had a science background with a focus on biology and was good at communicating clearly about complicated topics. I arranged for him to come to my office many mornings from 7:00 to 8:00. We went over every drug in the company's portfolio in great detail. We talked about the biology of the disease each one was intended to treat. We discussed the mechanism of action of various drugs—how and why they worked. We met for about a year. I became conversant with the science, but I still had the advantage of being able to ask questions in a confidential environment. I needed to win the respect of the company's scientists, and ultimately I had to understand the products so that we, together, could make some key decisions.

This is very important in the pharmaceutical industry, because the approach to R&D is unique. It generally takes 10 years and at least $1 billion to bring a new drug to market. That very long cycle makes it easy to delay making decisions within an organization. Most of the decision makers are physicians and scientists, who often want to hold out for more and better data. Novartis develops about 70% of its drugs in-house, and we license about 30% from other companies. When a licensed product doesn't do well in clinical testing, putting off a decision can be especially tempting, because pulling the plug would call into question the due diligence done when the deal was signed. For instance, one of the compounds we'd licensed ran into a problem in Phase II clinical trials. We thought we could formulate around the issue, so we continued working on the compound. I looked at the situation and asked, "Science aside, what are the odds that this drug is ever going to reach the market?" It turned out they were low. I pushed for a decision, and we shut it down and took a write-off of more than $100 million. I try to emphasize this message to our employees: If you're afraid to admit you made a mistake, you're not going to be successful in pharmaceuticals, because things don't always turn out the way you expect in science.

Three Ways to Restore Growth

After I took over the pharmaceuticals division, I convened a meeting with the members of the senior team. I said, "OK, show me the plan to deal with the Diovan patent cliff." I got a laundry list of 100 projects. There were many good ideas at this point in the process, ranging from new product development to potential acquisitions. However, it was clear that we'd need to prioritize and invest in the small handful of programs that held the most promise for replacing

Diovan revenues. At first we shortened the list to 25 ideas. We listened to project team presentations, and then we cut the list again to 10. At an offsite for the 100 top leaders, we debated the choices and ultimately focused as a team on three major initiatives.

First, we would accelerate the development of a group of oncology drugs that included Afinitor, which was designed to treat renal cell carcinoma and was almost ready for the market. The scientists involved believed that it could be used to treat a variety of other cancers as well, but testing it on a number of diseases would be prohibitively expensive. They had decided to move slowly, starting clinical trials in a sequential manner. But renal cell carcinoma affects far fewer people than some of the other diseases Afinitor might help treat, including breast cancer. So after discussions with the oncology team, we decided to make a significant investment to begin testing Afinitor in breast cancer and three other types of cancer. We also accelerated development of several other oncology drugs. It turned out to be a good investment: Afinitor received approval for the treatment of advanced breast cancer in July 2012, and it's expected to generate sales of more than $1 billion a year.

Second, we decided to take steps to expand more quickly in high-growth markets. Looking at China, Russia, Brazil, and India, I asked why our businesses there weren't growing as fast as the competition was. A key problem was that it's difficult and expensive to hire and train enough salespeople in those markets to fuel top-line growth. In 2007 the managers of our China business estimated that the maximum number of people they could hire and integrate into their operation in a year was 150 to 200. I told them I wanted to hire at least 500 people a year for four years. One idea that came from the China team was to set up a recruiting and training center called Novartis China

Commercial University, which would screen, hire, and train several hundred people. We decided to make some very big investments in the center in 2008, 2009, and 2010. It has worked out well: In 2011 our China business grew by 38%, and in the second quarter of 2012 our emerging growth markets contributed 24% of our total sales.

Third, we began to transition to an outcomes-based approach to selling medicine. Let me explain what that means. Insurance companies and government payers are tired of covering a new medicine when seven out of 10 patients may not respond to it. But right now that's how the industry works: It's transactional, and companies get paid for selling pills. I believe we're heading toward a day when pharmaceutical companies will be paid to deliver positive patient outcomes. So Novartis has started moving in that direction. For instance, we set up a unit in the pharmaceuticals division that is charged with developing companion diagnostics for our specialty medicines: Before a cancer patient is prescribed an expensive specialty medicine, we will offer a test to determine whether he or she is likely to respond to the drug. Tests like this should make third-party payers around the world more willing to approve reimbursement for new drugs, because we're taking steps to increase the odds that they'll be effective.

The outcomes-based approach has become even more important in view of changes in the way pharmaceuticals are marketed to physicians. Until a few years ago, companies competed to see who could hire the most sales reps to call on physicians, particularly in the United States. But that model is largely outdated. Physicians don't want to see seven pharma reps every day. Now we have fewer salespeople in developed markets, but the ones we have are often better equipped to understand the science. It's a very different skill set, particularly in the specialty medicines area.

The Benefit of an Outside Perspective

Five years after my executive team and I debated how to focus our strategy and moved forward to execute on this three-pronged plan, our efforts are beginning to pay off. The pharmaceuticals division management team that was named after I became the CEO of Novartis, in 2010, has done an outstanding job of offsetting the Diovan patent cliff. The results of their efforts are due to great team execution. We've told Wall Street analysts that we expect 2012 revenue to be in line with 2011 revenue, even as Diovan gives way to generics. Moreover, I am especially proud that Afinitor has now been approved in five indications, with the potential to help many thousands of women suffering from advanced breast cancer.

The teams within the company were generating many good ideas, but sometimes it takes an "outside in" view to gain clarity and focus. An outside perspective can add value and complement the great work that is under way. That's a lesson I talk about a lot: No matter how specialized your function, an external view of the way your industry is changing is very important.

Another lesson is the value of taking a very analytical, unemotional look at the solution to any problem. The solution to the Diovan patent expiration started as 100 different projects, but many of them weren't on a large enough scale. Even the three programs we prioritized initially lacked the investment they needed to succeed. People often think that failure is the result of poor execution rather than poor strategy. But sometimes people are just trying to execute against the wrong plan.

A third lesson I've learned at Novartis is that it's important to look to the junior people in an organization for ideas and to listen carefully to what they say. The culture in the pharmaceuticals division historically was top-down, and top executives had very strong points of view that were not easily altered.

It took some effort to make people throughout the company comfortable telling me what they really thought. Today we have a great team driving our performance with input at many levels and with junior people contributing significant ideas. This has been an important part of our success.

Dealing with patent expirations will always be a challenge. Some industries, such as technology, push for open models with limited patent protection, but that will never work for pharmaceuticals: We will never recoup the billions we spend on R&D every year if generic manufacturers can enter a market soon after we've created it. Nor will medical science advance. At the same time, the huge cost pressures in the health care industry are inclining governments and courts toward allowing earlier generic entry. We try to keep in mind that over the past 50 years life expectancy has increased dramatically, and much of the credit for that goes to pharmaceuticals. We all want those achievements to continue—so we need to find ways to keep funding our R&D pipeline even when the profits from a blockbuster drug come to an end. It takes a great team aligned around a common purpose to work through the challenges and deliver this.

Originally published in December 2012. R1212A

Encyclopædia Britannica's President on Killing Off a 244-Year-Old Product

by Jorge Cauz

Jorge Cauz is the president of Encyclopædia Britannica.

The Idea

By the time Britannica's top management decided to stop producing bound sets of the iconic encyclopedia, the company had made sweeping changes to put itself at the forefront of the online education market.

One year ago, my announcement that Encyclopædia Britannica would cease producing bound volumes sent ripples through the media world. Despite the vast migration of information from ink and paper to bits and screens, it seemed remarkable that a set of books published for almost a quarter of a millennium would go out of print. But in our Chicago offices this wasn't an occasion to mourn. In fact, our employees held a party the day of the announcement, celebrating the fact that Britannica was still a growing and viable company. They ate the print set—in the form of a cake that pictured the 32-volume, 129-pound encyclopedia. They displayed 244 silver balloons—one for each year the encyclopedia had been in print. They toasted the departure of an old friend with champagne and the dawning of a new era with determination.

We had no need for a wake because we weren't grieving. We had known for some time that this day was coming. Given how little revenue the print set generated, and given that we had long ago shifted to a digital-first editorial process, the bound volumes had become a distraction and a chore to put together. They could no longer hold the vast amount of information our customers demanded or be kept as up-to-date as today's users expect.

The reaction to our announcement was interesting and varied. Some people were shocked. On Twitter, one person wrote, "I'm sorry I was unfaithful to you, Encyclopedia Britannica, Wikipedia was just there, and convenient, it meant nothing. Please, come back!"

Of course, we didn't need to come back, because we hadn't gone away and weren't about to. But although most people seemed to know what was happening, some misunderstood. Commentators intimated that we had "yielded" to the internet. In fact, the internet enabled us to reinvent ourselves and open new channels of business. Reports cited Wikipedia as a disruptive force. In fact, Wikipedia helped us sharpen our business strategy. Our content model was dismissed as "vintage," but it is actually anything but: We update our content continually, with community input, reaching tens of millions of people every day—and they pay for it.

I relished the irony. If you relied on free, gossipy online channels to understand why we were ending the print edition, you got what you paid for: some jokes, some inaccurate observations about the state of our business, and maybe a 20% chance of seeing "Encyclopædia Britannica" spelled correctly. You may not have learned that by the time we stopped publishing the print set, its sales represented only about 1% of our business, that we have an increasingly significant presence in the K–12 digital learning space, and that we're as profitable now as we've ever been. Whatever ripples the announcement may have made, from a business perspective the decision itself was a non-event. It was just the final phase of a carefully planned strategic transition that had been 35 years in the making.

The Real Threat

For the *Britannica*'s first 200 years, editorial revisions were made with a variety of manual and mechanical tools. Preparing each new edition took years at first, and never less than a year. Then, in the 1970s, the contents of the encyclopedia were loaded onto a mainframe computer to streamline the process of making annual updates.

Prescient editors and executives recognized that although digitization would make updating more efficient for print, it was only a matter of time before the medium of publication itself would be digital. And that would represent a threat to the way we did business: selling multivolume encyclopedias to families door-to-door. So in the 1980s we began preparing for that day, experimenting with digital technologies and even publishing the first electronic encyclopedias. Meanwhile, sales of the print version grew throughout the decade, and in 1990 the company's overall business peaked: Our 2,000-plus salespeople sold more than 100,000 units of the iconic bound set in the United States.

Then the business collapsed.

The sales model started breaking down in 1991, as families became busier and had less patience for doorstep solicitations and as PCs began shipping with built-in CD-ROM drives— a potential knockout punch. The effect of CD-ROMs on the encyclopedia business can't be overstated. The spines of the *Encyclopædia Britannica* lined up on a bookshelf always had much more cachet than those of competitors such as *World Book* and the *Americana*. But CD-ROMs lacked this visual presence; they obliterated the physical evidence of the *Britannica*'s superior depth and size, an important part of our value proposition then. They also created a new demand for multimedia and interactivity, with which print-focused editorial and product teams had little experience.

In 1994 Britannica produced its own CD-ROM encyclopedia. It was originally priced at $1,200, about the same as the bound set. But by then Microsoft was bundling its CD-ROM encyclopedia, Encarta, with the vast majority of Wintel computers as a loss leader to increase the sales of home PCs by positioning them as a learning tool and a homework helper.

It was a brilliant move by Microsoft and a very damaging one for Britannica. Regardless of quality, it was hard for a $1,200 CD-ROM to compete with a free one bundled with a PC. Our direct-sales force was the wrong channel for selling the CD-ROM encyclopedia; moreover, there was no easy way to change the traditional encyclopedia business model, in which the multi-volume set was a break-even proposition and the profits came from ensuing subscriptions to the yearbook, a single volume of updates.

That same year, the company introduced Britannica Online, a web-based version of the *Encyclopædia Britannica* and the first such reference work on the internet. It was a bold move then: Few publishers had yet seen the web as a place to publish, let alone to put their entire flagship product. But it was a risky move, too. We knew that it would further cannibalize our own print market; we just didn't know by how much. Digital sales rose, but slowly, while print sales fell off a cliff. The decline was dizzying: From more than

100,000 units in 1990, sales fell to 51,000 in 1994 and to just 3,000 in 1996, when I arrived. This was surely the company's most vulnerable time.

Radical Change

Britannica was sold to the Swiss investor Jacob E. Safra in 1996, and I joined as a consultant helping to initiate the radical change Safra was looking for. To adapt to market shifts, we had to make several major transformations that would ultimately cost tens of millions of dollars. The most painful one involved changing the way we sold our products. The Britannica direct-sales force was at the center of the business structure; the vast majority of company revenue came from this door-to-door army that fanned out across the world. But that sales method had become obsolete, so we decided to abandon it and adopt other forms of direct marketing. We dismantled that part of the business in my first months on the job.

As we changed our sales focus to direct marketing, we tested price points on the CD-ROM encyclopedia and realized that our original price was too high. Like many content producers, we had assigned a value to our product on the basis of content and production costs. But customers were changing. They could get "good enough" content for much less—sometimes free. Within months we dropped the price from $1,200 to less than $1,000, then to $150, and eventually to less than $100.

We began seeking new online revenue sources from subscriptions and advertising, and we tapped resellers such as AOL to bring the CD-ROM encyclopedia to new consumer channels. Because our brand and the quality of our products were recognized and appreciated by educators, we focused on selling subscriptions to Britannica Online to colleges and later to the K–12 market as they came online.

Though we were headed in the right direction, our CD-ROM business was still problematic, because margins continued to be whisper-thin in our competition against the free Encarta. During this period there was one thing we didn't do: reduce our editorial investment. With our business declining, we could easily have justified eliminating long-tenured editors from a cost perspective. But editorial quality has always been intrinsic to our value proposition, and we knew that it would continue to differentiate us in a growing sea of questionable information.

One or two more years fighting in this market would have further debilitated Encyclopædia Britannica, and perhaps I wouldn't be writing this. But internet access exploded, as we had expected (and hoped), and the biggest threat to our company, the CD-ROM, was itself disrupted by online access, just when we needed it to be. Britannica was able to reestablish a strong direct relationship with consumers, and our digital subscription business took off.

Our Biggest Opportunity

Our next two major ventures on the internet—a free, ad-supported consumer encyclopedia and a misconceived learning portal for K–12 schools—ultimately bombed, but they allowed us to see that the internet was a far more favorable place to do business than CD-ROM had been. Margins were much better, and we didn't have to offer huge discounts to win business. When I became president, in 2003, I sought to transform the company once again in light of the opportunities that widespread internet access opened up to us.

What my staff and I realized was that we needed to go beyond reference products and develop a full-fledged learning business. Our growing K–12 customer base helped us by telling us what it needed: affordable lessons and learning materials, linked to the curriculum, that could be used in classrooms and at home. These educators wanted products that included assessment tools and that supported individualized or "differentiated" learning for various grade and reading levels. We knew we had the brand and the editorial resources to meet this need. We saw a looming opportunity in online education, and we caught the wave perfectly. We hired dozens of new people, and we now have curriculum specialists in every key department of the company: editorial, product development, and marketing.

As bad as our timing had been with CD-ROM, it couldn't have been better for the decision to focus on learning products, because something had arrived that would ultimately remake the consumer market for reference information: Wikipedia.

The Disruption That Wasn't

I had been following Wikipedia since the launch of its parent project, Nupedia, in 2000. At the time, I thought Nupedia was going nowhere, because it was trying to do exactly the same thing that Britannica was, and I knew how much editorial staff and budget it took to do that. Nupedia didn't have them.

When Nupedia adopted the wiki technology and became Wikipedia the following year, it seemed to me like an act of desperation. Needless to say, its success was a surprise, not only to me, but to everyone I've talked to about it. As Wikipedia's articles, contributors, and visitors skyrocketed in number, and Google's search algorithm continued to reward the site with top placement, I understood that this was another game changer for Encyclopædia Britannica.

But far from creating panic, Wikipedia's success actually reinforced our strategic decision to reduce reliance on consumer reference and accelerate activity in the K–12 market. Like many disruptive innovations, Wikipedia was of lower quality: If it were a video, it would be grainy and out of focus. But consumers didn't care about that, because Wikipedia has a vast number of entries and easy, free access. We couldn't compete on quantity or price. Did we believe that consumers preferred our reference material? Yes. Did we believe they were willing to pay for it? Not necessarily.

So instead of getting mired in a competition with Wikipedia, we focused on editorial quality with Britannica Online and used Wikipedia's quantity-over-quality approach and its chronic unreliability as differentiators in our favor. We knew that Britannica's long-standing mission to bring expert, fact-based knowledge to the general public met an enduring need for society. This resonated deeply in the education market (it's now standard practice for teachers to instruct students not to rely on Wikipedia as a reference source), and it helped boost sales there. Today more than half of U.S. students and teachers have access to some Britannica content, and globally we're growing even more rapidly.

Part of this effort was an aggressive overhaul of our editorial operation, a project we called Britannica 21. We engaged teams of scholars around the world in a wide range of disciplines to review, revise, and refresh the encyclopedia's content. We changed our editorial metabolism so that we could update content in four hours rather than the weeks it used to take. (Now we update every 20 minutes.) And we created a process for soliciting and using community input to enhance encyclopedia entries.

By the time Wikipedia took off, we weren't head-to-head competitors anymore. We maintain a world-class reference source with 500,000 household subscribers, and we take a clearly differentiated approach to informing society, but we're no longer an encyclopedia-only company.

Coming Disruptions

Over the past five years, we've seen 17% compound annual growth in our digital education services business and a 95% renewal rate, while sales of the print version of the encyclopedia steadily declined, from 6,000 in 2006 to about 2,200 in 2011. Producing the bound volumes wasn't passing basic cost-benefit analysis. It was, frankly, a pain. In February 2012 the management team had to make a call—either get the next revised printing under way, with all the work that would entail, or bring the print edition to an end. We chose the latter.

Today Encyclopædia Britannica is growing on all measures: revenue, margins, staff, content, and reach. We must be ready to adapt and quick to innovate; we must stay attuned to new challenges that could disrupt our business; but we no longer have a stake in the old education model of textbooks and printed classroom curricula. We are creating new digital solutions for math and science and in support of the Common Core State Standards. Here the entrenched players will get disrupted, not us.

There are no guarantees, of course, but I'm confident in Encyclopædia Britannica's ability to endure in the digital age. That's because our people have always kept the mission separate from the medium, which has allowed the company to handle one competitive threat after another. As long as I've been here, I've felt that my job was, first, to honor this deeply held sense of mission and to develop and apply business decisions that support it.

Even now, a year after the last bound volumes of the *Encyclopædia Britannica* were sold, people ask if we would reconsider and perhaps print limited editions as a kind of iconic collector's item. The answer is no. We don't want to be like an old actor trying to hold on to his youth. You get on with the times, and our times are digital. Some people may be nostalgic, but it makes no sense for us to print books. As an organization, we're over it.

Originally published in March 2013. R1303A

IMAX's CEO on How It Became a Hollywood Powerhouse

by Richard Gelfond

Richard Gelfond is the CEO of IMAX.

The Idea

The company experimented with business models to grow from its modest roots in nature documentaries into a major player in multiplexes around the world.

When I came to IMAX, in 1994, I had been an entrepreneur, a lawyer, and an investment banker. I didn't know much about the movie business, but I recognized that the moviegoing experience IMAX offered had great potential if we could find the right way to grow.

A partner and I had acquired the company through a leveraged buyout, and we took it public a few months later. On paper the transaction was a success, and the company's market cap grew rapidly. But at the time, most IMAX movies were nature documentaries shown in the theaters of science museums, and figuring out how to move into mainstream markets proved much more difficult than we'd expected. That was due in part to the technology constraints of the predigital era; it took years to find ways to make it easy and cost-effective to show

IMAX movies in a large number of multiplexes. We also faced cultural challenges. The Hollywood movie industry is an interconnected system of studios, directors, and theaters that has evolved over 100 years, and it has a traditional way of doing things. As newcomers we spent years trying and failing to persuade the industry to adapt to our model. Even after we began adapting our strategy to fit the Hollywood way of doing business, it took a while to find a model that benefited us and our partners.

Over the past five years, however, we've developed a business model that makes sense. Since 2008 our network of theaters has grown from 351 to 738. Five years ago eight movies were released in the IMAX format, and so far this year we've announced 27, including blockbusters such as *Star Trek into Darkness* and *The Hunger Games: Catching Fire,* both of which were filmed with IMAX's extremely high-resolution cameras. We're growing quickly in China and other new markets and releasing local-language titles in Japan, India, and Russia. Directors such as Christopher Nolan, J.J. Abrams, and James Cameron are huge fans of our technology—they have come to view IMAX as the perfect canvas on which to execute their artistic vision. We have a large base of "fanboy" enthusiasts who wait in line—and pay a $5 premium on their tickets—to see a release in an IMAX theater.

The biggest lesson I've learned in nearly two decades of leading IMAX is that you have to be flexible about your business model. It took us many years and several wrong turns before we found the right one, and that's not atypical. When I meet with entrepreneurs who want me to invest in a start-up, the first thing I look for is how attached they are to their business model: Would they consider a plan B or plan C? You're really lucky if your business model works well from day one. Iteration is key.

A Classic Chicken-and-Egg Problem

IMAX's roots trace back to 1967, when four Canadians, three of whom had been friends in high school, created a system for projecting movies onto a giant curved screen that seemingly immerses viewers. The initial public experiment with their technology took place at Expo '67, in Montreal. During its first 25 years, IMAX installed its system in museums, and most of its films were nature documentaries. The company chose that strategy because it didn't have much capital. By focusing on museums, it could get funding from the National Science Foundation and the National Film Board of Canada to build theaters. It produced nature documentaries because if you film whales, bears, or seals, you don't have to pay them. In those years IMAX was run almost like a nonprofit. Its culture felt like a university's.

When we bought the company, we thought we could send a few new people up to the Toronto headquarters and transform the culture into something nimble and entrepreneurial. It didn't happen—I overestimated the pace at which we could change. We had to replace more people than I'd expected.

The bigger problem, however, was the business model. We'd gotten involved with IMAX because we recognized the potential to shift from science museums to mainstream theaters showing Hollywood movies. But finding the right way to finance that shift proved really challenging. During the 1990s and into the early 2000s, IMAX was licensing its technology to theaters. Theater owners would pay us up front to install our projection and sound systems, and we'd receive a very small percentage of box office revenue. At that time it cost about $5 million to adapt a theater to IMAX—about $3 million to create the space and $2 million to put in the technology.

The huge up-front cost was an obstacle, but not the only one. Very few movies were being offered in the IMAX format. It was a classic chicken-and-egg problem. Studios didn't want to film a movie in our format (which required bulky, expensive cameras and lots of film) unless thousands of theaters were equipped to show IMAX films. Theater owners wouldn't convert to IMAX until many more IMAX films were available.

We attacked these problems as best we could. We brought the cost of the technology down from $2 million to $1.2 million, and we figured out how to retrofit existing multiplexes for IMAX, to eliminate the expense of building from scratch. But other disadvantages remained. In the predigital era, studios had to provide every theater with an individual print, and IMAX prints were horrendously expensive: The film reels for a regular movie might cost $1,000 and fill a couple of canisters, whereas each print of an IMAX film cost $30,000 and was much larger—you literally needed a-forklift to get it to the projection room. Although watching an IMAX film was enthralling, it's understandable why theater owners and studios were reluctant to sign on.

To increase the number of IMAX films available, at one point in the 1990s we even tried producing movies ourselves. It didn't work. I specifically recall a movie we made in 1998 called *T-Rex: Back to the Cretaceous*. We'd hoped it would have crossover appeal to both the science museum crowd and mainstream moviegoers. But the science museums hated it because it wasn't scientifically accurate (they said the dinosaurs had too many fingers), and mainstream theaters felt that it lacked excitement (they'd have been happier if the dinosaurs had eaten some people). Ultimately, we had to find a way to get both theater owners and moviemakers enthusiastic about the IMAX format.

Finding the Formula

Our first break came in 2001, when a computer scientist in our Toronto office figured out how to use computer algorithms to convert existing movies into the IMAX format. This was huge. Instead of persuading studios and directors to film with IMAX cameras, we could come in after the fact and turn a movie into IMAX. We paid for the conversions ourselves, and in return the studios agreed to give us 12.5% of the gross box office receipts on the IMAX versions.

By 2006 we'd begun to innovate on our business model as well. Rather than charging theaters $1.2 million for our technology, we started installing IMAX in them at no up-front charge. The theater still had to pay for renovating the physical space—typically about $150,000 per screen—but the conversion was now fairly affordable. In exchange for our technology investment, we received about 20% of the box office receipts for IMAX films shown on that screen.

This new business model works because consumers will pay a premium to see an IMAX movie, and we've found a way to divide that premium among the various players to create a win-win-win scenario. If it costs $10.50 or $11 to see a new release in a theater, a ticket to the IMAX version will cost about $15 or $16. That means that even if the studio pays us 12.5% and the theater owner pays us 20%, they still wind up with more revenue than if the moviegoer had bought a regular ticket. And theater owners see that simply having an IMAX theater installed tends to increase overall attendance at their multiplexes.

The final development that propelled us to success was the shift to digital. Since the late 1990s it's been clear that movie theaters were eventually going to shift away from old-fashioned film projection systems, just as homes were shifting from VHS cassettes to DVDs. There was a lot of uncertainty about when to make the change, however, because it would entail high costs, and theater chains had taken on a lot of debt building big multiplexes around that time. By 2006 this uncertainty was really hobbling IMAX: Theaters didn't want to install our film projection system because they figured they'd be converting to digital soon. So we decided to move aggressively into digital, and we began installing the new systems in 2008. The switch provided huge benefits to the company: Those $30,000 film prints that required a forklift were replaced by $150 plug-and-play hard drives. Showing a film in the IMAX format became cheap and easy.

We had all the pieces in place to begin growing, but IMAX almost didn't get to enjoy the success. We went through two or three periods of crisis along the way. In the early 2000s most of the major theater chains in America (and many around the world) filed for bankruptcy, and we were left with big receivables we couldn't collect. IMAX still carried a lot of debt as a result of the 1994 LBO, and sometimes we doubted whether we would earn enough to meet those obligations. At one point in 2001 our stock traded for 55 cents a share, and some of our bondholders began buying equity and trying to force us into bankruptcy. In 2006 we actively tried to sell the company, but our future was so uncertain that no one was willing to pay a reasonable price.

These were tough times: IMAX's existence was being tested, as was my resolve. This experience underscored the crucial role leaders play in inspiring and motivating teams through difficult situations.

Thank You, *Avatar*

We finally began demonstrating real traction in 2009. Our results improved, and we had money to pay down some of our debt. The stock popped, we were given a new bank line, and doubts about our survival faded. The moment I knew we'd make it came in December, when *Avatar* opened. The IMAX version was a global phenomenon. In China there were six-hour lines to get in, and scalpers were charging $100 a ticket. *Avatar* did $250 million globally on IMAX screens; because we shared in that revenue, it was a financial turning point for us.

That success helped convince theater owners that IMAX could drive business. Since 2000 the industry has been very concerned that as televisions become bigger, home theater systems become more affordable, and streaming allows viewers to access a wide range of movies anytime, people will become less inclined to pay to see first-run movies in theaters. To ward off that threat, theater owners have tried to create a more differentiated experience with bigger screens and better sound systems. (They also invested in 3-D, which generally hasn't lived up to its promise.) This trend has positioned IMAX quite well, as more of the world's leading filmmakers, studios, and exhibitors turn to the format to deliver experiences that audiences cannot find anywhere else. Our commitment to quality and providing a cutting-edge entertainment experience, combined with the differentiation we're able to create by working closely with these key partners, has enabled us to build IMAX into a globally recognized and sought-after brand.

Over the past few years we've been adding 150 to 200 new theaters a year to our network. We used to have to beg studios to make films in the IMAX format, but now a lot of Hollywood people say you can't really make a blockbuster except in IMAX. As a result, we've become much more profitable. Our business is a little bit like HBO's: Every new subscriber provides additional revenue but hardly any additional cost. It's been a long time getting to this point, but when I reflect back, I think that's probably a good thing. If it hadn't been so difficult to find a way to scale up this business, we wouldn't have been able to buy it for as little as we did. One of the studios would probably have beat us to it.

These days I spend a lot of time traveling overseas, where IMAX is experiencing very fast growth. I started going to China 15 years ago, and that market has always had an affinity for IMAX. Today our brand awareness in China is above 90%. When the 117 theaters awaiting construction have been completed, we will have 250 screens there, and demand is still exploding.

As our network has grown, so has the importance of our brand. From day one I recognized the significance of the IMAX name and communicating its values: quality, innovation, and providing exciting new entertainment experiences. By consistently delivering on these, we've earned substantial trust in the marketplace, which has allowed us to move beyond our traditional theatrical business.

For many years people have wondered whether we could re-create the IMAX experience in a home theater system. Our recent launch of IMAX Private Theatre will set a new benchmark for the ultrapremium home theater market.

When I first came to IMAX, my background was mostly in transactions. I'd started businesses and sold them, and I'd helped buy and sell companies on Wall Street, but I'd never run a business for a long time. I didn't intend to do that at IMAX—originally my partner and I figured that we'd hire a CEO to run it, or we'd sell it quickly. But I discovered that I really liked running this business, so I stayed. When I was a lawyer or a banker, people didn't understand what I did at work, but everyone likes talking about IMAX. My daughters are grown now, but for years I took them to movie premieres, which was very rewarding.

In this business I've met people with many different motivations—creative, artistic, financial, competitive. It's hard to keep everyone, internally and externally, focused on the bottom line and create win-win scenarios. I've also developed friendships with studio executives, exhibitors, actors, and directors who've become enthusiasts and boosters of our technology and brand. Running this company has had its share of thrills and has helped me lead a very interesting life, but none of it would have happened without experimentation and determination and a great management team.

Originally published in July–August 2013. R1307A

Index

About the Editors

The individual essays in this collection were edited by Alison Beard, Scott Berinato, Amy Bernstein, David Champion, Karen Dillon, Roberta Fusaro, Adi Ignatius, Suzy Jackson, Daniel McGinn, Gardiner Morse, Steve Prokesch, Anand Ramand, Katherine Xin, and Kite Xu. They were copy edited by Martha Spaulding.

This collection was edited by Daniel McGinn, a senior editor at Harvard Business Review Group.

www.ingramcontent.com/pod-product-compliance
Lightning Source LLC
Chambersburg PA
CBHW031416180326
41458CB00002B/392